FROM THE CINCINNATI REDS TO THE MOSCOW REDS

The Memoirs of Irwin Weil

D0874841

Jews of Russia & Eastern Europe and Their Legacy

Series Editor
Maxim D. Shrayer (Boston College)

Editorial Board
Ilya Altman (Russian Holocaust Center and Russian State University for the
    Humanities)
Karel Berkhoff (NIOD Institute for War, Holocaust and Genocide Studies)
Jeremy Hicks (Queen Mary University of London)
Brian Horowitz (Tulane University)
Luba Jurgenson (Universite Paris IV—Sorbonne)
Roman Katsman (Bar-Ilan University)
Dov-Ber Kerler (Indiana University)
Vladimir Khazan (Hebrew University of Jerusalem)
Mikhail Krutikov (University of Michigan)
Joanna Beata Michlic (Bristol University)
Alice Nakhimovsky (Colgate University)
Antony Polonsky (Brandeis University)
Jonathan D. Sarna (Brandeis University)
David Shneer (University of Colorado at Boulder)
Anna Shternshis (University of Toronto)
Leona Toker (Hebrew University of Jerusalem)
Mark Tolts (Hebrew University of Jerusalem)

FROM THE CINCINNATI REDS TO THE MOSCOW REDS

The Memoirs of Irwin Weil

Compiled and Edited
by **Tony Brown**

Boston 2015

Library of Congress Cataloging-in-Publication Data:
A catalog record for this book is available
from the Library of Congress.

Copyright © 2015 Academic Studies Press
All rights reserved

ISBN 978-1-61811-394-8 (hardback)
ISBN 978-1-61811-395-5 (electronic)
ISBN 978-1-61811-396-2 (paperback)

Cover design by Ivan Grave

Published by Academic Studies Press in 2015
28 Montfern Avenue
Brighton, MA 02135, USA
press@academicstudiespress.com
www. academicstudiespress.com

Contents

4. Social and Political Reform in the Soviet Union

5. Letters from the USSR

Preface

As a young boy in the 1930s, I became fascinated by the Cincinnati Reds, a team whose ownership rested for five years in the hands of my father, Sidney Weil. My father grew up in the service of the Weil-Mook Horse Stables, which provided an important part of local transportation. He had an unusual strength of personality, a great deal of kindness, and a gift for concentrated hard work—qualities that assisted him in navigating many different Midwestern institutions, including baseball, in which he left an indelible mark.

He was also the father of two girls, but he pinned his hopes on me, his only son, for carrying on the family business. At that time, he never dreamed that his offspring would enter academic life and then, as if that weren't bad enough, would become involved with the Russian language and its literary and musical culture.

Such is the unforeseeable nature of Cincinnati life and the events of the twentieth and twenty-first centuries. This book is an attempt to capture the predominant thoughts and feelings of that time and place by describing some of the happenings that shaped my experience and enabled me to affect—let's hope for the better—other people's lives in the United States and the Soviet Union/Russia.

The concluding chapter contains four letters sent to my parents within a week of my return from traveling to the USSR for the first time. They have all the naiveté of first impressions, in spite of the fact that I had previously studied the language and culture. They also have some of the freshness and vitality connected with first impressions.

The reader will notice extensive footnotes throughout. For those who are specialists in Slavic languages and literature and Jewish studies, such footnotes will simply present what they already know, whereas for non-specialists, they will provide helpful details.

The reader also will quickly notice that I have not presented all of the memories in strict chronological order. Rather, I have organized them according to my recollection of them over a life of four score plus six years. From Cincinnati to Moscow, I have participated in many institutions and have encountered numerous languages and cultures. Not without some defeats and disappointments, I have been fortunate enough to taste many of the world's delights. I hope that the following pages will arouse the interest and emotional participation of the attentive reader.

Acknowledgments

I could not have produced these memoirs without the loving support of my beautiful and intelligent wife of sixty-four years and friend for even longer, Vivian Max Weil.

It is also the case that this book would never have seen the light of day without the energetic, intelligent prodding, and continual help of my friend and colleague Tony Brown of Brigham Young University.

-Irwin Weil

Editor's Note

In 2012 I invited Irwin Weil to deliver two guest lectures at Brigham Young University. His lectures, titled "Pushkin: An Aristocrat of African Descent whose Reading of Shakespeare in French Profoundly Influenced His Febrile Imagination" and "Russian Composers and the Clash Over the Issue of Nationalism" were received enthusiastically by students and faculty alike. When the auditoriums emptied and we had a chance to talk in private, I asked Irwin: "You have such a wealth of personal stories involving cultural figures about whom most of us today can only read. Have you written down these accounts?" His reply: "Every time I attempt to write them down, they just don't come out the same as when I tell them." I couldn't help but propose: "Irwin, how about if you tell your stories to me and I record and transcribe them? Once they're on paper, I'll go back and edit them for the reader." I'm pleased to say that he accepted my proposal, which set in motion the events leading up to this book.

The following summer, I traveled to Chicago and spent several days interviewing Irwin. While I prepared some general questions in advance, I mostly tried to clue in on key points that would arise during our discussions and construct questions accordingly. Our conversations resulted in many hours worth of oral recordings, which I subsequently transcribed with the help of my research assistants, Lydia Roberts and Adam Rodger.

Stitching the transcribed material together into a cohesive narrative presented a number of challenges, including determining whether to follow a strict chronological versus topical approach. I think the reader will find that the resulting manuscript represents a careful blending of the two. The question of tone also arose, i.e., should the finished product preserve the spontaneity of the oral interview or adopt a more polished, academic tone? When considering this question, I recalled Irwin's words to me: "Every time I attempt to write them down, they just don't come out the same as when I tell them." Accordingly, I set about editing the text with the goal in mind of preserving, to the extent possible, Irwin's masterful oratorical voice. Ultimately, the reader will have to be the judge as to the success of such an ambitious and, perhaps, presumptuous endeavor.

After completing a draft manuscript, I highlighted people, places, and things for which I thought a non-specialist in Slavic and Jewish studies might appreciate having some background information. In order to ensure a consistent voice in both the text and footnotes, I brought Irwin to Brigham Young University where he recorded responses for each of the highlighted items. Thus, the footnote material that appears in this volume represents a transcription of the recordings made during his visit.

Transliterations of Russian dialogue follow the Library of Congress system; however, when transliterating names of persons, places, and things, I generally favored commonly used transliterations, e.g., Maxim Gorky versus Maksim Gor'kii, Suzdal versus Suzdal', and *Novoye Russkoye Slovo* versus *Novoie Russkoie Slovo*.

–Tony Brown

Chapter One

The Lives of Sidney and Florence Weil

Sidney Weil (23 December 1891-14 January 1966)
Florence Levy Weil (November 1891-15 January 1998)

In dealing with tough times, ya gotta use horse sense.
—Sidney Weil

Ancestry

My father's great-great-grandfather and great-grandfather both came to the United States from Surburg, a small town in Alsace—at that time, in the 1850s, a part of German culture (in France politically). Surburg is about forty kilometers (about twenty-six miles) north of Strasbourg, the most important city in the region. Gabriel Weil, my great-great-grandfather, made his living, like many German-speaking Jews of the time, by selling vegetables along a route between the large city and his small hometown. After the great European revolutions of 1848,[1] the currency collapsed and the Weils decided to try their industry and their luck in the American Midwest and South. They came to the banks of the Ohio River in Cincinnati, where economic development and commerce were proceeding vigorously. The Ohio proved to be no worse than the Rhine had been. Indeed, the future proved it a lot better and far less mortal for Jews.

---

1   In 1848, there were a series of revolutions that broke out across Western and Central Europe. These revolutions lasted for a year and caused the powers that be great anxiety; however, they eventually were put down.

My father's father, Isaac (after whom I received my Hebrew name, Yitzkhak), started peddling vegetables, like his grandfather, in Cincinnati. An oft-repeated story maintains that he was melodiously hawking his vegetables one day from a pushcart when a professor from the Cincinnati Conservatory of Music heard him and insisted on the spot that he study vocal music. Whatever the attractions of music may have been for Isaac, he soon gave up both his notes and his vegetables for a partnership in the main transportation business of the latter part of the nineteenth century— horse stables run by the Mook family, who had earlier come to the United States from Bavaria. Thanks to this partnership, Isaac married one of the Mook daughters, named Minnie, who was a very strong woman of old-fashioned German-Bavarian-Jewish stock; her personality left an indelible imprint on the family. Minnie went on to become the mother of three boys, the oldest of whom was Sidney. Thanks also to this partnership between my grandfather and the Mook family, Sidney was born into the business of buying, managing, and selling horses.

Sidney Weil

From almost his earliest days, Dad remembered with pleasure and passion his time working in the stables and the judging of good, as well as bad, horseflesh. He took to the tricks of the trade very quickly and ably, much more so than to those of formal schooling, which he found an utter bore, and this boredom with schooling continued throughout his life. However, he deeply believed in formal education, both Jewish and secular, for others but never for himself. He could read and pray beautifully in Hebrew and in English, but he left school after fourth grade, which he once flunked and then repeated; he never learned the third person singular of the verb "to do"—Dad always said, "He don't." He also learned a little "Cincinnati Deutsch." "Mit a bissel Englisch, das glinkt ja, so wunder schoen" (With a little bit of English, everything goes so well) is an example of a song in the Alsacian dialect that he repeated many times in his life. Dad didn't know German as well as his mother, Minnie, but attended public schools that taught in German for part of every day.

In 1914, when Dad was twenty-two years old, World War I started to kill its European young men in huge numbers in a fight that only increased the rapidity with which a social order was tearing itself apart. Dad was not much interested in European history or politics but he knew, as most Americans did, that sooner or later the United States would become involved. He also knew that some of his distant relatives with the name Weil in Alsace would be affected. By 1917 it was clear that the United States would enter the war on the side of the Allied powers. One eventual result of the war was that Alsace was made part of France instead of remaining part of Germany.

The US government was in the market for large numbers of horses for training soldiers and military transport. Dad was sent by his beloved father to Washington, DC to try to negotiate the sale of some fine horse-flesh. While there in DC, the young fellow also had stern instructions to find his female cousin at a dance and make sure that her card was filled up with partners for every set of quadrilles and foxtrots. He intended to do what he was told until he encountered a lovely and attractive young woman named Florence Levy. That meeting made him put his family's instructions out of consciousness. After learning why he came to Washington, she primly ordered him to do his duty. He scampered about the ballroom with his usual energy and force, and soon a whole list of cavaliers had been assigned to his cousin. When Florence saw the evidence, she graciously consented to dance with the Cincinnati bundle of energy.

Florence Levy

My mother was born as the eldest of six children. In 1893 her parents emigrated from a small town in Lithuania called Popilon to Charleston, West Virginia. With a pack on his back, her father traveled among coal miners to sell everyday necessary goods. When my mother was in the sixth grade, her father died. The burden of supporting the family fell upon her, since her mother spoke Yiddish and was illiterate in English. The Jewish community tried to set up the young girl with a small store, but its business turned out to be beyond her capacities to manage. Luckily, a local scion of an aristocratic Virginia family, Adam Littlepage, recognized in Mom the energy and intelligence necessary to help him in his practice of law. He also had empathy for the needs of her fatherless family.

After hiring her, he soon came to realize that he had made the right choice; she gave him the kind of help and support that his growing practice desperately needed.

Soon the attorney's little practice in West Virginia was traded for an office in Washington, DC. Shortly after the beginning of World War I, Mr. Littlepage ran a successful campaign to enter the US House of Representatives. He resisted the attempts of influential people to place one of their family members in his office, and Mom soon found herself ensconced as a very young and attractive woman working as chief secretary and assistant in the office building of the US House of Representatives. Often when Mr. Littlepage found himself harassed or burdened by a pesky constituent, he would dictate a very angry letter of response. Mom would ask him if he really wanted to send it off, and he would reply with a vigorous—perhaps even mildly profane—affirmative. On the following day he would come to regret his impulsiveness and say, "I wish I hadn't sent the blasted thing." Florence, after asking him if he really meant that, would produce the letter that she had put, not in the post office drop box, but in her desk drawer.

Mr. Littlepage came to depend heavily on the young person he affectionately called "Little One." Years later, in the midst of a solidly conservative group of Cincinnati citizens, Mom proudly reminisced about the fact that she had once danced with Franklin Delano Roosevelt when he was Secretary of the Navy, some years before he contracted polio. In the midst of a Republican family, she quietly mused that the man she had danced with could not be entirely bad!

When constituents would come to the Littlepage office, they would sometimes say to Mom: "We know what a good West Virginia girl likes best," and they would produce a delicious sandwich crammed with fine, West Virginia ham. Florence, who came from a religious Orthodox Jewish family, would never even think of consuming non-kosher meat. She, therefore, had the task of diplomacy: With deep thankfulness she accepted the *treyf*[2] goods and assured the donor that she anticipated a magnificent lunch. Later, she would give the sandwich to a colleague who was delighted

---

2   The word *treyf* in Hebrew is the word for "non-kosher," that is to say, the kind of food that should not be consumed by those who are obeying the biblical laws of kosher.

to receive it and who would then consume it with West Virginia enthusiasm.

There was a dilemma in Mom's life: to continue working in Mr. Littlepage's office so she could send money to her family, or to allow my father's courtship to advance. Initially Mom tried to block the horse dealer's advances, including a box of chocolates that he attempted to send her. She indignantly refused the gesture, which she considered improperly forward, but she, from an Eastern-European background (her parents had emigrated from Lithuania, which was part of the Tsar's Russian Empire), did not at first appreciate the reality of German stubbornness. Dad would never let a mere refusal interfere with his well-laid plans. But when he later popped the vital question, she replied that she couldn't possibly consider an acceptance. After all, how would the family survive without the money she sent them? Dad replied that he would bring the whole gang to Cincinnati, send her younger brothers to college, and find good, respectable work for her sisters. (In those days, it wouldn't have occurred to Dad that the young women might get a higher education. In later years, that mindset had changed mightily when he demanded that his own daughters enroll as students at the University of Cincinnati, whether they wished to or not.)[3]

However, there was one more obstacle to the proposal: Mr. Littlepage was not eager to lose his important assistant. He demanded to see the

---

3   When my two sisters, both older than I, went to college, the oldest went with great pleasure. She was both brave and very creative. The second oldest, Margie, loved fun. "I don't want to go to college," she would say, to which my father would reply, "You're going to go to college if I have to drive you with a whip!" She didn't have the nerve to say, "But you quit school!" so she went to college. Conversely, my two aunts had to go to work. The younger one eventually worked for a bank that was in the Federal Reserve System. During the war, the men had to go and the boss realized that my aunt was a woman with some brains. He said, "Look, you should become an inspector. What you should do is take a couple of courses in statistics at the local university, and you can become an inspector in the Federal Reserve System." Soon thereafter she became (I'm pretty sure) the first woman inspector in the part of the Federal Reserve System that included Ohio, Indiana, and Kentucky. She would go around inspecting banks. When she came to town, by God, they had to show her the books, and she did all of the things an inspector does, which was quite remarkable for a woman in her position who had never received a higher education. And yet, she was very skillful in this line of work. After retiring, she became a tutor for kids in the local public school. She lived to be 103 years old.

young fellow. Little did the estimable gentleman know that he was facing the best horse salesman west of the Appalachians. At the end of an hour's conversation, Mr. Littlepage emerged from his office and exclaimed: "What a wonderful young man, Little One. Marry him at once!"

Joining the Army

But marriage would have to wait until after the war. In the army, Dad served as a quartermaster sergeant and was responsible for feeding the men around him. His description of those days included quite a few times when men got a special treat (thanks to supplies that he had wrangled), often having to do with sweets or ice cream. From the sound of his voice in reminiscing or singing about those days, I gathered that he loved the army songs of World War I.

However, he had at least one source of dissatisfaction: Dad tended not to order bacon for the soldiers' breakfast since bacon is not kosher. According to later stories told by my father, the men would grumble about the absence of bacon. Several replied that Weil was Jewish, didn't they know that? How could they expect bacon? Dad's reply (in his own words, many years after) was, "What's the matter? Aren't you eating well under me?" The pitch of his voice would go way down—the way it often did when he suddenly got very serious. The soldiers would reply, "Yes, but bacon is a good thing, too, you know!" "All right," Dad retorted. "From now on you'll have some bacon." But you can be sure that this particular quartermaster sergeant never touched it. Abstention from non-kosher meat and fish was something Dad continued for his entire life, and all his friends and business associates—Jew and Gentile alike—knew about it.

Not only was Dad loyal and kind to his troops, he also cared about his own family in Germany. He tried to look up some of his relatives in Alsace to see if they had experienced difficulties. After finding out that they were not in bad straits, he left matters at that. Evidently seeing his relatives was less important to him than helping them if they had needed his aid. That was characteristic of him for his entire life: Dad was the one to give help and support. Simply visiting relatives whom he had never seen, in a country whose language he knew imperfectly but from whose boundaries and customs his own beloved family had come, did not arouse his curiosity or strong interest.

Any talk of fighting or killing in the War to End All Wars was never discussed in our home. It was as if Dad's spirit was completely separated from the mass killing and trench warfare of World War I. Politics did not seem to affect his memories of the war either. When I was much smitten with French culture, he told me that the impressively clean German houses he saw after the war appealed to him much more than the less-than-clean French houses he saw. It was hard for me to accept, especially in view of the fact that France was our ally in both world wars, but he insisted on German cleanliness.

After the War

After the end of World War I, Dad was very eager to get back to his business in Cincinnati. He sensed that American business would change drastically, and he wanted to jump into the situation with his characteristic verve and energy. He could not do this as long as he was a soldier, and he ached for demobilization. Of course he had not forgotten the comely secretary to Congressman Littlepage. Many letters and telegrams came to Miss Florence Levy, and she tried as hard as she could to prevail on the US government to demobilize a soldier from Cincinnati.

My parents were married on 1 July 1919. After Florence added Weil to her last name, the two of them departed on a honeymoon to the western states. National parks were important to my parents. Conversation about the great parks, especially Yellowstone, was staple around the house for all the eighteen years I spent growing up there; it became a kind of folklore for the family.

The Roaring Twenties

During the 1920s, Dad was full of ambition and energy, but he was not completely ruthless or as aggressive as the famous business tycoons are often pictured. Dad set out to become a real tycoon: rich, influential, creative, and helpful to others in need. He realized that his beloved horses were on the way out and that the new mode of popular transportation would be automobiles. His experience in buying and selling horses and providing transportation for the area prepared him admirably for what would become the commercial vortex of the storm of buying and selling automobiles. He managed to get involved with the sale of the elder Henry Ford's products, and he soon became a general agent for Ford in Cincinnati in the early 1920s.

The stories about this time when Dad sold cars were legion. It soon became clear that Dad knew how to control costs and prices in a way to make the business thrive. It also became clear that he was a person of unusual directness and honesty. I heard many stories from other people about how Dad would return money if he got more for a trade-in than he expected—he would go out of his way to find the person and return the excess. When I would ask him about this transaction, he would literally snort and say that of course he did that—it was only good business! His favorite story was about the loaves that grew after being thrown in the water: "When you throw loaves of bread upon the water, they come back to you in greatly increased numbers."[4] He may even have distorted the story, but his point was the increase this action brought about. "Don't ask me how it happens," he said, "but it happens. I see it happen every time."

His honesty had a very rough side that offended some people but was legend among all. If a person came to him with a business proposal, he said exactly what he thought. If he thought the proposal was nonsense, sparing the person's feelings did not occur to him. This often drove my mother, who was more soft-spoken (but no less tough), to distraction. But not even she could get him to change his public manners. The insulted person would often redden with anger and hurt and leave the office. Later, however, that same person would return for more advice because he or she knew that advice represented Dad's honest opinion, built on a great deal of energy and thought. Dad could be wrong, but he would never say what he did not believe.

A few years later came one of those central episodes that expressed Dad's character. Henry Ford learned that my father, the marvelous general

---

4   This story represents an admixture of Old and New Testament teachings. From the Old Testament, "Cast thy bread upon the waters: for thou shalt find it after many days" (Eccles. 11:1, Authorized [King James] Version). From the New Testament, the miracle of "The Feeding of the 5,000," which appears in all four canonical Gospels: Matt. 14:13–21, Mark 6:31–44, Luke 9:10–17, and John 6:5–15 (AV).

agent in Cincinnati, was Jewish. Ford then decided that Dad would have to go. The auto mogul and inventor of both mass production and the assembly line told Dad in no uncertain terms where he could and should go. Dad told Ford to take the matter to court and "show the judge" exactly where in the contract it stated that a Jew could not be a general agent. "If," said Dad, "the judge of an American court decides in your favor, I'll leave immediately and quietly. If he decides in my favor, I'll sue the pants off you!" Mr. Ford may have been a bigot, but he was no fool in business and he backed away.

Dad went right on with his vigorous business dealings and did not stop with automobiles. In very many of his activities, his brothers were closely involved. One of his early actions was to buy a piece of real estate on favorable terms in North Avondale, still far from where Jews lived in Cincinnati. He wanted to use this house to establish a Jewish part of the city's burial business. The result was the beginning of the Weil Brothers Funeral Home to offer burial services in a completely Jewish way (they would also do it in a partly Jewish way if the family wanted). The business became very profitable, and Dad had many reasons later on to be happy with his initiative. As he became more and more successful during what came to be called the Roaring Twenties, Dad got bolder and bolder and considerably more reckless with the investment of his and his brothers' money. He acquired controlling interest in a bank and helped establish garages, cleaners, and other business establishments in Cincinnati. He also joined in the national madness at that time: he bought stock on margin, paying only for a part of its value, hoping to maximize profits in a constantly rising market.

Faith and Family

Yet one of the deepest parts of Dad's life, and certainly the center of his faith, was his attachment to Judaism and to the Isaac M. Wise Temple in Cincinnati.[5] His personal feelings were attached to traditional, Orthodox forms of prayer and behavior. Every morning, except on Saturdays (*Shabbos*[6]),

---

5   The Isaac M. Wise Temple is a reformed Jewish temple in Cincinnati, Ohio. It is named in honor of the major figure who established Reform Judaism in the United States.

6   *Shabbat* (Hebrew: שָׁבַּת, "cease, rest," the Ashkenazic pronunciation is *Shabbos*) is the word for "Sabbath." It's a day that starts at sundown on Friday and continues until

he put on his *tefillen*, or *phylacteries*.[7] Dad followed tradition: he went through the traditional prayers in exactly the traditionally prescribed form. On Friday and Saturday nights, he would make *kiddush*[8] and *havdalah*[9] with the wondrous spice box and plaited three-wick beeswax candles, which he made himself, together with our whole family. His deep voice rendered the prayers in what I can only describe as Dad's own personal Cincinnati Hebrew. He made an unforgettable picture and sound. This was true largely because his feelings were so clearly consonant with the sounds.

As Orthodox as were his feelings, however, he gave his complete organizational loyalty to the American Jewish Reform Movement, whose founding leader, Isaac Meyer Wise, gave his name to the congregation that Dad made an important part of his life's work. In Jewish community life, Dad dealt with many interesting people, including one Rabbi Shmuel Vul, who was born in the Ukrainian part of the Russian Tsar's Empire and at the age of fifteen had exchanged a letter with Leo Tolstoy.[10] When the young man came to the United States, he called himself Samuel Wohl. He

---

sundown on Saturday. On this day, Jews are not supposed to travel by vehicle or do any work. Rather they are simply supposed to pray, eat, and study religious works.

7   *Tefillin* (Hebrew: תפילין, the English word is "phylacteries") are leather straps that observants use six days a week, excluding the Sabbath. They wind them around their arms and also around their forehead to fulfill a famous prayer: "And thou shalt bind them for a sign upon thine hand, and they shall be as frontlets between thine eyes" (Deut. 6:8, King James Version). There is a small box that has the prayer inside of it that is attached to the leather that you wear between your eyes. The straps on the arms eventually form Hebrew letters when they get to the hands. These straps are to show that you are aware of the most important divine commandments.

8   *Kiddush* (Hebrew: קידוש, "sanctification") is the blessing for sanctifying wine or the fruit of the vine before the Sabbath, and the introductory blessing also is recited before any holiday or season when partaking of the fruit of the vine.

9   *Havdalah* (Hebrew: הַבְדָּלָה, "separation") is the separation of the holy time that is celebrated on the Sabbath and the time that comes after it, which is the week. There is a famous *Havdalah* service involving a three-pronged candle that observants light every Saturday night at sundown when the Sabbath is going out and the secular week is once again coming in. It's a division between the sacred and the secular.

10 Lev Nikolayevich Tolstoy (9 September 1828-20 November 1910) was one of the most famous writers in the world. He was a Russian novelist who wrote incredibly powerful novels, the two most famous ones being *War and Peace* and *Anna Karenina*. He was a very important figure, not only in Russian literary life, but in Russian social and political life as well.

was as Russian in his temperament as my father was German, and the two became instant friends. Some of the more hoity-toity members of the congregation resented his Russian accent when he spoke English, although after my studies in Russian, I now know it was rather light.

Such attempts at snubbing Rabbi Wohl by certain members of the congregation infuriated Dad and further inclined him in the Rabbi's favor. The fact was that Samuel Wohl was a hardworking, sincerely feeling Rabbi, who had all kinds of new, reforming ideas that were on the move at the time. Rabbi Wohl had a very pleasant wife, and soon the two families were close to one another. Rabbi Wohl felt the helping side of his new friend in many practical areas of life. He also had an instinctive appreciation of the rare kind of Jewish spirit in Dad and realized what that energy could do for Judaism in Cincinnati. Above all, he liked and valued Dad's passion and sometimes childlike nature.

Over the span of eight years, my parents had three children. My sister Carolyn was born in 1920 and Marjorie in 1922. Dad, however, was still eager to have a son. Finally, after several miscarriages, I was born in 1928.

In that same year of 1928, Dad was organizing a campaign of stock buying, engendering all kinds of cartoons and gossip in the Cincinnati newspapers that would end in the spring of 1929 with him as the majority

Sidney and Florence Weil family. Father Sidney (standing), (left to right) Irwin, sister Carolyn, maternal grandmother Mary Levy, mother Florence, and sister Marjorie.

stockholder and titular owner of the Cincinnati Reds. The Reds club was the first professional baseball team in the United States, and Dad was the first Jew ever to own a major league baseball club. The newspapers were calling him Mr. Money Bags, and Mom was deeply frightened that someone might kidnap one of the children for ransom, perhaps because she was influenced by the famous Lindbergh case.

Great Depression

The spring of 1929 was, alas, all too close to the fall of 1929—the time of the great stock market crash and the beginning, at least in psychological terms, of the Great Depression. Like thousands of Americans, Dad was suddenly stung by a stock market that had previously increased almost consistently (with only minor downturns) and in which he had increasingly invested on margin. This catastrophic decrease and call in of debt could not have come at a worse time for him, since he had to expend large amounts of capital in order to build a good baseball team.

As if that personal economic collapse were not bad enough, his bank soon collapsed, taking with it other large amounts of capital. From the material and financial point of view, it could not have been a more depressing, gloomy time. It was especially difficult for Mom, who winced every time she read in the newspapers about how a previously wealthy financial investor, now wiped out, would throw himself out the window of a high building, seeking death as the solution to his problems. Those were fervent days for her in prayer in the I. M. Wise Temple.

Dad later told me: "I got greedy, and God punished me for that greed. Irwin, never work only for money. It's great stuff to have, but as life's only goal, it is the most horrible goal possible. Always work primarily for the good that work can do. Then, the money will come in a sufficient amount to support you and your family."

Yet Dad did not later seem to remember those years as generally grim. He knew the problems, probably better than most people at that time, and he certainly made no attempt to hide them, either at the time or in retrospect. After all, he was dealing with his beloved baseball, his second religion after Judaism. He had loved it since childhood when he watched the scores chalked up outside the Cincinnati Beer Steuben.

He loved every minute of the game, which he watched in rapt and concentrated silence, drinking in every move.

Baseball Players

Dad got to know closely at least two major and dynamic personalities. The first of them subsequently played a powerful role in my father's life and vice versa. Bill Veeck was a youngster cutting hot dog buns at the Chicago Cubs stadium where his dad, William Veeck, was the general manager. Although Dad's business was with the elder Veeck, he soon became captivated by the exuberant effervescence of the young man, as did most of America fifteen to twenty years later. Dad and young Bill became close friends. I will go one step further: I will say that the two very best human beings in baseball came together at that time. If I am overstating, mea culpa—*Khotonu, avinu L'fonekho!* (I have sinned before you, O Father!)[11]

The second of Dad's closest friends and peers in those years of club ownership, and for at least two decades afterward, was Branch Rickey. Branch was the general manager of the St. Louis Cardinals and, later, the Brooklyn Dodgers. He was famous for many things, including the signing of Jackie Robinson, the first of many great black athletes to play in the major leagues. Branch, the so-called Mahātmā of baseball, was an extraordinarily canny manipulator and trader of players; his reputation for acumen was sky-high. He was also a very religious Methodist. When Branch's mother was on her deathbed, he promised he would never go to a baseball game on Sunday, the Christian Sabbath. That promise was never broken.

Branch Rickey was almost immediately sympathetic to the former horse trader and very religious man. It made no difference to Branch that Dad was not a Christian. He correctly perceived that heaven did not exclude kosher hot dogs and that the temperaments of truly religious people touched each other. My father kept his World Series bags packed during the *Yom Kippur*[12] day-long services so he could leave as soon as

---

11 Bill became Catholic, with a great love for Jews, so he would love that linguistic connection.

12 *Yom Kippur* (Hebrew: יוֹם כִּפּוּר) means "Day of Atonement." It comes ten days after the Jewish New Year, *Rosh Hashanah*. It's a day when you're supposed to fast and try to make atonement for the sins that you've committed during the year—the idea being

N'ilah[13] was over. Of course, he didn't object if some of the prayer readers kept him abreast of the score and the number of innings completed! No questions were asked about where such secular and non-repenting information was obtained.

Above all, Branch Rickey, a gentleman of humor and sensibility, recognized in Dad a man of quality and bedrock integrity. Branch loved to make jokes with, and sometimes at, his Cincinnati religious friend about precisely those vices. A putative "letter of recommendation" from Branch hung on Dad's wall for over fifteen years; it described him as shiftless and irresponsible, but nevertheless likeable and arid, with a wonderful wife! When Branch and Dad talked, it was like the backyard of all the basses in the choir with their Midwest twangs bouncing at each other in a mellifluous lower register. Branch also sympathized with Dad's growing financial difficulties and tried to help him where he could.

The Move

After five years of ownership of the Reds, the bank foreclosed on Dad's debt, thus forcing him into total bankruptcy, including the funds he had managed for his younger brothers. He remembered that as a very, very dark day, and he swore he would never set foot in that bank again. (I believe he kept that vow.) Mom again worried deeply, remembering the suicides of the early Depression years.

Dad struggled hard for several years after this event, which played such a somber role in the family's collective memory. He had lost his capital, his business, his house; in a material sense, he had lost everything. He had formerly been the seemingly all-powerful senior advisor to his brothers. Now they and a few close and loyal friends were giving him money so his family would not be in total penury and so he could get started again. The family lost the house in North Avondale, which had become the most desirable section of the Cincinnati Jewish community in

---

that you first concentrate on past sins and then hope to commit fewer such sins in the future.

13 *N'ilah* is the last part of *Yom Kippur* day. In the ten days since the New Year, God's book of life has been open and inscription is available for all genuine repentance. At the service's end, the book is closed.

the 1920s and '30s. Members of my family often reflected on those years as a lost, golden paradise. For decades after, Dad pointed out our old neighborhood with nostalgia and longing memories as we drove past.

On the other hand, the move was not entirely negative by any means. We moved into a modest but comfortable apartment in a different part of the Jewish community on one of the major north-south US routes at that time, Nos. 25 and 42, Reading Road. The building was right next to the apartment of my mother's mother and her two single sisters and single brother. All of them had played a large part in our lives, as Dad had in theirs. They were tremendously supportive in everyday ways, and I am sure all of these things were crucial in helping Dad to weather the 1930s.

Dad tried very hard to reestablish himself in the business world of the Depression. He went back to the automobile business, this time with General Motors. We kids used to love to watch the gaudily painted advertising automobiles in which he would sometimes drive home. But the '30s were not a time for gaudiness; most business people were in a somber, money-clenching mood, and they were not easy customers for such major, expensive merchandise as automobiles. Dad himself had become very conservative in the use and investment of money, although he never lost his impulse for generosity toward those in dire need, and he shuddered at the very mention of debt or buying stocks on margin. The financial burn he had suffered went deep within him.

Within a few years, Dad had to admit that the selling and buying of automobiles was no longer a viable occupation for him. He then experimented in the mid-1930s with various schemes of buying and selling goods. This experiment gave only indifferent results. Several of his friends tried to tempt him with the business of commercial real estate. However, Dad was cautious; he had learned a lesson he couldn't forget. He told me later, "I would have become a millionaire, but I couldn't see it for myself."

Life Insurance

Then in 1937-38, a real career break came for Dad. Sam Sturm, a business friend, convinced the man who still loved baseball and had a world of friends that he could do very well in the world of life insurance. Dad loved to help people. Others knew this quality about Dad and trusted him. You could say that persistence and doggedness were his middle names. Sam was sure that life insurance was just right for him. Dad was not so sure; he and Mom visualized insurance salesmen as inveterate pests who pulled a signing pen on you just as you thought a personal friendship was starting. But Sam was no less stubborn and convincing than Dad, and the latter sat down to something new for him: studying for exams, whose successful passing was necessary to receive a license to sell insurance. This remarkable graduate of the fourth grade (twice repeated), fortified by his extensive life careers, began his exam with this statement: "I am answering these questions not so much on the basis of what I know from books as on the basis of thirty years of experience in many different parts of the world of business." He passed the exam and received his license.

The rest is insurance company history. Shortly thereafter Dad became the national leader in sales for his company for quite a few years. He also became a member of the euphemistically named "Million Dollar Round Table"—those who sold over a million dollars in life insurance at a time when the dollar was not yet devalued by inflation, as it was from the mid-1950s to the present. It is important to repeat here: He cared deeply about the money but not as an end in itself. He was happy to be in a position to be generous on a larger scale. Countless numbers of people came to him for help, and he rarely refused. He would not sell life insurance to people who in his opinion couldn't afford it. One prospective buyer, Bill Veeck, called Dad "the only insurance man to refuse to sell me a policy. He said I shouldn't do it. If I insisted, I'd have to buy it from someone else."

Raising Money

Perhaps the best indication of his attitude toward the use of money appeared in the literally thousands of hours he spent on charitable fundraising. He always aggressively fought to feed financially the I. M. Wise Temple and the local and national Jewish charities. His greatest praise was for his friend who "made fifty thousand dollars a year (a huge sum in those days) and gave away fifty-two thousand." On the other hand, I can't even begin to count the ways he knew how to curse the "cheap bastards" (a mild rebuke, under those circumstances, in Dad's mouth). By his definition a cheap bastard was one who could afford a nice Florida vacation for himself and his family but only gave a paltry sum, in Dad's eyes, to charity. A few years later, during World War II, when Midwestern American Jews were vaguely beginning to sense the reality of Hitler's horrors—full knowledge came later, in 1946—the moral and mortal significance of giving grew stronger.

On the basis of his fund-raising reputation, Dad was made chairman of the All-Cincinnati Community Chest. Suddenly, dismayed Christian businessmen were being solicited by their best customers. The Christian business executives had never experienced this kind of pressure before; they had not, thank God, gone through the agony of losing eighty percent of their European community. It seemed to them the fund-raising had gotten out of hand! No less a personage than Neil McElroy, president of Procter and Gamble and later Secretary of Defense under Eisenhower, called Dad and tried to urge diplomacy tactfully: "Please, Mr. Weil, we don't want to antagonize people, even for a good cause." I can almost picture Mom's relief when she heard those political words of common sense. Yet Dad did not heed them. He said, with some characteristic choler, that they should decide whether they wanted to raise money for good, charitable causes and help people in real need or whether they wanted to spare the feelings of a few no-good, cheap bastards. Dad was soon removed as chairman of the All-Cincinnati Community Chest.

Dad saw what he considered an ideal chance to pay off the mortgage on the I. M. Wise Temple building. Right after World War II, new automobiles were scarce because production of civilian cars had been drastically curtailed during the war. Through his automobile dealer connection, he obtained a rare, new automobile. He ordered the dealer to put it on display in front of the temple with a sign that told people to buy chances on a lottery. The proceeds would go to pay the mortgage on the temple building, and one lucky person would win a new car. The dealer filled the order and Dad walked off, proud and satisfied.

Shortly thereafter, Rabbi Wohl came by the temple and experienced horror and mortification at the sight of a grubby raffle right in front of the holy sanctuary. Indignant at the idea of a market in such an inappropriate place, he angrily called the dealer and demanded immediate withdrawal of the disgraceful vehicle. Such was the prestige of the Cincinnati clergy in those days that the dealer saluted and complied posthaste. Dad later came by and discovered only thin air where an example of Detroit's finest automobile had rested earlier. Angry at the contravention of his benevolent scheme, he called the dealer and asked what idiot or thief had taken the vehicle. The dealer stuttered but eventually replied that the idiot was Dad's close friend and coreligionist, the eminent Rabbi Samuel Wohl.

Dad's reply has not been recorded for the ages, happily for the gentility of our American English language. But the fact of the matter is that he did not countermand the Rabbi's order. In his opinion, the Rabbi was a holy man and must reign in the temple. This doesn't mean that at home Dad didn't grumble and mumble in his best bass voice about business ignoramuses who were destroying the financial possibilities for the temple. At that point I piped up with the wisdom of adolescence, "But Dad, he was right. It's not nice to sell things in front of the temple." The reader can perhaps imagine how this sage remark was received. Dad replied, "Well, so what if he is right? What does that prove?"

By the 1950s and '60s, an increasingly larger amount of life insurance was being provided in large corporate pension plans run by new corporate bureaucrats who were more technologically sophisticated. They were referred to as "brain trusters" by the new breed of men who ran the agency (I heard this term from them myself, and they explicitly excluded my father from this category). Of course, they still valued Dad's tremendous prestige among individual clients who were growing older, and they were not so blind as to ignore his remarkable warmth and colorful personality.

I have a picture of my father standing with two of these bureaucrats, and the difference is clear at first glance. He is dressed in an older, rumpled suit with a vest; they are spruced up in what look like tailored suits. They are holding drinks in their hands (Dad almost never drank alcohol, except wine for Jewish prayers). They fit immediately into any corporate bureaucracy whereas he, with his sore back, braced himself against the wall in an individualistic stance. These corporate bureaucrats were mid-twentieth-century products; Dad, a nineteenth-century product.

Zionists and Education

In the pre-1948 days, my father and almost my whole family, like many Midwestern Reform Jews, were anti-Zionist. Midwestern Reform Jews believed that Jews formed a religion, not a nation, and they were unmoved by the prospect of a Jewish national state in what they called "Palestine." Of course my parents were almost completely ignorant of East European Jewish history. Conversely, both rabbis in the I. M. Wise Temple—unlike Isaac M. Wise himself—were passionate, fervent partisans of Zionism. Rabbi Wohl, who had stuck by Dad through thick and thin and who was so loved and respected by Dad, loved the doctrine of Theodor Herzl[14] and Ahad Ha'am[15] with all the power of Wohl's essentially Russian soul. In the immediate post-World War II years, he lived and breathed for Zion—*Ahavas Zion*! (The love of Zion!)

I found Rabbi Wohl's enthusiasm contagious, and soon I got deeply involved in the Zionist network of youth organizations: Socialists, schmocialists, capitalists, schmapitalists—it was all the same to me. But there were great songs, lots of poetry and drama, and intelligent and beautiful young women—*enthusiasm*! It never occurred to me that there could be really complex political problems; it seemed simple and straightforward to a naïve Cincinnati Jewish teenager. When my dad saw some examples of my ardent new faith, he was repulsed by its inexperience and what he regarded as stupidity. As usual, he minced no words and told me just how stupidly the Zionist youth leaders and I were behaving. He didn't quite

14 Theodor Herzl (2 May 1860-3 July 1904) was an Austrian Jew who was the founder of political Zionism. As a correspondent for an Austrian newspaper, he went to Paris to attend the Dreyfus trial where a Jewish officer was unjustly condemned for something that another man had actually done, and when Herzl saw the anti-Semitic outburst that happened in France at that time, he decided that the only solution to anti-Semitism was for Jews to have a country of their own just like everyone else had. In those days, that country was called Palestine, and now it is called Israel. His book, *The Jewish State*, together with his actions played an essential role in the eventual establishment of the State of Israel a half-century later.

15 Asher Zvi Hirsch Ginsberg (18 August 1856-2 January 1927) took on the pseudonym Ahad Ha'am, which literally means "one of the people." He was contemporary with Theodor Herzl and with the upsurge of Zionism that took place at the end of the nineteenth century. His idea was that if Zionism was only political and not cultural that it would do something terrible to Jewish culture. Instead, he envisioned a revitalization of Jewish culture.

dare to oppose Rabbi Wohl openly, however, and he never tried to stop me from joining the Zionist youth groups and expressing my enthusiasm. Perhaps some part of him admired my spunk!

Rabbi Wohl could be rigorous and emotionally pressing when it was a matter that touched his heart, grounded in love for the Jewish tradition, yet he was also a pioneer in social and ritual reform. He was very strongly in favor of educating all young people, and my wife will testify to his heartfelt encouragement for young women to study and learn—not only Jewish subjects, but also education in any field. Throughout my young life, all the way through college and beyond, Rabbi Wohl was concerned that I get a good education and make connections with the widest assortment of ideas and experiences, including what he considered the most interesting new books in my field of Russian literature. He had a genuine feeling for the beauties of Russian literature and music, and he combined this with a deep and genuine love for the people in the Wise Center Temple. My wife and I owe him a great deal for his communication of profound human feeling and sensitivity.

In general, Dad began to understand that his son was beginning to look at a somewhat larger world with considerably different eyes than those usually produced in Cincinnati in the 1940s. In the spring of 1946, Harvard University unceremoniously told me I was not the proper raw material for its delicate New England maw (causing some squawks at my high school, which had encouraged me to apply). Dad was half disappointed and half relieved that I would not become a "Hahvahd" man, although he tried unsuccessfully to pull strings at Princeton later. It was one of the few times when his stubborn attempts at manipulation failed.

After being turned away by Harvard, I enrolled at the University of Cincinnati. But when Dad heard my disappointment at learning in the same city where I grew up, in the fall of 1946 he offered to support me in any way necessary to get what I thought was a good education. He deeply believed in its importance, and he implicitly trusted the judgment of the same kid whose ideas he had considered naïve and stupid. I am almost sure he was unaware of the paradox. When my friend Howard Schuman (later to become an eminent sociologist at the University of Michigan) showed me an article on R. M. Hutchins' highly regarded plan for the University of Chicago, I decided that program was for me. Dad immediately set out to help me get in, and he rejoiced when I was accepted for January of 1947. I will never forget his face as he took me to the train at beautiful art deco Union Terminal in Cincinnati. He was ashen-faced, barely containing the tears that would veil his sight of the kid going off to learn how to be a Chicago intellectual—light-years away from baseball, as Dad knew it, and from the experience that had produced the remarkable character of Sidney Weil.

The Horrors of World War II and Life After

My parents' reaction to the horrors of Nazism that occurred around World War II would eventually lead them to the Zionist cause. Dad and Mom were aware of them. I can well remember the frightened pallor in their usually rosy and confident faces when they would listen behind closed doors and curtained windows to the ugly radio broadcasts of Father Coughlin, the American Fascist and Hitlerite. They also listened to the increasingly agonized sermons of Rabbi Wohl, who watched with infuriated impotence while Nazi butchers mangled European Jewry, especially those from his childhood world of the Ukraine. Whatever political and temperamental differences my father had with the man were utterly drowned by the Rabbi's deep and obviously true feelings for the perishing of Jews and European Judaism.

My father had extraordinary successes in fund-raising. He often repeated his favorite slogan: "A Jew has to have a heart" (strange how that parallels the oft-expressed idea of Christian charity, *caritas*). His efforts were obviously connected with feelings of solidarity with Jews suffering under Nazi barbarism. At about the same time, however, he saw to it that people in the Cincinnati Jewish old folks' home got the same gourmet dinner that he and his family ate on the day of his thirty-fifth wedding anniversary. He never told anyone about this publicly—empathy simply came naturally to him. But the feelings of solidarity for Jews in Europe became welded on one unforgettable day in 1946 when the whole neighborhood received leaflets with an article by the well-known journalist Dorothy Thompson[16] about the Nazi death camps.

For the first time in our Cincinnati lives, the names Dachau, Auschwitz (Polish: Oświęcim), and others became engraved in our minds. My parents had heard, in general, about the Nazis and their program to make Europe *Judenrein*.[17] But here was specific evidence, details that have since become common knowledge but which, at the time, produced a very deep trauma. In many important ways, no one conscious at that time ever outlived that trauma.

These events were a major factor in changing my family's and our community's views toward Zionism. After the State of Israel was declared and established in 1948, all of these groups gave it enormous psychological and material support. The old anti-Zionist slogans were quickly forgotten. In Dad's view, who could oppose a homeland and state for the remnants of the people who went through the Nazi Holocaust? Just as they had been ignorant of East European Jewish history before, now they were equally ignorant of the history of the Middle East, of Islam, of the Arab peoples, and of all the incredible complications of politics and human feelings in that part of the world.

When all this information was coming forward in the year 1948, my father suffered his first major heart attack. I was still a student at the University of Chicago when I heard my mother's frightened and shocked voice over the telephone, and, within a few days, I heard Dad's uncharacteristically weak and fuzzy (but still deep in the bass register) voice. He was obviously determined to fight his way back to strength and life.

Despite my father's heart attack, he continued to work with full force. With no small amount of courage, he determinedly continued his life in the world of business, of Jewish affairs, and of baseball (last but not least!).

---

16 Dorothy Thompson (9 July 1893-30 January 1961) was a very popular American columnist back in the days of World War II. It was her columns right after the war that played an enormous role in arousing peoples' consciousness of the hideous things that had happened under the Nazis.

17 *Judenrein* is a German expression, meaning literally a territory completely free of Jews. It was a slogan of the Nazis who intended to make Germany *Judenrein*; they either threw them out of the country or executed them. The term is connected with one of the terrible, tragic chapters in Jewish history.

When Bill Veeck, Branch Rickey, the head of the Mutual Benefit Life Insurance Company in Newark, New Jersey, or the head of the Union of American Hebrew Congregations in Cincinnati and later in New York City (there was a battle royal over the move, with Dad championing his beloved hometown) heard the phone ring at seven o'clock in the morning, they immediately knew who was calling. Dad was famous for his love of the telephone and of the early morning hours when he was raring to go! His office had all the latest (for the 1950s) telephone equipment and he loved to talk directly into the loudspeaker, without using his hands for the phone. He was one of the first to use a car phone, and God knows how many accidents he barely avoided while fiddling with the damned thing.

Although Dad loved his car phone, Mom was not a fan. Mom, after enduring many a call from his business friends in his car, who were *oohing* and *ahhing* over the new toy, finally issued the only threat she knew always worked with him: "Choose! It's either me or the phone, not both!" The phone was yanked out of the car, and traffic safety in Cincinnati improved dramatically. To my knowledge, Mom used this tactic on only one other occasion: Bill Veeck tempted Dad to come back into baseball with him in the 1940s or '50s. Mom remembered the dark days when a misplayed ball or an unexpected rainstorm could mean financial catastrophe. "Choose! It's either me or baseball." The world of insurance could rest easy in the knowledge that its star would remain stable in its firmament.

I used to visit Dad's office on the thirty-fifth floor of Cincinnati's highest building, the art deco Carew Tower. Out the window, one could see the Ohio River snaking its way around the many curves its course made in the landscape. Dad loved it there, right in the heart of the business district of Cincinnati, not far from the house where he was born. His office was absolutely clean and neat with the small file of potential clients at his elbow. He had a humorous photograph on the wall, showing him sleeping, feet on the desk: the opposite of reality.

In the summer of 1949 I used his office, at his invitation, to study the Russian text of Tolstoy's *War and Peace*. During that time, I learned something about his working milieu. His work pace did not surprise me, but what did surprise me was the jealousy some of the other salesmen felt toward him. I was accustomed to hearing grateful words from the national administrators of the insurance company. In my naiveté and inexperience, I hadn't considered how this would play with other salesmen. Dad made no attempts, as far as I know, to socialize or even chat with them, and they considered him cold and distant. This was a dissonant picture compared to what I knew of him, and I didn't let it get close to my consciousness.

Baseball versus Academia

One time in Chicago, Dad tried to introduce me to Bill Veeck, no doubt remembering how William Veeck Sr. had once introduced the young, hot-dog-bun-cutting Bill Jr. to Dad. Alas, the introduction didn't take! Bill was far too upset and absorbed; at that moment he was going through a divorce and selling his interest in the Cleveland baseball team, which he had brought to championship competition. He was very much interested in helping young men with an academic bent, but at that instant, he just could not concentrate on extraneous people or issues. Dad was disappointed but knew how to bide his time, in spite of his normal impatient attitude.

Some years later, in 1955, my father sent his then Washington-based son to visit Bill Veeck in eastern Maryland where the baseball maverick chose to live in temporary, self-imposed exile. Bill greeted me with words of welcome: "You must be hungry." He signaled to his daughter, and she automatically brought ham and bread to the table. Bill quietly said, "Honey, I think the man likes turkey." He immediately remembered that my father kept kosher, and he had no idea whether or not I did the same. He simply showed his sensitivity to my father's custom.

Bill's sensitivity along these lines came out a few years later in the late 1950s when Dad invited me, by that time a Harvard graduate student, to come to a Yankees World Series game in New York City. As usual, Dad's friends and clients—numbering in the hundreds—were pressing him for hard-to-get tickets. Dad deeply loved this time of year, and the wheeling and dealing around the tickets satisfied him at a profound level of his soul. One man in particular was angry about not getting a ticket, and Dad could only throw up his hands and explain that he had no more.

I worried about his heart condition and the strain and said, "Dad, let him have my ticket." This man immediately refused: "Good heavens, no! I wouldn't think of taking your son's ticket. I'm not that kind of person, please! Don't think badly of me!" I replied, "It's all right. There's a Soviet film in town, and I would rather see it than go to the World Series." When those words came out of my blasphemous mouth, Dad gave a look that combined the agony of Prometheus bound to the rock (with a bird pecking at his liver) with the anger of Achilles after the death of Patroclus. Then he sighed and said, "Go ahead, take the ticket; that young idiot really would prefer to see the goddamned Russian film."

That evening, Bill Veeck invited everyone to a party. Word had gotten around that Dad really did have one weirdo of a son. Only Bill Veeck understood my non-baseball passion, and he asked in an utterly straight tone of voice, "Irwin, how was the film? Was the plot suspenseful?" (In a Soviet film, yet!) "Did the action play well?" He was quite willing to admit the theoretical possibility that a Soviet Russian film might be just as absorbing as a Yankees World Series baseball game. Dad knew that such a possibility simply didn't exist.

During the 1950s, when I was in Washington, DC, and then in Cambridge, Massachusetts, I had to watch and learn about my father from a distance—not only geographically but also psychologically. I was already a young man, developing along very different lines from those in my father's life and experience. Yet we both valued our contact, and he went to great lengths to keep our relationship strong: he always wrote twice a week, although all too often with haste and about trivial matters. He was sometimes puzzled, sometimes bemused, by the fact that his son, for whom he had foreseen a glorious career in the insurance business, was becoming a specialist in, of all things, Russian studies. Still, Russian and Soviet politics would burst out in public view from time to time, and he once cut through the usual trivia in his letters when Beria, former head of the dreaded Soviet secret police, was suddenly convicted of what they called "treason" and quickly murdered. My father wrote to me that I, as a specialist, "had of course long seen this coming." His letter crossed one of mine in the mail, in which I had written: "I was never so surprised in my life."

Rabbi Heller

About this time my father went through an episode that I would call one of his shining hours. The other rabbi at the I. M. Wise Temple was a publicly revered figure, Rabbi James G. Heller. A large, imposing figure, often in a robe with PhD bars on it, a real connoisseur of classical music, he spoke in well-organized sentences and in stentorian tones (unlike Rabbi Wohl's meandering talks). His voice was deep, and his language sounded to my young, inexperienced ears like the Oxonian English of a British aristocrat. I often heard him thunder, "The congregation is in apostasy!" Aside from my realization that it was something bad, probably not listening to enough of his sermons, I hadn't the foggiest notion what the congregation was in, nor do I suspect did ninety-nine percent of the good Cincinnati Jewish burghers sitting around me and nodding their heads.

Dad, closely allied with Rabbi Wohl, was temperamentally unable to understand Rabbi Heller with sympathy. Perhaps that was his fault; his intellect never reached those high spheres so knowingly embraced by Rabbi Heller, especially in realms of music. Eventually, there came to be a kind of suppressed dislike, or coolness, between my father and Rabbi Heller, although they both were willing to work for the good of the congregation and Judaism. The most prominent people in the congregation admired Rabbi Heller and considered him an ornament to all Cincinnati Jews, a jewel in their collective crown, so to say.

Then in the 1950s, Rabbi Heller announced that he was divorcing his wife of many years, the mother of his beloved daughters about whom he always spoke with eloquent pride, to marry the wife of a prominent congregant, one of his longtime supporters and partisans. In the relatively small and compact bourgeois Cincinnati Jewish community of the 1950s, the news fell with almost the impact of a bomb. Almost all of Rabbi Heller's earlier supporters quickly distanced themselves from the unhappy man. They became even more furious when he indicated that he would go to New York and position himself among the powerful politicians in the American-Israeli establishment, unlike the provincial Cincinnati milieu he had previously served.

After this shocking news from Rabbi Heller, the congregation gathered to prepare their response. Almost all of them wanted to cut Rabbi Heller off from the congregation without a dime. Although my father had fought with Rabbi Heller for close to thirty years, he stood before the mob thirsting for Rabbi Heller's livelihood and reputation, held up his arm, and said, "Stop! You are acting like a lynch mob! Are you Jews? Shame on you!" Dad, the inarticulate man who barely finished fourth grade, told them in his raspy, ungrammatical bass articulation, that "He don't [*sic*] leave here without a full pension and a decent settlement for the innocent children who still need an education. This man served the congregation honorably for decades. If you try to do anything else, you'll do it only over my dead body." To this day I can imagine the "ponim fun dizer yehudim" [the faces of these Jews] at the sound of Dad's words spoken for the benefit and welfare of this man.

Jewish Traditions

My father joyously participated in all of the many religious ceremonials during the Jewish year. Perhaps his most joyous time was during *Hakkofos*,[18] around the autumn holiday of *Sukkos*[19] when all of the Torahs from the largest to the smallest (perhaps fifteen or twenty of them) were carried around the congregation of the lovely Plum Street Temple in Cincinnati, one of the real American gems of synagogue architecture. In the midst of those wonderful, deep colors and the complicated arch work and beam work that made up the interior—and the lusty singing of the choir—men and boys would carry the Torah to signify the exaltation of having completed a year of reading through the complete Hebrew scrolls of the Pentateuch and of starting a new year's cycle of again reading the same Hebrew scrolls. It represented the wonderful, compulsive, book-drenched essence of the conventionally defined Jewish soul.

---

18 *Hakkofos* is the joyous procession with the carrying of many Torah scrolls around the synagogue. The holiday calls for the construction of open-roofed booths decorated with fruits of the harvest (Abraham Lincoln formalized Thanksgiving on the basis of his biblical reading about *Sukkos*). The holiday also involves a palm branch with sprigs of willow and myrtle—all together called a *lulav* (Hebrew: לוּלָב). It is held together with an *esrog* (Hebrew: אֶתְרוֹג)—a lemon-like fruit with fragrance, but no flavor. The whole unit is shaken while reciting a Hebrew blessing—an invocation for favorable weather and a symbol of the whole human personality: willow for humility, upright palm branch for righteous pride, and *esrog* for fragrance of moral decency.

19 *Sukkos* (Hebrew: סֻכּוֹת, "Feast of Booths, Feast of Tabernacles") is a weeklong Jewish holiday celebrating the harvest and the annual end of reading passages of the Torah (first five books of the Old Testament). It also is the time to start again with the reading of the world's beginning in Genesis.

My father and Rabbi Wohl saw to it that I was included among the Torah carriers, especially the smaller Torahs. At that point father and son felt very close together, and Dad liked that. At the end of the procession, a few Torahs were placed on stands on the *bimah*, the raised space in front of the congregation. Of course, people tried to be careful, but there was a tremendous atmosphere of excitement that could—and sometimes did—lead to clumsiness. Lo and behold, on one of those occasions in the 1930s, Dad's hands slipped and the Torah, instead of slipping into its stand, fell on to the floor with a great clatter, followed by an almost immediate "ooh, ahh" from the congregation. Dad immediately picked it up, kissed it, and finally put it in its stand. Everyone started buzzing because there is a well-known Jewish tradition that he who drops a *Sefer Torah*[20] must fast for thirty days. Everyone was as sure as I was that he would not do that. The event proved us correct. Dad assiduously went about his ceremonial duties, as if to apologize for the accidental insult to the Torah, but that was the end of it.

Dad was accepting of all Jews. On *Rosh Hashanah*[21] and *Yom Kippur*, Dad spent many hours in the I. M. Wise Temple, a place of Reform Judaism. But he also spent many hours among his friends in the Conservative and Orthodox synagogues. His own traditions and memories were very close to the way they practiced *davening*,[22] and he felt very much at home among them. He was truly a person who, at the emotional level, could easily transcend the divisions among Jews: Orthodox versus Reform, German Jews versus Polish and Russian Jews, skullcap wearers versus non-skullcap wearers, Hebrew language prayers versus English language prayers, etc. On the other hand, whenever he ran into Orthodox

---

20 *Sefer Torah* (Hebrew: ספר תורה) is literally the "Book of Torah." The Torah, together with the extensive commentary of the Talmud, forms the basis of Jewish law. The Torah scroll is carefully inscribed by hand following detailed rules of procedure and its completion calls for a special celebration.

21 *Rosh Hashanah* (Hebrew: ראש השנה, "Head of the Year") is a celebration of the New Year according to the Jewish lunar year. The Bible calls it the first day of the seventh month. The ancient celebration of the first month (in spring) celebrated the birth of new lambs for nomadic people. When Jews turned from being nomads to farmers, the seventh month (in autumn) celebrated the harvest.

22 *Davening* (Yiddish דאַוונען *davnen*, "to pray") is the Jewish form of prayer chanting. It is a beautiful sound when done by a person who can carry a tune.

condescension or sneering at Reform custom, he became extremely angry. There was something inside of him at an emotional level that simply could not abide snobbery. To me, that consideration of others was perhaps his most endearing and admirable trait.

Although Dad was very accepting of all Jewish divisions, he had little sympathy with the Yiddish language and its culture, much to my sorrow. Whether it was a vestige of the old Germanic prejudice—or perhaps his resentment of some Jews who insisted on trying to force it on him at public meetings—he kept it out of his life and consciousness. It was not from him that I learned to respect and love Yiddish and even teach its culture later on. I can still hear the resentment in his voice when he told me, "They asked if they could speak Yiddish. Of course there are always loudmouths who will yell in such a situation, and they did so. The result was that I couldn't understand a thing."

Dad's Greatest Pleasures

One of the congregational customs he liked most—it could hardly have been called a traditional ceremony—was the annual fathers and sons dinner. He liked it for the idea it represented: he adored the memory of his own father and always carried my grandfather's photo inside a large pocket watch. He hoped for a similar relationship with me even though we couldn't work together in the horse business, as life had permitted in the 1890s.

Dad liked the evening because he was able to bring baseball players over to talk after dinner. To people at that time and place, few things could have been more exciting than to meet the Cincinnati Reds baseball players who were in the center of civic attention and emulation. Many of these men had spent evenings at our house when I was young, and I shared the general feeling. A few of them were even interesting gentlemen. I remember Bill McKechny, the astute manager, and Frank McCormick, a fine gentleman married to the daughter of the official hunter of the Austro-Hungarian Hapsburg dynasty. Bill Veeck also was an extraordinary individual and a fine speaker. Somehow the Jewish fathers and sons assembled there felt that nobility rubbed off on them, a little bit, and Dad always felt proud and happy at these events.

There were hundreds of times when he saw to it that groups of people could attend baseball games. Whether it was orphanages, religious groups of any persuasion, schoolchildren, scholars, rabbis, or any other configuration of individuals who came to his attention—Dad knew that their proper pre-taste of paradise lay in the baseball park. I can hardly count the number of people, some of them very far from your usual association with baseball watchers, who came away—numbly or otherwise—entranced with new concepts of a curve ball, park attendance numbers, managerial slyness, foot position for outfielders, Branch Rickey's coup, etc. All this went on with a steady stream of purchases from the food vendors who always experienced joy passing Dad's box. I wonder how the hot dog and ice cream manufacturers are doing now?

Dad was also a welcome visitor to the Cincinnati Reds dugout before the games. The players and managers knew him as a source not only of information about the game, based on years of hard-earned experience, which they respected, but also as an advisor on family and financial problems. They would often take him off to a corner of the dugout or along the walkway to the players' showers and lockers and engage him in obviously earnest conversation. He always seemed to give them a positive word, or at least they looked relieved after talking with him. As in many places, he took an obvious relish in being among them and being part of their ongoing lives.

My father got his greatest pleasure from the late 1940s onward in his grandchildren. Marjorie and her husband, Orren, had three; Carolyn and her husband, Victor, had two; and my wife, Vivian, and I had three. Whenever Dad came into a room where the grandchildren were, he would immediately stimulate them to louder and more boisterous play, and they would respond to him with lots of real joy. As far as I know, that was true when the grandchildren were small. They seemed to sense immediately in him the directness and emotional honesty of a small child.

I shall never forget his visit to Cambridge, Massachusetts, when my oldest son, Martin, was about four or five years old. Dad gave himself completely to the desires of Martin, who was thrilled with streetcars, buses, and subway trains. The two of them went all over Boston, taking enormous numbers of public vehicles. Dad came home pale and exhausted but deeply satisfied with himself. Martin was in seventh heaven, barely satisfied with the first dent he had made in trying out the public transportation system and was eager for more.

Later on, as the grandchildren grew up, I think it was harder for my father. For all of his wonderful childlike spirit, he could not help but look at the radically changing 1960s as a fantastically different time and society from what he knew of the 1890s and first decade of the twentieth century. He tried very hard not to let his feelings of alienation show—he really felt the old family love—but his every statement to the young people betrayed his old-fashioned ways of evaluating business and family life.

I remember his amazement at how my own kids opened presents that he purchased for them. He wanted them to open the presents swiftly, agog at the abundance that he loved. Instead, Martin and his sister Alice opened each one slowly, determined to play with and master each, before turning to the next. Indeed, they didn't even suspect there would be a "next." Dad found this baffling and even incomprehensible. His childish impulsiveness was more powerful than theirs!

Later Years of Life

In the late 1950s or early 1960s, Dad had a sudden onset of very uncharacteristic, long-lasting depression—for at least six months, maybe longer. He suddenly became listless, uninterested in work or activity, and very sad. The only times I could remember that were in any way similar were the early mornings in the 1940s when he would drive me to school at a quarter to seven on his way to work. He would bite his nails to the quick, wordlessly, with groans and sighs. I had assumed this just reflected the high tension and stress of his daily work. But the longtime depression was very upsetting to everyone around him. We all tried to buck him up. I wrote several long letters in which I told him what he already knew: how much he always meant to me and how much I wanted to see his old, energetic self come back. He thanked me for very good desires, but he indicated that he still felt listless and limp. Whether or not this had anything to do with his perception of the changed ways of the generation of the 1960s, I don't know. I can only speculate.

However Dad felt about the changing times, he snapped out of the depression fairly suddenly, as far as I could tell. He returned to several years of hard, energetic work in the 1960s. Unfortunately, at that time his troubles with his back, what he called lumbago, got worse, and he was often flat on his back for days at a time. For him, the enforced idleness was pure hell; after his family, work was his greatest pleasure in life. I urged him to take time to write his memoirs. He replied, with some impatience and annoyance, that he was no writer, and who in hell would be interested, anyway? I said we'd all like to learn, from his direct and firsthand experience, about horses, World War I, early Fords, baseball, the Depression, insurance, Judaism in America, etc. His only reply was "Aw, stop bothering me, I hurt!" So I stopped.

About six weeks later, Dad called and said, "Well, did you finish your book [my dissertation] yet? I finished mine." "What book is that?" I asked. His reply: "*The Life of Sidney Weil.*" He had gotten himself together, cancelled all appointments, and, after a one-sentence false start with a tape recorder, had written down what he remembered. I am very proud to have it today, and I'm proud that I nagged him into doing it.

In the latter years of his life, he thought very highly of two associates, both of them religious Catholics whose conviction deeply resonated with his own sincere religiosity. One was his longtime secretary and assistant, Aileen Ryan, who was a fine person of profound culture and who immediately saw past Dad's rough manners and speaking. Many times she forced me to see the strength and sense behind everything he did. She had a thoroughly conservative, traditional mentality and understood how Dad was looking at the world of the 1960s. Dad said many times that without her, he would have been at least fifty-percent less effective than he was.

The other person Dad highly admired was George Fee, a lawyer and political figure in Cincinnati. George was highly educated for that time and place, and he was deeply repulsed by all sham and high-flown rhetoric and hypocrisy. In my father, George saw a rough and direct man, pushed by the hand of God. George was amused at his friend Sidney for having produced a pup with pretensions to education and scholarship. Dad always pushed me, whenever I was in Cincinnati, to talk with George Fee and Aileen Ryan. They gave me the intellectual and emotional challenge that he would have liked to articulate.

In the beginning of January 1966, I moved to Evanston, Illinois to start teaching at Northwestern University. Dad loved to hear about my autumn 1964 conversation with Northwestern's old-fashioned businessman dean, Simeon Leland—a man similar, in some ways, to my father. Dean Leland talked in a rough, Hoosier way, and his tone brooked no nonsense. He was also a kind and generous man, interested in other people. Dad loved the fact that, in spite of my utter lack of business sense, I made what sounded to him like a good business deal (at last!).

Shortly after Vivian and I moved to our new home on January 14, 1966, I returned to Evanston following an afternoon and evening at the University of Chicago to find about ten urgent messages to call Cincinnati. The true import hit me like a stone to the head: my father was dead. Never again would I feel the live emanations of that great heart.

A thousand people attended the funeral service at the I. M. Wise Temple. One man came across the country, as a special funeral guest, and he beautifully articulated his very real feelings for my father. His name: Bill Veeck. In a nationally syndicated article that appeared in many newspapers on Sunday, 23 January 1966, Bill Veeck wrote:

> Sidney Weil: Remarkable Man, Friend
> I had the Phoenix sports page before me.
> It was a one-column story one inch long.
> "Former Reds' owner dies on Parkway." It was about Sidney Weil, who was owner of the Cincinnati Reds from 1929 to 1933.

Sidney Weil.

(From left to right) Irwin's sister Carolyn and mother with Irwin behind them. Celebrating Irwin's mother's ninetieth birthday in Cincinnati.

As the dimly-lighted plane sped on through the darkness, I thought of Sidney, for I was on my way to Cincinnati to attend his funeral.

One column inch was all they gave the man who along with Harry Grabiner, Satchel Paige, and Casey Stengel made up my cast of "most unforgettable men."

I'd like to tell you about my Sidney Weil, the man I knew for almost forty years, about kindliness, piety, thoughtfulness, generosity, humility, intelligence and courage.

I'd like to tell you about a remarkable man.

He was my daddy's friend first, from the day he bought the Reds back in 1929 before the market crashed[.] Sid owned the biggest Ford agency and the first multi-level garage in Cincinnati. The earth was young and everyone knew the market would never stop going up.

It did.

Sid lost his agency and his multi-level garages, and finally his ball club. That was the last to go because he was a baseball fan. Not the publicity seeking, glamor-bitten kind.

He was the real 24 carat article. The entire National League tried to help him hold on, not that it had any success (a bank sold him out, behind his back, while he was getting the clubowners' support), but it did try.

You might think such an experience would embitter a man, or at least corrode his interest just a little. You might think that, but you'd be wrong. At least you would have been wrong about Sidney Weil, as Bill DeWitt, present Reds' owner, can attest. You see, Sidney was his best customer—33 seasons later.

While Sidney's romance with the game never ended, his interest in ownership was never rekindled. When I offered him a piece of Cleveland, St. Louis, and Chicago, he just laughed.

"I like it better this way," he'd say. "I have all the fun and none of the headaches."

But he sent me to his friend, Mark Steinberg, when I desperately needed extra scratch in St. Louis. And Mark bought, more on Sidney's say-so than my pitch.

After 1933, Sid became my friend. The next year, for instance, he hunted me down in Wrigley Field. He finally found me hidden behind casks of mustard, rounds of beef, and a mountain of red-hot rolls. As we sliced buns, we talked. We spoke of baseball, my Daddy, Branch Rickey, and Leo Durocher, of World War I and the prewar days when Sid crisscrossed the Middle West buying horses and mules. Although he never said so, I'll bet he was a good horse trader. We spoke of how important it was to keep looking forward. Mostly I listened (unusual in itself) for Sidney was an example of the "forward look." He had made the transition from horses to automobiles. He had flown to Chicago.

He was heading a new established insurance school. The crash may have diminished his assets but not his zest and enthusiasm. At 43 he embarked on a new career in insurance. And that, my friends, takes guts.

Years later, when things were better for both of us, I asked him to sell me some insurance (I asked him). He wrote the policy for half as much as I thought I wanted.

"Don't get carried away, Bill," he said. "I want to sell you insurance, want you to have enough, but if you want more now, you'll have to buy it from someone else."

This was from a perennial member of insurance's million dollar round table, from the man who led his company in sales more times than any other man in its history. Maybe this was one of the reasons why.

I remembered so many little things, nice things, the sort of things that take time, energy, and thoughtfulness. They were the things the rest of us always talk about doing, but somehow forget. He didn't. (He wrote himself notes and stuck them in the buttonholes of his coat until he was festooned from head to foot with ivory slips of paper.) Seemingly nothing was ever too much trouble.

He called me once a week—more often, when I was in trouble—sometimes just to say hello, usually with advice (good) and encouragement.

He sent me saltwater taffy from Atlantic City (a weakness) and an out-of-print copy of Van Loan's "Easy Pickings," which I needed to complete my set. "Just happened to stumble over it in a book store," he said. "Put in an order with every bookseller in New York," said the dealer. "Then called up once a week to see why nothing had happened."

To Sidney, friendship was a two-way street. You did things for friends and expected them to do likewise—no, not really expected, hoped. Finding hotel rooms when there were none was routine for Sid. He asked nothing for himself, except World Series tickets. And here at least, Sidney was as other mortals. He could only sit in one seat.

I'll make a wager, even give odds, that Sidney Weil had more friends than anyone in the country, in the strangest places. And wealthy or broke, if you asked them: "Why?" their replies would sound like a broken record. "D'ya know what Sid did for me?"

This is the man who got a one-column, one-inch note. But do you know something? He didn't need more ink because those who knew him will never forget.[23]

---

23   Bill Veeck, "Sidney Weil: Remarkable Man, Friend," *Pittsburgh Press*, January 23, 1966, http://news.google.com/newspapers?nid=1144&dat=19660122&id=y2ocAAAAIBAJ &sjid=SU8EAAAAIBAJ&pg=7531,3109750.

After Bill died, I attended his memorial service in a Catholic cathedral. The priest related a story to the assembled mourners about Bill's final hours. He mentioned that, as a precautionary measure, he administered the last rites to Bill. Afterwards, the phone rang and it was Bill's inquiring wife. Bill informed her, "The good Father just administered the last rites to me. Now I'm completely kosher." The priest conceded that this was not quite the word he would have used, but he understood what Bill meant, as my dad would have.

Chapter Two

Early Years and Education of Irwin Weil

Youth is a disease that can be cured.

—Irwin Weil

Introduction

George Washington had a terrible temper. When roused, he could make a genuine fuss. Consequently, when his veteran officers came to him with the usual eighteenth-century demands for title and landed estates, he blew his stack. He wanted to establish a republican democracy, not a new territory for newly ennobled landowners. However, when our country's Father calmed down, he generously offered them land on the new Ohio River bank settlement called "Losantiville" (literally, "city opposite the mouth of the Licking River"). Since the veteran officers had organized a society named after a Roman general, Cincinnatus, who after the war returned to the plow, they renamed the settlement "Cincinnati," using the Latin plural form.

Namesake

It was into this city, beautiful in its hills overlooking the river called Ohio—the native American Indian word for "Beautiful"—that a Jewish baby was born on baseball's opening day in 1928. His advent caused his mom to do something very rare for a patriotic Cincinnatian, and something she otherwise never did from 1919 to 1990—she missed the opening game; it's hard to give birth when you're at a ballgame! Dad heard my first cries, and reportedly said, "Ugh, I can tell by the cry—it's another girl!"

I had a grandfather named Isaac, or Yitzkhak. I never knew him; he died before I was born. But from what my father said and the way other people talked, he must have been quite the diplomat. He was a much-loved figure in the Jewish community, very highly respected, and my dad thought the world of him. So, when I was born, they naturally wanted to give me his name. However, had he been alive, my parents couldn't have given me his name. In the Jewish tradition, you don't have a junior as long as the person is alive, because the *Malach HaMaves* (Angel of Death)[1] might make a mistake and get the wrong guy (apparently, this angel of death isn't good at using names). But since my grandfather had died before me, then I could be given his name.

Although my grandfather had already passed away, my parents didn't want to name me Isaac because they were afraid of anti-Semites. In my father's generation, Jews didn't quite feel comfortable in the United States. So instead, my parents used the name Irwin, which still sounds pretty Jewish. Anybody named Irwin is automatically pegged as Jewish. Most people, when they hear my name, mispronounce it as "Irving," because they're so accustomed to that. But since Irwin is a little bit less Jewish-sounding, they gave me that name.[2]

When I'm called to the Torah, I'm Yitzkhak. When you're called to give one of the blessings before they read the Torah, they call your name, and there's a special ritual name when they say your name. I'm Yitzkhak ben Schlomo, that is, Isaac the son of Solomon (my father's name was Sidney, but his Hebrew name was Schlomo).

Growing Up

Although my experience in Russia is a long story, with many meanderings, my beginnings started as I grew up in the late 1920s and '30s in the

---

1   *Malach Hamaves* is the Hebrew word for the angel of death. In Jewish folklore, a son is never named with the same first name of a living father—the idea being that the *Malach Hamaves* might come for the wrong person when it was time for death.

2   Irving Howe (11 June 1920–5 May 1993), a wonderful critic who was also one of the most truly socialist socialists in the United States, yet an anti-Stalinist, tells the story of when the magi came to Jesus, one of them tripped over the doorsill, and said, "Jesus Christ!" When the magi said that, Mary turned to Joseph and said, "You know, it's not a bad idea. It's better than Irving."

city of Cincinnati, Ohio—a very conservative place when it came to issues of national or international politics. Suffice it to say that in 1940, Cincinnati was the only large city in the United States where a majority of the voting population cast its ballots for Wendel Wilke, the republican opponent of President Roosevelt. As one might imagine, there were not many friendly voices to be heard there about the reality of the USSR.[3] Most people in Cincinnati would have had no idea of the distinction to be made between the political term "Soviet" and the national term "Russian."

I can well remember the signs in Cincinnati store windows that proudly proclaimed: "America: love it or leave it!" This sign was openly addressed to anyone who might have sympathies toward the Soviet Union or to any kind of socialist or communist ideas. I also remember the accusatory articles in the local newspapers toward a few young, presumably misguided people who were plastered with the label "communist." One of them happened to be a teacher of mine, whom I had always found to be a rather sympathetic person with a reasonably sensible head on his shoulders. Naturally, I saw all of this with very young and uneducated eyes. I think it very likely that such an atmosphere was typical of the United States at that time.

In the 1920s, when my father was doing very well financially, the family moved into a nice house in the Jewish part of Cincinnati. It was in that house that I spent the first five or six years of my life. My first memory takes me back to the early 1930s. It was a typical, extremely hot, Cincinnati summer day. I was on the porch rolling a small toy truck around the floor when I suddenly saw a caterpillar wiggling along the floor. "Aha!" I thought. "My first customer!" I put the poor insect in the truck and proceeded to give it a real excursion around that part of the house. It wiggled mightily, but the body stayed in the truck. I was quite proud of my work as a chauffeur and that may have contributed to my first

---

3   The Union of Soviet Socialist Republics (often known as the USSR) was the governmental entity set up by the Bolsheviks after the 1917 Revolution. The idea was that it should be nationalist in form and socialist in content. Each of the sixteen internal republics would have its own Soviet (a word for "council" or "congress"). Originally it was supposed to resemble a democracy run in a parliamentary manner, but it very quickly dissolved into a dictatorship in which the Soviets simply followed the orders of the Party.

ambition: to become a loyal and skillful bus driver and provide mobility to both caterpillars and people.

But I did have sense enough to make my world entry into a place with a history analogous to the country of my future professional interest: a city whose name had been changed for political reasons, and whose baseball team bore a name friendly to Soviet Russia: the "Reds." In spite of my almost immediate co-natal arrival with the Great Depression, 1930s Cincinnati remained a haven of political conservatism, and I often heard the complaints: "That man in the White House [F. D. Roosevelt]— his New Deal program is ruining my business!" When, at the advanced age of eleven, I objected that the Weil Funeral Home of my uncle's was doing rather well, I was unceremoniously instructed to keep my foolish immaturity private.

But politics really didn't enter too deeply into my early upbringing. Much more immediate and more important were two powerful social dynamics that our family experienced almost in entirely local terms. The first one revolved around the exciting world of a baseball park housing what Cincinnatians proudly called the oldest established professional team in the United States. What my father had lovingly known as "Redland Field" had been changed (much to my dad's disgust) into the namesake of a local mogul—Crosley Field—and I was regularly transported there to watch a game whose rules and fine points were not explained to me as a very young child. It was always exciting to watch the crowd—in all its multifarious forms and sorts—react with bellowing (if sometimes profane and sometimes mellifluous) sounds to the dramatic events surrounding a hand-thrown ball solidly smacked into the air, and often into the held up mitt, in the midst of gracefully moving athletes. It was a special thrill when our beloved Redlegs got the advantage in the game.

But my real pleasure, as a very young kid at the park, was when my Aunt Fran—who for many years worked for the team's general managers— took the seventh inning as a time to invite me to partake of the food in the journalists' pressroom. To this day, seventy-five years later, I see genuine romanticism in a box of Cheez-its!

My baseball experience was also made warm by one of the players who became my friend and sharer of emotion—Ernie Lombardi,

Irwin Weil, age 4, with father Sidney Weil. Cincinnati Reds spring training.

a lumbering, slow moving giant of a catcher, whose bat could make the ball soar in a dramatic arc, slamming against the outfield fences. He had a particularly Italian sympathetic quality, which showed itself in his every movement. Of course, it didn't hurt that Fran, and her sister Leah, outrageously spoiled me: I got a wonderful, chocolate ice cream soda if Ernie got a hit in the game that day. My loving mother would tell them, "Don't spoil the child." I, of course, effectively subverted this maternal command by telling my doting aunts, *sotto voce*, "Don't listen to her—spoil me!"

Early School Years

Perhaps the deepest feelings in my professional life came through the medium of music. In my early years, this area was most strongly affected by the experience gained through activities at the Wise Center Religious School. The melodies and words we learned through Jewish holiday songs gave us a sense of life's joys. Only later did I learn that many of those melodies were poetic words grafted onto tunes that were crafted in many parts of the world.

One of our favorite songs connected with the holiday of *Purim*,[4] which celebrated the courage of the Biblical Queen Esther. Had it not

---

4   *Purim* (Hebrew: פּוּרִים, "lots") is a Jewish holiday that takes place in early spring. It celebrates the story of Queen Esther in the Bible who was married to the Persian

been for her, the villain named Haman would have executed a plot very similar to Hitler's evil madness. The song starts with the lines:

"Once there was a wicked, wicked man
And Haman was his name sir . . ."

I learned much later that these lines were applied to the melody of an English song:

"O landlord come and fill the bowl
Until the cup runs over . . ."

In addition to the mostly rollicking holiday songs, there was the musically peppery personality of the choirmaster at the Wise Center services, a German-born man appropriately named Herr Hugo Grimm. When I was very young, I sang for him a song connected with the Sabbath. I thought I had the melody and words under perfect command. Imagine my shock when I heard his passionate, German accented reply: "Vat's a matter with you, dummkopf ["dumb head"]? Don't you know how to count? Eins, zwei, drei, vier—now zing it right!" I soon learned, at a very tender age, that for Herr Grimm, the second-worst crime in the world was murder; the unforgivably worst crime was "zinging out of count," pronounced with an ominous *sforzando* on that last word.

Not the least of the attractions at the Wise Center was a group of very attractive girls. They added a very special kind of liveliness to our activities, usually expressed in a kind of mockery or teasing toward us boys. They would take advantage of any opportunity to make fun, especially if we did anything the least bit clumsy or stupid. Needless to say, we gave them many such opportunities.

Among the girls at the Wise Center, the most spirited soul appeared in a vivacious face and highly intelligent girl named Vivian Max. Viv and

---

king. Her cousin was Mordecai, who urged her to go to the king and explain the plot of the villain, Haman, who wanted to exterminate the Jewish people. It was an evil plot and it was to be stopped. Thanks to Esther and Mordecai the Jews were spared mass murder at that time. *Purim* means "Feast of Lots," and it's a joyous holiday often involving a theatrical dramatization of the events and costumes that show the beauty of Queen Esther.

I met in Sunday school when we were in seventh or eighth grade. It didn't hurt matters that she was very attractive—flashing eyes, beautiful figure, and a very sharp tongue. At an early age I found myself involuntarily thinking about her. Furthermore, she was bright as hell. Every academic honor that there was, she pulled it down. You couldn't argue with her because her logic was impregnable—you couldn't break it or go around it. She was the prettiest girl in the school, too. (She still is pretty, I think.) And what could I do? So, I went after her with all my force. From very early adolescence on, we have been close.

When I reached the age of twelve, I encountered a Cincinnati institution that gave some credit to the city's long ingrained conservatism at that time. There was a publicly supported six-year school for ages twelve to eighteen, Walnut Hills High School. It was college preparatory, attracting youngsters from all parts of the city. They had to pass an examination to enroll. The students and teachers of the school were demanding, but most of the teachers were understanding and sympathetic to young people. What sticks in my memory was the statement of a Latin teacher (we all had to take Latin): "Don't write this down in a notebook; put it in your head! If you lose such a notebook, you lose your education. If you lose your head, you have no need for an education!"

In addition to such capricious advice, we learned to handle the grammatical forms of a language that looked at the world in a non-English speaking way. After our work on Biblical Hebrew at the Wise Center, the study of Latin and Hebrew proved a highly complementary eye opener, the force of which was not reduced by a saying that I heard more than once in Cincinnati: "If English was good enough for Jesus Christ, it's good enough for me!"

The school also had a policy of annually presenting a play by Shakespeare. At the age of sixteen, I learned the lines of Master Ford in *The Merry Wives of Windsor*. The angry exclamations of a man who was trying to keep his wife from the would-be lecherous machinations plotted by Falstaff, one of Shakespeare's most wickedly charming characters, was a new experience for a Cincinnati youngster. The vocabulary introduced me to the incredibly broad imagination of the greatest poet in the English language.

What cannot be eschewed must be embraced.

> Why, then the world's mine oyster
> Which I with sword will open.

This was a harmony and a linguistic force I had not previously encountered, except in the powerful Hebrew words of the Biblical Psalms, and Shakespeare was doing it in my mother tongue.

A year later, at the age of seventeen, I experienced an even deeper impression of the beauty of Shakespeare's language. We took on the poetry of a much more mature Shakespeare: I was given the role of Prospero in *The Tempest*. Here was a chance to memorize some of the greatest and harmonious music of the English language. How could a raw, Midwestern American youth insinuate himself into the mind and soul of a powerful man who had been thrust from comfortable ducal power by familial treachery, cast together with a young daughter on a primitive island, together with some of Prospero's books? Through Prospero's incredible mental skills and mastery of the sounds and natural resources, Prospero manages to control the elements of weather and the island. Not only does he regain power and mastery of his life and that of his daughter, he also learned that:

The rarer action is in virtue than in vengeance. . . .

> We are such stuff as dreams are made on;
> And our little life is rounded with a sleep.

This was heady stuff for a seventeen-year-old, and it grabbed my mind and spirit in ways I never previously believed possible.

One very important way such an appreciation of the English language became possible was presented by one of the most influential teaching personalities I ever encountered. She was Frieda Lotze, an American woman who spoke a dialect close to British English. To my young ears, it sounded like the most elegant kind of spoken music. She listened with a strange power to every syllable I spoke, and somehow, without even consciously thinking, I came to realize the power and gorgeousness of the words that the text put in front of my eyes. There was a certain special kind of human mobility in her every move, gesture, and tone of voice.

It was simply impossible to even imagine anything crude or ignoble in her presence. When I think of her, I recall the Hebrew tradition of the existence of the *Lamid Vovnik*—one of the thirty-six totally righteous ones, for whose sake God refrains from destroying the world.[5]

The most lasting and permanent high school experience came in the presence of that same vibrant spirit whom I had met in religious school. Vivian Max was a very energetic and active figure at Walnut Hills High School. Her high intelligence and unusual energy was quickly recognized, and she became a strong and prominent personality in student life. I began to learn more about her family background, which was very unusual and striking.

Vivian's Family Background

Viv's family lived in a shtetl, or mestechko (little village),[6] where Jews had to live in those days. The families of Steven Spielberg and Leonard Bernstein also came from the same shtetl. Viv's maternal grandfather, Moshe Alter, was a fairly successful businessman, by standards of the Pale of Settlement.[7] He had a domestic leather-making enterprise. It had to be domestic—if it had been commercial, he never could have owned it by Tsarist law. He was rather successful that way and was well known in the *mestechko* called Sudilkov. Then came the 1917 Revolution.

Ukraine tried to separate itself, and there was a democratic socialist at the helm whose name was Petlyura. His idea was that everybody should

---

5   *Lamed Vovnik* is a term used in Jewish folklore. Although humanity in general was a pretty sorry sort that committed all kinds of sins and crimes, there were certain special people who lived saintly lives. There were thirty-six of them alive and it was their presence that caused God not to destroy the world. *Lamed Vovnik* was one of these thirty-six characters for whose sake God did not destroy the world. You could never know exactly who they were; the most unlikely-looking person could be a *Lamed Vovnik*.

6   A *shtetl* (Yiddish: שטעטל; Russian: *mestechko*) was a tiny village in Tsarist Russia that Jews were forced to live in. These little towns were located outside the large towns of Russia.

7   The Pale of Settlement ("pale" meaning a line drawn on a map) was a region designated for Jews that included a good part of Ukraine and White Russia, but excluded some of the major cities of Russia. The average Jewish person could not leave without special permission; however, there were people, such as members of the first or second merchants guild, who could travel outside the Pale of Settlement freely, but these represented a small percentage of the Jewish population. In February/March 1917 (old/new style calendar), the short-lived Provisional Government abolished the Pale of Settlement.

live together in Ukraine in equality, that there should be voting, that there should be a parliament, and so on. He really was what should be called, with a small "d," a democratic socialist. He saw to it that Jews would not be persecuted and subjugated to the kind of repression that had been the case in Russia. He got an army together that fought the Bolsheviks in the name of Ukrainian nationalism. The problem was that things eventually became so bad that he began to lose control of his people. The so-called *Petlyurovtsy* became *pogromshchiki* (those who carry out *pogroms*[8]) and were responsible for some awful *pogroms*, killing thousands of people.

Because so many people were killed, Petlyura himself, rather unfairly, got a bad reputation as a mass murderer. While in exile in Paris in the 1920s, he was assassinated by a Jew named Schwartzberg, who was tried but acquitted, even though he had murdered Petlyura, because his death was seen as justified revenge. But it was actually not Petlyura who had committed the *pogroms*; rather, it had been followers who got away from him. However, the judges weren't interested in such small details. At that time, a peasant hid Viv's grandfather under a barn for a week in order to protect him from the so-called *Petlyurovtsy*.

Viv's mother and her four sisters survived the turmoil of revolutionary times, 1917–1922. The bloody conflicts between the Red Army and the White Army[9] came down especially murderously on the Jewish population. Part of the family, including Vivian's mother, managed to emigrate through Amsterdam and New York to settle in Chicago. Two sisters escaped to Poland; Viv's mother urged them to come to the States, and they finally agreed. She got practically blood money; she worked very hard in a factory and saved money to pay for their travel expenses, which

---

8 *Pogrom* is a Russian word that refers to violence that broke out when mobs of sometimes intoxicated peasants would attack Jews, burn their houses, rape their women, and even murder people. They were hideous events that took place in Russia from the 1880s and became widespread during the murderous years of the Civil War (1917-1922).

9 The Red Army comprised the armed forces of the Bolsheviks who carried out the October Revolution of 1917 and overthrew the Tsarist regime. The Red Army was in opposition to the so-called White Army that was made up of people representing various political views spanning the far right to moderate left, many of which supported the February/March Revolution of 1917 (old/new style calendar).

was immediately pocketed by the man who had promised to arrange their trip to the United States. This happened twice, and by the time she'd gathered the money for the third time, the immigration law was passed, and Viv's sisters could not come. So they were in Poland when the Nazis came. What happened to them is what happened to many of the Jews in Poland; they were lost. For Viv's mother that was a terrible trauma. She went through some terrible times, and for anybody in the family, naturally, it was a trauma as well.

Viv's father, Moshe Max or Matsevich (in America his name was Morris Max) was born in Shepetovka. Most Russians know a little bit about this town because it was a railroad junction just about a mile and a half from Sudilkov. Her mother and father had never known each other there. Viv's father decided to emigrate in 1913, the year before the outbreak of World War I; he went eastward through China and Japan where he got involved in some commercial activities. After Moshe traveled through the East, he went across the Pacific Ocean and ended up in Cincinnati, where his brother had already settled. There, he opened a small clothing shop and was what was called a *jobber*, which means that he went around picking up men's clothes that were of high quality but odd sizes that would not easily sell. He would sell them to people in Cincinnati at bargain prices, but he would make out okay because he had also bought them for bargain prices. On one of his buying trips to Chicago, he went to a *landshaft*[10] gathering—where Jewish immigrants from the area including Sudilkov and Shepetovka gathered in a kind of mutual aid society. It was there that he met Viv's mom. So, Viv's folks were born about a mile and a half apart and both went around the world before meeting each other. They married and had two children: Vivian and her sister, Beatrice.

Viv's family spoke Yiddish, which was a normal language for Jews. My mother-in-law spoke a special kind of Russian. I later would realize, when she'd write to me, that it was sort of a mixture of Russian and Ukrainian. Vivian grew up understanding that colorful and rich culture.

---

10 In Yiddish *landshaft* refers to an immigrant community originating from the same region.

When they didn't want the kids to understand, they spoke Russian. The only Russian Viv later learned from me were the following phrases: "Da, ia ego zhena. Ochen' priiatno." (Yes, I'm his wife. Very nice to meet you.) "Akh, vy govorite po . . ." ("Oh, you speak . . .") and "Net, ni odnogo slova." ("No, not a single word.")

In Cincinnati, Viv's dad had a store right near the courthouse where a lot of lawyers and policemen gathered, and he got a very good reputation among them. For one thing, customers could buy very high quality clothes at low prices, and he was totally honest. He made a lot of friends among those people in Cincinnati. He died when Viv was a junior in high school, so I only knew him from maybe two or three encounters. When he spoke English, it was with a very heavy accent.

Vivian and I were on a camping trip when news came that her father had died. Naturally, that was quite a trauma for the whole family. Eventually Viv's mother had to go to work to support the family. Viv pretty soon got a scholarship to go to college. She got a job when she was a student at the University of Chicago. Her mother had to support the younger sister and herself, and life was not so easy for them. Then Viv's aunt in Chicago died, and her mother married the widower, whose name was Finkelstein. Viv's mother changed her name to Finkelstein when she remarried.

Viv's mother was really a rather interesting personality. She had a wonderful sense of humor, in spite of losing two sisters during World War II. She would say, "[President] Carter had no luck." When Hinckley tried to assassinate Reagan, she said, "If that had been Carter, he'd have got him. He just had no luck." If you asked her who the vice president was thirty years ago, she could tell you without hesitating. She kept her money under the mattress.

Viv and I would say, "Ma, you just can't do that. You've just gotta open a bank account." "I'm not going to open a bank account," she would say. Well, we practically had to beat her, but eventually she opened a bank account where she put her money. She wouldn't keep a ledger, but if you asked her, she could tell you down to the last penny how much she had. She had a remarkable mind.

Unfortunately, when she was in her nineties, she had a fall and broke her hip, which is terribly painful for someone at that age. A nurse came to give her therapy and asked her to throw a ball. Now, she had never thrown a ball in her entire life. "This is crazy! What do you mean, throw a ball?"

During *Seder*,[11] the meal for Passover, we always took turns reading, and she would read in Hebrew. Her Hebrew was a riot; it was a mixture of God-knows-what, Yiddish, and this and that, and the other. But, by God, she read it! She could be annoyingly obsessive at times, but to be with her was always a pleasure. That humor was absolutely unique. Viv got her brains from both her parents.

Musical Background

Nelle Custer Murphy was another teacher at my high school, who did for music what Shakespeare did for non-melodic harmony. What Herr Grimm had done for a small child, she did for an adolescent. She gathered together both a large a cappella choir and a small boy's octet. In each case, she enforced a musical and behavioral discipline that produced musical sounds capable of expressing the most moving kinds of youthful enthusiasm. Singing in that choir opened up for me the whole panorama of Christian experience—in some ways it evolved from my previous Jewish education and experience, and in some ways it opened a different take on the world.

The first experience of this type occurred around Christmastime when the carols made their presence known. Suddenly I found myself in a group that quite easily and naturally fell into the singing of melodies and words familiar from early childhood—"Oh come all ye faithful, joyful and triumphant …" I had never heard this before, and the melody and harmony were both quite attractive. Mrs. Murphy wanted all students to lift their voices and join in.

Although I could pick up a simple melody quite accurately and quickly, I had no idea of the words and found myself completely on the outside of an attractive musical experience. I decided then and there to learn the carols quickly and true to the melody. Since we all had to study Latin for

---

11 *Seder* (Hebrew: סֵדֶר, "order, arrangement") is a Jewish ritual feast that takes place during Passover. On the first and second night of Passover, many special prayers are said and songs sung before and after the feast. The *Seder* includes four glasses of wine based on ancient Roman traditions—quite unusual for a Jewish feast.

several years, this led me to a treasure house of Christian songs, both oriented toward Christmas and toward other parts of the Christian tradition. Naturally, Bach and Beethoven were not far behind.

This musical study of my early education was then expanded when our choir was invited to sing during Sunday worship services at various Cincinnati Protestant churches, most of them Presbyterian. In the beginning, it was quite a shock for me to find myself singing at a Protestant service; it was in many ways different from the Jewish services I knew so well. These feelings were especially strong when they passed around bowls containing what they called *communion*—then a new word for me. To my surprise, the contents were filled with what I immediately recognized as Jewish *matzo*, the unleavened bread I remembered from the Jewish Pesach-Passover. If anyone had told me then—what I later learned—that this *matzo* and grape juice represented (or even literally became) the flesh and blood of a Jew named *Yeshua* ("Jesus" in Greek), I can barely imagine what would have been my shock.

This connection with the Christian tradition was broadened when I became friends with Rabbi Wohl's elder son, named Theodore Herzl. Ted, as we called him, was named in honor of the founder of political Zionism and inspiring forefather of the state of Israel. He induced me to join him in attending some Baptist Revivalist services taking place in Cincinnati storefront churches. It was in the wartime 1940s, when many people came from Kentucky and Tennessee to work in the wartime factories. Ted had a magnificent bass voice—one would think he had a Cossack[12] background—and my baritone backed him up nicely.

---

12 Cossacks are people whose ancestors had run away from serfdom into the southwestern parts of the Russian Empire, just north of the Caucasus, where they set up independent farms. Eventually, up until the emancipation of the serfs in 1861, they became the only Slavic-speaking working people in the Tsarist regime who could have independent farms. They also learned from Arabic peoples, with whom they came in contact in the south, how to ride horses, and they became extraordinarily skillful and powerful horsemen. On the battlefield, they were a force to be reckoned with. The Cossacks eventually became the backbone of the Tsarist Russian Army. They were very loyal to the old regime and strongly opposed the new revolutionary army, so in Soviet times they suffered greatly. Since the fall of the Soviet Union, there have been efforts to try to reinstitute the famous Cossack soldiers.

When the people in the Baptist congregation heard our combination, they rushed us into their tiny choir. We lustily joined in their rhythmically pounding Christian revivalist music. It also had the flair of Kentucky folk music, with its southern US dialect in the words—"wind" rhymed with "end" and "friend." At that time, I obtained a virtual storehouse of Baptist tunes with strong elements of the Kentucky and Tennessee folk traditions.

In what ways could my Christian, choral experience be combined with my extensive emotional and intellectual grounding in the Jewish tradition? It was an interesting question. I can only say that after the initial shock of discovering the Christian ways, it came to feel only natural to put the experiences together. As I grew older and faced exposure to many different cultures far distant from my own grounding, I decided it would be a mistake to look down with condescension on anyone's religious traditions or beliefs. This perspective doesn't change the pleasure and inner strength I received, and continue to receive, from my original grounding in the Jewish temperament and character. It only strengthens my hold on the world. I would never use the word *pagan* as a derogatory term.

My father was particularly fond of my singing and often asked me to sing his favorite songs connected with our army and air force, whose members were fighting the Nazis. When I was fifteen years old, he said that I should get some professional help for my voice. My mother made some inquiries and found out that a former opera singer, Madame Kruse, was giving voice lessons in our neighborhood, so she took me to meet her. Mme. Kruse was amused to see how confidently I behaved in the first interview and agreed to take me through the necessary exercises to develop my voice.

I became most grateful to her for introducing me to the music of opera. She took me through many baritone arias composed by Verdi, Gounod, Mozart, Wagner, and others. To this day, when I listen to classical music on the radio, I suddenly recognize arias she taught me and can hardly resist the temptation to sing along. She taught me the proper pronunciation of French, German, and Italian, and she provided the basis for my later learning of these languages. I sometimes entertained the fantasy of becoming a professional opera singer, but common sense prevailed. I have a very pleasant amateur voice, but Chaliapin[13] need have no fear of competition!

Adolescent Politics and Experiences

In the 1940s, each Cincinnati public high school elected a representative to serve on the municipal City Council, and it was this group's responsibility to elect the boy mayor of the city. Consequently, the high school group of youngsters had the privilege of electing the "Boy Mayor for a Day." Walnut Hills High School selected several students to address an assembly of the whole school, and each one was supposed to deliver a campaign speech on how that student would represent the institution in front of a wider world.

I was chosen as one of the students to speak at the assembly. To my considerable surprise, I realized that my fellow students reacted very favorably to my words. I don't think it was necessarily a matter of intellectual agreement with any program that I would propose. It was rather a kind of emotional response, as if I hit a note that resonated pleasantly in their spirits. For whatever reason, I was sent forth to represent Walnut Hills on the day set up to establish the boy mayor.

The next step was a meeting of all the students elected from the various high schools. We got together and talked with each other for perhaps a half hour or so. Then came the moment when we would vote to select the one who would become mayor for a day. The result was a tie: the two highest candidates were another young man and myself. At that point, I made my first and last political deal. Another fellow came to me and offered to add his vote to my column if I would commit myself to vote for him as Vice Mayor. As a result of sealing that deal, I became Boy Mayor of Cincinnati for a day. As you can imagine, my executive powers were a bit limited. I could sit beside the florid-faced real mayor of the town. As speakers came to address the municipal Council, they would start by

---

13 Fyodor Ivanovich Chaliapin (13 February 1873-12 April 1938) was one of the great bass voices of the early twentieth century who became close to Gorky and other revolutionaries before the Revolution. After the Revolution, he went into emigration and was often heard in the United States. His voice was tremendously powerful and whenever you hear a recording of Chaliapin, you understand the force of music.

addressing the real mayor and then turn to address the boy mayor. I, of course, would sagely acknowledge their courtesy and discernment.

Things like this made my father very proud, and he always wanted me to call him at the office just as soon as they happened. On the other hand, attending Shakespearean plays was torture for him, a determined low brow. He even announced after my wordy evening as Prospero in *The Tempest* that he would never attend such a long-winded play again. This tension was made more complicated by my growing estrangement from watching professional baseball. He had taken great pride in taking me with him to the ballpark as a very young kid—in fact, perhaps as a kid who was too young. Although I retain some early and precious memories and deep associations with the park, I was only bored when I watched the game. It was hurtful and inconceivable to Dad that his only son, the flesh of his flesh, could not be interested in Dad's beloved game. After all, he was counting on me to follow in his footsteps and carry on his business and his name. He was convinced that I would make a cracker-jack life-insurance man because he saw that I was ambitious and could work hard.

In any case, it was through these various activities that I became a kind of adolescent celebrity to my fellow students and to some of the teachers at Walnut Hills High School. It didn't come, of course, without a certain amount of resentment and disdain from some students and teachers who wondered who this kid was who sat so confidently on his high horse. Many people in the school, including the principal, predicted that I would gain entry into the most prestigious university in the land, fair Harvard. But, there's an old and trustworthy cliché: Pride goeth before a fall. Soon enough, I was to realize the truth of that statement.

First Impressions of Russia

In 1941, the Nazi armies invaded the Soviet Union. Suddenly, it turned out that Russia was a country of heroes, who with their terrible and bloody sacrifices were opposing the hideous Nazi ideology and army. Especially around the time of the Battle of Stalingrad, the choruses of praise for our great Soviet ally reached a tremendous crescendo. Newspaper articles, popular songs about Soviet resistance, Hollywood movies—all of these things portrayed the USSR and Russia in the most flattering possible light.

The General Secretary of the Soviet Communist Party suddenly turned from an ogre into a friendly, pipe smoking "Uncle Joe." In our local high school, we learned English language translations of Soviet patriotic songs, the melodies and words of which, in both languages, I still bear in my head. Shostakovich[14] became a popular idol whose works filled the airways, yet we never dreamed that he might have had some difficulties with the mighty Soviet regime.

Furthermore, this perception of the Russians affected my family quite personally, since both husbands of my older sisters were in the US Army fighting first in France, then in Germany. My sisters hung on the daily news reports. You can perhaps imagine their joy when they read about the heroic Soviet exploits that relieved some of the pressures on their dear husbands. Pamphlets were left on our doorstep at least weekly vaunting the virtues of our great Soviet ally, even while they pictured the depths of Nazi barbarism in places with names we began to learn: Auschwitz, Dachau, Theresenstadt, and many others. Needless to say, names of Soviet camps like Magadan and Kolyma in the far northeast, and the murderous forest of Katyn, in the west, were never mentioned.

Flying

During World War II, at the age of sixteen, I decided I wanted to pilot a plane. As a younger kid, I was obsessed with airplanes and would build models out of pieces of balsa wood, stuck together with glue and covered with tissue paper. They were powered in flight by a tightly twisted rubber band attached to the tail and extended to a wooden propeller in front. To watch them fly brought great satisfaction. With remembered shame, I have to admit that I sometimes put a lighted match to them in order to produce a dramatic crash. A destructive impulse was certainly there.

---

14 Dmitri Dmitriyevich Shostakovich (25 September 1906-9 August 1975) was one of the greatest composers of the twentieth century. In many ways, his music broke with traditional Russian music that had been popular in the nineteenth and early twentieth centuries. At the outset of the Soviet regime, he was held in tremendous esteem. The Soviets would say: "You see, we in the Soviet Union also can produce great music." Later on, the government turned against him and he suffered greatly in the 1930s, but he nevertheless survived. He was an extraordinarily powerful composer and a very interesting individual.

To my mother's horror, my father thought that my getting a pilot's license was an excellent idea. He envisioned me as a salesman, travelling by air near and far, beating the competition to all customers, since I would travel by airplane while other salesmen would take surface transportation. Convinced that flying was both safe and efficient, my dad signed a contract, and my time as a student pilot commenced. I was put into the instructive hands of a woman pilot named Jo. While my mother spent additional hours at the I. M. Wise Temple earnestly praying to keep her foolish kid and the plane in the air, I went through the hours of instruction and practice necessary to receive a pilot's license.

Jo was stern, loud voiced, and thorough in her instruction. While we were flying in a small Piper Cub, not much faster than a car on the open highway, she showed me how to avoid danger. Most dramatically, she showed me how to avoid a spin, in which a plane can fall to the ground like a corkscrew going through a cork. She also demonstrated what a spin felt like—the ground seeming to turn like a carousel under your falling plane—and then showed how to recover. Since a plane can revolve around three axes—vertical, horizontal, and front to rear—the

Irwin Weil as pilot of a Piper Cub, age 18.

Irwin Weil as a student pilot.

pilot has a wonderful feeling of freedom of motion, just like a bird. It was a tremendously liberating feeling.

While all of this was going on, Jo watched how I concentrated on mastering the process. When my attention was completely focused on the problem at hand, she would unexpectedly cut the throttle so the engine was idling and say: "Okay, the engine has gone to idle, as if it stopped. Show me how you can make an emergency landing." I would have to pick out a flat farm field and glide the plane (with no help from the idling engine) to a height of about twenty feet off the ground. She would then give the engine full throttle, and we would fly away. The first few times this happened, I was surprised and anxious, but over time it became routine and almost automatic. I learned soon enough how important this training was.

It was my first solo flight, without Jo's presence in the plane. All went well until almost the end, when the engine really did conk out, and I was alone in a glider in the sky. Almost without thinking, I put the plane into a glide and eased my way safely onto the airport runway. Jo was watching, and I noticed that her normally ruddy face was a deathly pale white! To this very day, I fantasize on commercial airplanes what I would do if I suddenly had to take over the flight of an aircraft much bigger and more complicated than that primitive Piper Cub.

University of Cincinnati

In 1945, World War II came to a victorious end and larger parts of the world shared the sentiments expressed in a hymn dedicated to the newly formed United Nations. The words were attached to a melody previously composed by Shostakovich:

> The sun and the stars all are ringing,
>> With song rising strong from the earth;
>> The hope of humanity singing,
>> A hymn to a new world in birth.

> United Nations on the march
>> With flags unfurled;
>> Together fight for victory,
>> A brave new world.

Little did we know that the original Russian words set to Shostakovich's melody[15] were composed by a poet,[16] who was executed in the course of the Stalinist purges.

The atmosphere was one of high anticipatory hope—Nazism was at an end and forces of liberation were ascending. Never mind that other dictators were on the scene! I shared in this hope, thinking that the great Harvard University was about to propel me toward a life full of creativity and humanity's highest pleasures; however, the rude awakening was not long in arriving. That great university made me aware that my good services would not be needed in its august New England halls. My only alternative was to enroll in McMicken's less-than-august halls at the local municipal University of Cincinnati, whose "magical name" I was "to the world proclaim"—in the words of its anthem composed by one of my high school teachers.

Snobbery has never been a quality that earned my admiration. The teachers in my freshman year at UC, as we all called it, were intelligent, very decent academics. The Italian man, Mr. Marni, who introduced me to French, was a delightful example of an intelligentsia whose traditions went back to Imperial Rome. Full of a skepticism laced with biting humor, he kindly attempted to cut through some of my naiveté. His gravelly voice and tightly pressed lips have for sixty-seven years remained clear in my memory.

---

15 The lyrics to *The Song of the Meeting*, penned by Boris Kornilov, and set to music by Dmitri Shostakovich:

> "The morning greets us with a chill,
> The river greets us with a breeze.
> Curly headed girl, why are you not pleased
> By the merry sound of the factory siren?"

16 Boris Kornilov (29 July 1907-20 February 1938) was an enthusiastic communist poet. He was the totally genuine type; there was nothing about him that was either totalitarian or repressive. He sought the joy and freedom that he thought could be found in socialism and communism. Although Shostakovich set one of his poems to music (*The Song of the Meeting, Pesnia o vstrechnom*) that for many years opened morning radio broadcasts throughout the Soviet Union, Kornilov fell afoul of the Stalinist purges and was executed by the very communists whose ideology he so enthusiastically had supported.

University of Chicago

But Cincinnati really wasn't ready to fire my imagination into the conflagration I yearned for. This young, would-be scholar was snagged by a rather popular American educational figure at the time: Robert Maynard Hutchins, the boy wonder, President of the University of Chicago at age twenty-six. In his early twenties, he had become Dean of the Yale University Law School. Mr. Armour, of Chicago meatpacking fame and an important trustee of Chicago's named University, had become intrigued by the young administrator's charm and audacity. Mr. Hutchins declared that he wanted no less than the destruction of American higher education and its replacement to be brought to life in his image. Mr. Armour and his colleagues took the bait, and Hutchins was off running at a gallop!

By the time I was eighteen years old, Hutchins had made the University of Chicago a bastion of higher educational changes, with classes full of almost breathless enthusiasm for such undoubted worthiness as Plato, Aristotle, Aquinas, Locke, etc. Every single student had to face the force of passionate argument with classes engaged in Socratic-like (or so Hutchins wished) dialogues. The U of C was sometimes called that Baptist place[17] where atheist professors taught Jewish students Catholic doctrine.

My friend, Howard Schuman, who much later became an eminent sociologist at the University of Michigan, showed me an article in the *Reader's Digest* (at that time, a high example of American popular journalism) expounding Hutchins' ideas with breathless vigor. I was hooked in thirty seconds. Both Howard and I made eager supplications to the gods controlling admission to paradise *à* la Hutchins.

I still remember the pain clearly expressed on my father's face when he put me on the crack train,[18] "The James Whitcomb Riley" (then a

---

17 John D. Rockefeller Sr. (8 July 1839-23 May 1937) was a devout Baptist and a famous capitalist in the United States whose image is that of the extremely rich and religious magnate. He made his fortune in oil and also was the financial backer of the founding of the University of Chicago. Eventually he gave millions to the man who founded the University of Chicago.

18 In the days of my youth there was a crack train that used to run between Cincinnati and Chicago called the James Whitcomb Riley and in those days it was one of the fastest means of transportation around. Commercial passenger aviation was still

popular Indiana poet), from Cincinnati to Chicago, the "City of the Brawling, Brawny Shoulders." I also found out that it was the stomping grounds of Al Capone, the famous gangster, and of Yellow Kid Weil,[19] a famous Chicago con man and slick robber who purportedly wore yellow kid gloves while fleecing money out of older women. Because Yellow Kid Weil and I shared the same last name, I was to hear no small amount of talk about my infamous namesake.[20] That was Chicago. We were Chicago. We were the greatest in the world, and we were radical as hell!

By January of 1947, the year I entered as a lowly freshman, the U of C had become the scene of a red hot series of polemics between the Student Communist Club and the American Veteran's Committee (AVC), a collection of young veterans returning from the aftermath of World War II and representatives of the liberal, non-communist left, but also opposed to the conservative American legion. The AVC was very much opposed to the notion that the Stalinist government of the USSR could in any way be seen as an ideal model for the United States. To the members of the Student Communist Club, this seemed like evil reactionary propaganda, and the blast furnace heat of the public debates between the two factions reminded a person of the early political attacks from Bolshevik times in Russia.

Stalin was not the only dictator whose actions caused a large emigration that included a remarkable number of first-rate talents. No one could ignore the hideous actions of Hitler and his Nazis. A flood of great German-speaking scholars had fled their native land; many of them came to the United States and raised remarkably the level of American scholarship and artistry. Many American universities and colleges were reluctant

---

young, so I boarded that train many times to travel between Cincinnati and the University of Chicago where I was a student.

19 Joseph "Yellow Kid" Weil (1 July 1875–26 February 1976) was one of the best-known American con men of his era and is reputed to have stolen more than $8 million.
    In regards to his nickname, Yellow Kid Weil wrote: "There have been many erroneous stories published about how I acquired this cognomen. It was said that it was due to my having worn yellow chamois gloves, yellow vests, yellow spats, and a yellow beard. All this was untrue. I had never affected such wearing apparel and I had no beard." Quoted in Brannon, W. T. (1957). *"Yellow Kid" Weil: Con Man*. New York: Pyramid.

20 The shared last name was somewhat softened by my curious resemblance to the well-known photo of the young Kafka!

to accept them. Hutchins was an admirable exception. His university, the University of Chicago, welcomed these immigrants with open arms. Consequently, I was among the young high school graduates who got the advantage of the best of European scholarly sophistication. Ironically, Europe's worst dictators furnished us with an excellent education.

Between the *fortissimo* harangues of the warring political factions on one side and the highly abstract dialectical cleverness of the newly acquired ancient Athenian sages on the other side, I hardly knew which way to turn. It also was Chicago's worst January—the snow banks made me think of Siberia. Perhaps, by some kind of fate, I was struck by the writings that a man had produced after a close-up connection with that very Siberia just mentioned. Although I had read some powerful literature in Biblical Hebrew and in Elizabethan iambic pentameter, I had never before experienced this kind of explosive writing and emotion. This ex-Siberian chained guy bore a name I had never heard before: Fyodor Mikhailovich Dostoevsky. The text covered what initially seemed to me the wild shenanigans of some fraternal characters named Karamazov.[21]

In my most articulate literary critical mode, I exclaimed, "Wow! Who the hell is this guy?" My sophisticated fellow students, many of whom had been matured by warfare in France and Germany, replied, "Oh, some Russian writer. If you liked that stuff," they told me, "get a book called *Crime and Punishment*." I moved as fast as my legs would carry me to the university bookstore and, in my excitement, barely got out the words of the title. The salespeople, amused by my clumsiness, got the book for me.

After finding my prized book at the university bookstore, I was back in the dormitory on a Saturday night and I immersed myself in the book that introduced me to a certain nervous Nellie named Raskolnikov (only later did I learn that his name connected him with the historical Russian *Schismatics*).[22] The next thing I noticed about the time was that it was

---

21 The root *kar*, I came to understand, meant "black pitch," which might well have applied to parts of the characters' souls.

22 *Schismatics* (Russian: *raskol'niki*) date back to the fifteenth and sixteenth centuries in Russia and practiced a version of Christianity that differed in some details from Eastern Orthodox Christianity. At one point, the *schismatics* were very powerful and

afternoon on Sunday, and Raskolnikov was now in a Siberian prison. In short, those hours of reading Dostoevsky changed my life.

I decided that the only way to experience the full love of Dostoevsky's power was to read the actual words he wrote in his own language. Russian had been taught at the University of Chicago by Samuel Harper, the son of William Rainey Harper, who founded the institution in 1891, with extensive financial help from John D. Rockefeller.[23] Samuel Harper was an early American pioneer in the study and popularization of Russian language and literature. But in the 1930s, Slavic Studies had languished and become almost non-existent at the University. When I became a student in 1947, people had begun to realize the importance of the USSR, and in 1948, the university again offered a course in beginning Russian. I was one of five rather unusual and capricious students who signed up for a course taught by Riga-born[24] Morris Halle, who later became a well-known scholar in the Slavic field.

My previous work in learning Hebrew and Latin had prepared me to handle the study of an inflected language,[25] and the prospect of learning a new alphabet with some letters the same as I already knew was not particularly daunting. Nevertheless, what initially seemed to me a capricious Russian use of language forms, which I had already learned, caused

produced many works of literature, poetry, and music that became important in Russian culture.

23 Harper went to Rockefeller who gave an initial grant of ten million dollars—the Midwest would have an institution of higher learning. Shortly thereafter, Harper came back to Rockefeller with hand extended and asked for more millions. Rockefeller (the famous giver of infuriatingly tiny dime tips) coughed up more millions, albeit grudgingly. This scenario repeated itself many times. In the end, Rockefeller's copious wallet became thinner by over a hundred million dollars (in late nineteenth-century dollars!) and the University of Chicago did not have to chase the wolf from its door in the era of the robber barons. As students, we sometimes sang a parody to the famous hymn of the doxology: "Praise God from whom *oil* blessings flow."

24 Riga is the capital of Latvia—one of the Baltic States that belonged to the Tsarist Empire. It became independent after the 1917 Revolution, then was annexed by the Soviet Union in 1940, and once again became independent in 1991.

25 An inflected language is a language that defines relations between words by adding endings to them. It has what are called "cases." There's the nominative case for words that are the subject of a sentence or predicate nouns or adjectives, the accusative case for words that are the direct object of certain verbs or prepositions, and so on. Modern Russian has six cases (Old Russian had a seventh—the vocative).

Irwin Weil standing in front of a set of Russian-English and English-Russian dictionaries.

considerable toil and hand wringing. I found myself studying Russian, with all its attendant grammatical horrors, such as the various uses of the instrumental case and the battle of the verbal aspects, perfective versus imperfective. I won't even go into the irregular twisting declensions of personal names ending in -ov, -ev, and -in. Why was the word for student different from when that person was no longer a student (*student* versus *studentom*)? Why was the description of going on a journey differentiated between a single and a repeated action (*idti* versus *khodit'*)?

Like French and German, the Russian language has some words borrowed from a common stock, e.g., *literatura, politika*, but the amount of such recognizable vocabulary is much smaller than in French or German. The Russian mentality looked at time progression and word relationship in a way that was considerably different from what I knew in other languages that I had learned previously. The result allowed an extraordinary sharpness and beauty in the hands of a genius like Pushkin,[26] but it required a lot of work and mind stretching from a raw youth brought up in Midwestern America.

---

26 Aleksandr Sergeyevich Pushkin (6 June 1799-10 February 1837) is considered to be the most famous Russian poet. He beautifully combined many elements of Church Slavonic and spoken Russian. He was also a master of Gallicisms in Russian. His

This new pursuit plunged me into abstract grammars like the one written by George Birkett, a Scottish Slavist, and into books that took a more gradual approach like the one by Helen Jakobson, the sister-in-law of the famous Slavic scholar Roman Jakobson. These preceded by perhaps a generation and sometimes several generations the more sophisticated texts of Alexander Lipson (remarkably original and challengingly different), and the texts produced by American and Russian scholars working in tandem, sponsored by our national professional association, American Council of Teachers of Russian (ACTR). All of them were eager to present the language precisely and at a level spoken by highly educated Russians—a kind of direct gateway to the glories of Russian literary culture. Only somewhat later did they tend to concentrate on the spoken variant of the language, which changes markedly over several generations, particularly in a time of intimate, international, commercial contacts, as has been the case since the early 1990s.

Although I was beginning to acquire the ability to handle sources in the Russian language, most of my reading was in English translation. The three history books I remember most vividly were the ones by the British scholars, Sir John Maynard and Bernard Pares, and the one on the Soviet Union by Frederick Schuman. Maynard concentrated mainly on the role of the Russian peasantry and how the country attempted to manage the questions of land ownership after the emancipation of 1861. He introduced us to the concept of the *mir*[27] and continued some of the speculation about how this might play out in the general Russian psychology concerning problems of individualism versus a sense of the collective. Schuman was very much interested in the development of Soviet society and generally took a rather friendly approach to the reality of the USSR

---

poetry serves as the basis of much of the classical music of the nineteenth century that came out of Russia. His sense of rhythm, sound, and poetry is virtually unmatched by any other poet in the world with the possible exception of Shakespeare. As a matter of fact, Pushkin did discover Shakespeare and Shakespeare's writing greatly influenced Pushkin's poetry.

27 *Mir*, in Russian, has several meanings. Its usage here means the "world," i.e., the world of peasants. It's their small, restricted world that they lived in when they had to live on the estates of the aristocracy. The *mir* had its own rules, its own culture, and its own language, and became very famous in Russian culture.

and its plans for building a different kind of society. For this reason, more conservative American publicists and scholars often attacked Schuman.

Even at that relatively early time in my life, I began to understand that Russian reality was at the center of strong debates concerning big problems of politics and sociology. The post-World War II era produced the beginnings of the "Cold War" between the USSR and the US with its Western European Alliance. The U of C campus bubbled like a cauldron on a hot stove. The Communists called their opponents bourgeois reactionaries, who replied with denunciations of Stalinist murders and repressions. In the beginning, I simply felt amazement (and a certain amount of attraction) when I saw and heard the passing, historical, and political knowledge of the combating sides.

In retrospect, it seems to me that our professors at the University of Chicago tried to take as objective a stance as humanly possible toward such hot topics, since they wanted to train us, or perhaps push us, toward the ability to engage in thoughtful and critical dialogue. In this sense, they were rather far removed from the more popular sources of public opinion like newspapers, magazines, radio, and films. In those venues, one could feel the ever-growing tensions of the Cold War, the most convenient villain of which was Russia. Again, most of these people could not separate the historical reality of Russia from the ideological tendencies of the Soviet Union. While the two were certainly connected, in some ways they were hardly identical.

This confounding of historical reality with ideological tendencies was forcibly brought home to me by a placard that I saw in front of the Chicago Opera House in those years. It was the evening of a performance of Mussorgsky's[28] famous version of *Boris Godunov*. The placard was a stirring attack against horrible Communist propaganda and Marxist events that, according to the naïve notions of those sponsoring the demonstration, were a part of the opera. Mussorgsky's first name was deliberately

---

28   Modest Petrovich Mussorgsky (21 March 1839-28 March 1881) was one of the greatest Russian composers of the nineteenth century who combined the spoken language, the musical language, the Russian nationalist idea of music, and the western idea of opera into incredibly powerful works of music. His most famous work is probably the opera *Boris Godunov*. He was an incredibly powerful and talented composer.

changed from Modest to Immodest! Can you imagine Tsar Boris Godunov in the late sixteenth and early seventeenth centuries as a Communist? As a young student, I was somewhat baffled, to put it mildly, by the connection between the False Dmitri[29] of the early seventeenth century and the twentieth-century world of Communist ideology. Alas, such stupidity and ignorance were not rare in those days.

Experiences with Russian History and Literature

In my studies of Russian history, I began to gain some context for the political and ideological noise. To a considerable extent, this developing understanding was facilitated by the fact that the head of the Russian Department was George Bobrinskoy, an aristocratic émigré from Russia at a time when bloody civil war was raging between the insurgent Communist revolutionaries and the representatives of the old Tsarist regime, together with the non-Communist liberals and moderate socialists. We also heard the story that the Bobrinskoy family was actually the offspring of an illegitimate birth by the Empress Catherine—one of her many reported love affairs.

I was initially a bit skeptical about my professor claiming to be related to the Empress Catherine, because Lord only knows how many con men in the US claimed to be former Russian Grand Dukes. But, fifty years later, my friends in St. Petersburg took me to Gatchina, the palace built by Catherine's legitimate son, who became the Emperor Paul. In that palace was a long corridor with portraits of Catherine's many lovers. Imagine my amazement when I saw a portrait remarkably similar to my former U of C

---

29 The False Dmitri was a character in *Boris Godunov*. Boris Godunov was a Tsar who was accused of coming to power by arranging the murder of the Tsarevich Dmitri. There's some dispute over whether or not he indeed had the heir murdered, but in those days it was taken as fact. There was a monk in a Muscovite monastery who heard the story and realized that he was the same age as the so-called murdered son of the previous Tsar, so he decided that he would claim to be the resurrected Tsar. He managed to escape from Russia to Poland where he convinced some of the Poles to back him in an invasion of Russia. The False Dmitri went on to defeat Boris Godunov's army and sat on the Muscovite throne for just under a year (21 July 1605-17 May 1606). At the end of his short-lived reign, he returned to Poland faster than he came—his ashes were shot out of a cannon pointed in the direction of Poland.

teacher. It was all I could do to restrain myself from shouting, "Professor! What are you doing on that wall?!"

Bobrinskoy had the very kindly manners of the old aristocracy. When I was a student in his course on Soviet literature, one of the assigned authors was Ilya Ehrenburg. He wrote a novel, *The Second Day*, which described the early years of Soviet efforts to build an industrial economy in Soviet Russia. The novel was clearly in sympathy with the Soviet five-year plans, although it was not entirely void of some critical passages.

In my naiveté, for Bobrinskoy I wrote a paper that was somewhat on the left about Ehrenburg's *Second Day*. I said we shouldn't criticize the novel until we have our own First Day. Little did I know that my professor had been an officer in the White Army, which fought with ferocious (although ultimately unsuccessful) vigor against the Bolshevik Red Army. I'll never forget Bobrinskoy's comments on my paper: "Mr. Weil, you write nicely and argue impressively. But, my dear student, one can look at this question from a different point of view." Only years later did I fully understand the force behind those elegant, courteous words!

As time went by, my understanding of Russian literature grew. In addition to my first love (Dostoevsky), there were Tolstoy, Gogol, Turgenev, Chekhov, and, somewhat later, Pushkin, whose poetry captured me no less than Shakespeare's. In those years, the major translations—many of them re-published by the American series entitled *The Modern Library*—were the work of a remarkable English lady of the nineteenth century, Constance Garnett. To be sure, there were the beginnings of more precise and nuanced translations by people like the British scholar Bernard Guerney. His anthology, *A Treasury of Russian Literature*, has been used for many generations as a sterling example of well-translated literature.

While a graduate student at the University of Chicago, I witnessed the beginning of Vladimir Nabokov's[30] popular work in the United States.

---

30 Vladimir Vladimirovich Nabokov (22 April 1899-2 July 1977) was one of the most powerful Russian writers of the twentieth century. He was the son of a liberal Russian politician, a famous aristocrat in his own right. At the time of the Revolution, he and his father had to leave the Soviet Union and he had to write in emigration, first of all in Germany and France, and later in America. During the fifties and sixties, Nabokov became one of the most famous writers in the United States, writing in perfect English,

We read his early book about the Russian exemplar of the comic and grotesque, Nikolai Gogol. To catch the atmosphere of the subject, Nabokov wanted to print, not a portrait, but rather a picture of the nose of the man under study. After all, Gogol created the unforgettable story of the uppity nose![31] In many ways, the book, published by the New York Publishing House, New Directions, was so extreme that it was difficult to accept. Nabokov's strikingly unconventional approach to literature was sure to create in the readers a strong reaction, either positive or negative—or perhaps a curious combination of both.

And then, Nabokov published the so-called translation of Pushkin's *Onegin*. In his *Partisan Review* article, Nabokov quoted the line from Pushkin's *Onegin*: "Devy, gde vy?" (Maidens, where are you?) Since it took so many years to have the whole four-volume set published, with its long, meticulous commentary, I often raised the query, "Gde vy?" (Where are you?) When the translation came out, I was terribly disappointed because it was a pony, that is, a word-for-word, literal translation. Nabokov said, "That's exactly what it is, it's a pony. To translate it into rhyme is to reduce it." That's a very nasty thing to say about others who translated it into rhyme. Nabokov took great pleasure in putting other writers down. It soon became apparent that the only one who really appreciated literature, especially Pushkin's poetry, was—V. V. Nabokov! Most others were slain by the cannon shots of Nabokov's murderous prose.

As far as Nabokov was concerned, the only person who knew anything was he himself. Anyone who went slightly outside of that was no good, and Nabokov put him down very cleverly. In his classes at Cornell, he would criticize Dostoevsky. That's his privilege, and he did it very intelligently. But when students would try to defend Dostoevsky, he'd flunk them, which

---

and yet in an English behind which you could see the Russian. Nabokov became an incredibly powerful figure in American literature and world literature, and after the fall of the Soviet Union, he also became very popular in Russia. He had his own particular ideas about what literature should be.

31 *The Nose* is a famous story by Nikolai Gogol in which a man wakes up one morning to discover that his nose has disappeared, and it turns out that the nose has taken on a separate identity: it becomes a bureaucrat in the Russian regime—a bureaucrat one rank higher than the man from whose face he escaped. It's a wonderfully fantastical and powerful story and one of Gogol's most famous.

I couldn't forgive. That to me was Soviet. I mean, how could Nabokov criticize the Soviets when Nabokov would do something exactly like what
they would do? So, there was a part of me that didn't like Nabokov, but I
had to admit, my God, he was an incredible talent. Such unique and sometimes extremely capricious works started me toward an understanding of
the kind of powerful stylistic novelties and deep human insights produced
by Russian writers of both the nineteenth and twentieth centuries.

While much of this education was going on in the form of English
translations, I was also beginning to read some of the great Russian novels
in the original. First came Tolstoy's *Voina i mir* (*War and Peace*), which
text I literally slaved over for two months with the help of a well-worn
copy of Smirnitsky's *Russian-English Dictionary*. Suffice it to say, it took
me several years to work my way, linguistically, into the Russian twentieth
century. Somewhat later, I was able to get through the Russian texts of
several novels by Dostoevsky and Turgenev. The poetry of Pushkin came
still later as my grasp of the language and the general reality of Russian
culture began to expand.

All of these experiences took place in an American environment
where the mere mention of the word "Russia" or "Russian" brought about
a strong emotional reaction on the part of the listener. Such a reaction
could sometimes be one of mild curiosity stimulated by the notion that
something new and very different was happening in the country that had
been our staunch ally during the war against Nazi Germany. They were
also aware that some people within that country were boasting about the
creation of what official propaganda called an entirely different—and
more just—social order. Much more often, the typical American reaction
was one of hostility toward a country that many perceived as a threat to
our way of life. Such reactions, as naïve as they sometimes were, often
found resonance in Soviet anti-American propaganda that could be crude
in expressing its own kind of ignorance. Hostility on one side more often
than not fed and grew upon the hostility from the other. Still, in the midst
of all these emotional currents, I have to state objectively that no one ever
tried to stop me from pursuing my growing and sympathetic interest in
Russian language and culture. On the contrary, almost everyone near to
me encouraged what I was doing.

Life in the Theatre

In addition to my slowly growing knowledge of Russian language and literature, I found another outlet for my passions and ideas. The U of C had a very interesting and vital student theatre that specialized in improvisation and that later produced many of the founders of nationally known theatre in Chicago and New York. One theatrical group became the well-known Chicago bunch of actor-improvisers called "Second City."

They included quite a few graduates from our U of C theatre who would go on to have other accomplishments. The actor who played King Agamemnon later broke the bank at Las Vegas with his whiz-kid knowledge of math (without a computer!). The woman at the U of C who played the role of Lysistrata (who abstained from conjugal sex until her increasingly comical husband ended the war) also became a well-known actress in Chicago theatrical life. There was also the incomparable Severn Darden, the half mad, half brilliant scion of Louisiana's Attorney General, who later made something of a splash in radio and Hollywood film. As a student, he rode around Chicago in a late 1920s model of the southern state's official limousine. Viv and I, royally ensconced in the spacious rear section of the vehicle, saw in front of us a panel bearing three signaling buttons for the driver's attention. Their notations read: "Turn left," "Turn right," and "Go home." His maladroit charm struck an unforgettably U of C eccentricity on stage, screen, and radio. After watching the plays and interacting with the actors, I enthusiastically immersed myself in the translated versions of Aeschylus' *Agamemnon* and Aristophanes' *Lysistrata*—I had not forgotten my early loving brush with Shakespeare.

I pestered Mr. Blair, the theatre director, to let me direct a production of my beloved *Tempest*. With a group of student actors, I threw myself, heart and soul, into making iambic pentameter Shakespearean lines into spoken dialogue that would stir the hearts of U of C students, who were steeped in the language of Aristotle's *Poetics*. Alas, those weeks of full-blooded attention powerfully distracted me from the classroom assigned reading of that same Aristotle.

At the end of my first undergraduate experience at the U of C, I possessed two important things: a Bachelor's degree earned after two years of college-level work—one of the results of Hutchins' attempted reorganization of education in the US, and a burning desire to make a mark in the American theatre. Encouraged by my work both as an actor and director in the university theatre, I strongly desired to spread my thespian wings in New York. My friends told me there was a very important figure with a worldwide reputation in the "Dramatic Workshop" of the New School for Social Research—a continuation of what had been founded as The University in Exile.

This university was established as an academic haven for German scholars exiled from Hitler's Germany. Their theatre was under the direction of Erwin Piscator, the man who had first put the work of Berthold Brecht on the stage of the famous *Volksbühne* (People's Theatre) in the Berlin of the 1920s. Both Brecht and Piscator were convinced Marxists and Communists, and they understood the theatre as a powerfully expressive esthetic instrument for propagating ideology. Piscator had served in the Kaiser's German army in World War I, and he openly boasted that he had never actually aimed his rifle at a British soldier. When he returned to Berlin in the years after 1918, he became a Communist; hence, the name of his workplace can be accurately translated as "The People's Theatre."

When the Nazis came to power, Piscator, as a publically renowned Communist, had to escape. As a loyal Communist believer, he chose Soviet Moscow as his refuge. So he went to Moscow, where among other things, he went two million rubles over budget shooting a film called *Rybaki (The Fishermen)*, which didn't make Stalin happy. In spite of the fact of his Marxist loyalties, he also had a modicum of commonsense. He soon realized that it was safer to be a loyal Bolshevik in New York, the great bastion of capitalism, than it would be to stay in Moscow, with its deadly Stalinist purges. That is why I was able, in 1948, to meet and work with him in the belly of the great American capitalist Leviathan.

Piscator was deeply convinced that the true purpose of any artistic endeavor was to promote the cause of the people in the *Marxist* sense of that often mangled word. While Piscator stuck loyally to his own, private sense of dialectical materialism,[32] as a manifesto for Communism, he also

---

32 Dialectical materialism was a theory that Karl Marx proposed to explain the course of all history. According to Marxist dialectics, each phase of history produced a ruling class, the thesis, and an underclass that inevitably became stronger, the antithesis, and

had a highly original theatrical style that he called "Epic Theatre." Since the classical definition of epic meant covering the activity of the epic hero from his birth to his death, Piscator's theatre would do the same for his own hero, that is, Marx's definition of history, which inevitably led to Communism, although Piscator defined these Marxist terms somewhat less dogmatically than official Soviet literary ideology. Piscator was determined to use all ultra-modern techniques to achieve his effects: revolving stages, projected movies, transnational dialogue and effects, and strange dim lighting. It was often said that he had more lighting equipment and less light than any other theatre in the world.

In Piscator's notions about dramatic art, the worst possible mistake, or even sin, was represented by the kind of theatre so admired by the leading American directors: the system developed by the famous Moscow Art Theatre, founded by the theatrical gods of the twentieth century, Konstantin Stanislavsky and Vladimir Danchenko. Ironically, these were the figures whose work and ideas were most supported in Moscow during Stalinist times. Stanislavsky's famous "method," developed in his two major books, *My Life In Art* and *The Actor Prepares*, was almost universally considered by actors and directors either as gospel truth or the devil's own handiwork—but it was never ignored, except by Piscator. Some of the most emotional and useful discussions I heard in my youth occurred in the seemingly endless debates between Piscator, with his emphasis on the intellect of the artist and the ideological effect of the stage, as opposed to the ideas of our teachers, many of them Russian émigrés and their American disciples.

Stanislavsky campaigned tenaciously against the famous artists of his time, especially the star celebrity Sarah Bernhardt, who dramatically, almost operatically, poured forth gestures and sounds whose effects were obviously carefully planned as such. According to the Muscovite[33] master, Bernhardt's performance was obviously emotionally false. The only path to genuine emotion on the stage, according to Stanislavsky, would be found by the actor who carefully understood the psychology and previous

---

overthrew its oppressors. Synthesis would result in full communism and the end of pre-history.

33　"Muscovite" is the word for a person who was either born or lives in Moscow.

experience of the dramatic character and then found in his or her own life an emotional experience parallel or identical with that of the character in the drama. By reliving that experience, the actor would bring truth to the stage, and the audience would immediately catch on.

The productions of the Moscow Art Theatre, especially of Chekhov's work, became world famous, and all the teachers of the Dramatic Workshop promulgated this gospel, except Piscator, who stood like a boulder in the middle of the road. Piscator was totally disinterested in the actor's personal emotions; he cared only for the brain. According to him, if the brain worked right, then the scene worked properly, and the proper idea would get across (an idea close to the truth of Marxism), which would then make the audience think seriously about the play's progressive message. It was Chekhov's *Seagull* that we studied almost religiously, and which had been hissed off the Petersburg stage, only to be famously brought to life by Danchenko and Stanislavsky in Moscow. That work became the rallying cry of the teachers in Piscator's school, only to be preemptively dismissed by Piscator, the supervisor and chief of these very pedagogues!

In Chekhov's play *The Seagull*, there is a scene in which the administrator of the Russian country estate, Shamraev, is trying to placate his ultimate boss, the owner of the estate and also a famous actress, Mme. Arkadina. She wants horses to provide transportation for one of her flings, and he cannot release horses needed for urgent work in the fields. She shows her artist's temperament by expressing her anger at his philistine lack of understanding for her desires. He is no less angry, although he tries to show respect for her talent, and absolutely refuses to give in. It is a typical Chekhovian situation where both sides of a miscommunication are right and wrong, each in their individual way. The followers of Stanislavsky and his method tried to get the actors to experience the situation by using episodes from their own memories that would reproduce the authentic emotions of the situations. These emotions would be so just and true that the audience would not be able to resist getting emotionally involved in the scene.

In contrast to Stanislavsky's interpretation of *The Seagull*, Piscator relied on a rational and intellectual understanding of the situation in his interpretations of various plays. In *Romeo and Juliet*, the actor playing

Romeo was trying to go through the famous scene where he stands beneath his young lover's balcony.

The director was not satisfied with Romeo's stance, so he asked him, "Where are you standing?" The reply: "I'm standing at the base of a wall, under a balcony." "And who owns that wall and balcony?" "The Capulet family" came the reply. "And what family do you come from?" "I'm a Montague." "Well then, how would you approach the wall of a hostile, passionate, and well-armed family?"

The actor, of course, got the point and went into what he considered a more fearful and cautious mood. For Piscator, it was a matter of understanding and plotting the dramatic effect; he was disinterested in the emotional history of the actor.

I began to understand that arguments could be made, both for and against, both systems. Each approach could produce moving and interesting drama, if used properly. If misused, or used excessively, either one could degenerate into dry pedantry and produce the exact opposite of good drama. Even Stanislavsky once is reported to have said, "I don't care which hook you use, as long as you catch the fish." And I understood further that often it was the very existence and heat of the debate that, at least partly, produced the high quality of the work. It seems to me there is a great deal in Russian intellectual history from the nineteenth as well as the twentieth and twenty-first centuries that bears witness to this issue. It was this argument that was brought back to the United States by young American directors who went to the Moscow Art Theatre in order to learn from Stanislavsky. In New York, they established the Actors Workshop that produced much of the powerful art that went into some twentieth-century Broadway productions and Hollywood cinematography. They also inspired the continuation of the debates around the "method" arguments that continue to the present day.

The University in Exile eventually became The New School for Social Research, still operating in New York. Such scholars had an enormously positive effect on the development of the American intellectual world, and I, like many of my young colleagues at that time, owe a great deal to the teachers at The New School regardless of their ideologies. They brought a whole new world of the mind into my consciousness.

For some reason, Piscator took a liking to me, in spite of the fact that our reactions to Shakespeare's *Coriolanus* were diametrically opposite. I thought that Shakespeare's protagonist lacked a certain necessary empathy with the Roman people, whom General Coriolanus considered a totally ignoble rabble—and he didn't in any way conceal his disdain. Piscator said, "No, no, no. He was a great and noble leader like Stalin." And he turned to me and delivered the ultimate Communist denunciation. He said, "You are a Sozialdemokrat." Piscator's strong German accent made it seem the ultimate end of my potentially moral authority. Although he spoke English with an almost comically German accent, his mastery of our language's grammar and syntax was superb. His favorite curse to an actor was: "Do you want to be an artist or a goddamned dilettante?" Of course, he totally mixed up the phonetics of the "g's" and "k's," the "t's" and the "d's." What a festival of Germanic phonetic mangling of consonants. It was almost all I could do to keep from an outburst of laughter.

But one accusation was often raised against Piscator's work—his critics accused him of a certain Germanic heaviness. They were not favorably impressed by his use of technology and what they labeled as a "dry, intellectualized style of acting." I always felt this was an accusation that ignored the impressive results of his talent and his work. But I did feel the extreme quality of his views, and in a particularly parodistic mood, I decided to write a satire on the idea of "Epic Theatre."

I handed the paper in to my teacher and then went away—I had worked off my parodistic mood in the writing of the paper. Little did I realize that my teacher would show the damned thing to Piscator. Our General Director had the habit each week of gathering together everyone connected with the Dramatic Workshops and talking about a particular issue that interested him.

On this particular occasion, Piscator began the session as follows: "It seems that we have in our midst a wise young man who graduated from the University of Chicago (the last word sarcastically drawn out.)" "Uh oh," I said to myself. "What is coming now?" Piscator continued, "Our student wrote this very interesting paper that I would like you all to hear."

With that introduction said, Piscator read aloud my whole opus. I quickly realized that my attempts at irony were totally sophomoric, not to mention stupid. My fellow students filled the hall with laughter. At the end, Piscator said, "Now what grade has this gem earned?" Shouts came in at all levels. Piscator said, "Clearly, it's an A or an F."

After Piscator's declaration, there followed total silence. Then he continued: "My dear young fellows, tell me—what is theatre (he dramatically mangled the "th")? Theatre is truth (again, the dramatic phonetic mangling). And our Chicago friend has expressed the truth as he sees it—therefore, *A!*" That was the high point of my career in theatre. What followed was all-downhill.

At one point in my short theatrical directing career, I did set up an unusual combination of Shakespearean scenes. The idea was "the development of Shakespeare's heroes." Romeo was a hero overcome by events in his world. Hamlet made his strength known, but he eventually succumbed. Prospero suffered initial reverses but eventually overcame them and triumphed in his world. When I put the scenes together, some of my fellow students performed them in New York's Rooftop Theatre. Piscator liked my rendering of the voice of the ghost of Hamlet's father. Another rotund spectator came up and informed me that he didn't like disconnected scenes. I later learned that I had been addressed by none other than Orson Welles.[34]

Marriage to Vivian

While I was living in New York (1948–49) and working in the theatres of Piscator's Dramatic Workshop, Vivian was working on a Master's degree in philosophy at the University of Chicago. She was, understandably, getting more and more impatient with the young man who called himself her boyfriend but lived a thousand miles away. Finally, her patience snapped, and I heard an ultimatum: "You're going to come back to Chicago, and we're going to get together, or this is going to be the end. It's either me and Chicago or forget it all." Whatever my foolishness was at that time, I had enough sense to realize that I would never find another woman with her combination of spirit, sense, and beauty who understood exactly who I was.

34 George Orson Welles (6 May 1915-10 October 1985) was a famous writer and director who had a special reputation in American cinematography.

Irwin and Vivian Weil in early married days.

Consequently, at the age of twenty-one, I came back to do what the University of Chicago called graduate work, and in 1950 Viv and I got married.

The two rabbis from the Isaac M. Wise Temple officiated our marriage. Rabbi Wohl emanated his usual warmth and pride in the young people he had nurtured. Rabbi Heller, who had astounded me as a child with the word *apostasy*, had learned that Vivian was a student of philosophy. In the course of the ceremony, she repeated the expression "I do!" several times. He said to her, "You're not an idealist—you're an idoalist!"[35]

Kulischer

In 1951, a year after marrying Viv, and with the possession of an MA degree in Slavic Languages and Literature from the University of Chicago, Viv and I moved to Washington, DC, where I worked under a remarkable Russian émigré, Evgeny Mikhailovich Kulischer, who was born in Kiev and grew up in St. Petersburg. He had been a young member of the Kadet

---

35 Interestingly, I recently had to get a copy of our marriage license for insurance purposes. Our license certifies in writing that neither of us is a congenital idiot or alcoholic and the license is signed by two rabbis and a judge. Now how many people, I want to know, in this country have a marriage license signed by two rabbis and a judge that shows that neither is a congenital idiot or alcoholic? Those were the good old days.

(Constitutional Democratic) Party in pre-Soviet Petrograd[36] and was a protégé of one of Tsarist Russia's leading liberal lawyers, Nikolai Karabchevsky. My boss also had been a close associate of another well-known Russian liberal, Vladimir Dmitriyevich Nabokov, (father of the aforementioned writer, Vladimir Vladimirovich Nabokov), who was assassinated in the 1920s in pre-Hitler Germany by Russian Fascist sympathizers. As a matter of fact, Kulischer went to the Nabokov's house every Friday night in St. Petersburg. This interaction occurred long before the 1917 Revolution.

When the 1917 Revolution came, Kulischer had to get out of there, as he was a fairly well-known Social Democrat. He had to cross the Romanian border, and the Romanian guards wanted to send him back, but he said, "Wait a minute. I know a relative of Nabokov's (who had married a Romanian noble at that point)." They called her and she vouched for him, so she saved his neck and he got to stay in Romania. He then became a docent at the University of Berlin. When Hitler came to power, Kulischer had to go to France. He became a docent at the Sorbonne.[37] Hitler came there; Kulischer had to cross the occupied/unoccupied part of France.[38] After Kulischer escaped on one of the last boats, he arrived in the United States, where he became a professor at Columbia, and one of the leading demographers.[39] It was he who was responsible for the figure of six million Jews killed by the Nazis.

While I was looking for a job, someone told me to go to the Library of Congress. I said, "Look, I'm not a librarian!" But the person told me to go anyway. Well, I went to a sign that said, "Authorized Personnel Only," and above it was the name Jakobson, about whom I had somewhat heard. The most courageous thing I ever did in my life was going past that sign!

---

36 Petrograd originally was named Saint Petersburg after the patron saint of Peter the Great. During World War I, Russians were not pleased that the city bore a German name so they changed it to the Russian equivalent: Petrograd. The city name remained unchanged until 1924 when it was renamed Leningrad in honor of Vladimir Lenin. In the early 1990s, its inhabitants voted to restore the original name of Saint Petersburg.

37 The Sorbonne at that time was a college of the University of Paris, located in the Latin Quarter in Paris, France.

38 Unfortunately, Evgeny Mikhailovich's brother was caught by the Nazis trying to cross the occupied/unoccupied part of France and was killed.

39 A demographer is a specialist in the study of populations and their effect on society.

It turned out it was not Roman Jakobson,[40] it was his brother, Sergei Jakobson. He told me that there was a project that involved demography and that I could possibly be of use.

After meeting with Sergei about the demographic job, the first step in determining whether I qualified was to take a language exam. The person who administered the exam showed me texts in Russian and in French, and I translated them for him. I later learned he knew neither Russian nor French, but he was impressed that I knew the languages. Shortly thereafter, I met Dr. Kulischer, who then gave me an assignment. Two weeks later I showed him my analysis and conclusions. He looked over my submission and said, "You don't think much of this project?" I replied that I was ready for correction, but he was right in assessing my attitude. He asked why I felt so negatively about the project, and for the next fifteen minutes I launched into my argument, similar in style to what I would do at the U of C.

As I argued my opinion, I could see in Dr. Kulischer's eyes a change of attitude toward me. It seemed as if he were thinking, "Maybe we can make something out of this young man." Much to my surprise, he started to pound my arguments into dust! Dr. Kulischer demonstrated how a real argument had to be constructed. He then gave me some valuable advice: "Now, go out and do some real work." In short, he taught me what serious research was all about. I remain eternally grateful to him for the lesson. Evgeny Mikhailovich was somewhat skeptical that a youngster from Cincinnati and Chicago could really handle the Russian language, as well as other European tongues. His skepticism, expressed in the very old-fashioned Russian style, was a kind of goad to me, and I soon found myself deeply

---

40 Roman Osipovich Jakobson (11 October 1896-18 July 1982) was one of the greatest scholars in the Slavic field of the twentieth century, and also a proponent of the idea of formalism in literature—the idea that if you really wanted to understand literature you had to understand its form, which was much more important than its content. Jakobson was a great teacher who, after his emigration first to Czechoslovakia and then to the United States, became a very polemical professor at Columbia, then Harvard, and finally at MIT. An entire generation of Slavic scholars, especially in the United States, came out of Roman Osipovich's teaching. Eventually he became very respected and popular in the Soviet Union, in spite of the fact that his ideas about formalism were anathema to them.

involved in Russian demographic sources, as well as issues of the Soviet press gathered from far-flung parts of the huge geographic mass that was the USSR—a country that I soon learned had space enough to include three countries the physical size of the US, which also was not exactly Luxemburg!

For three years, I worked for Dr. Kulischer at the Library of Congress. We made a partial census of the Soviet Union. I soon learned that in the Stalinist USSR, the usual census figures about the country's population were considered to be a closely guarded secret. Consequently, we researchers at the Library of Congress were supposed to work out the actual figures that would have been published in a normal, open census. At one point, we were really stuck on a particular figure and said that we should try something crazy: we decided to call the Soviet Embassy in DC to ask if maybe they could give us the figure. To our surprise, the Soviet Embassy said, "We're depending on your figures!" They knew that we were aiming solely at the truth of the matter, and they knew the world reputation of Evgeny Mikhailovich Kulischer.

We had to work on the basis of two brilliantly conceived and executed multi-volume census publications, one of them from 1897, and the other from 1926. We also had exactly two pages from the national Soviet press published in 1939, three years after the second Soviet decentennial[41] census was supposed to have been published—according to Soviet law, the next census should have been ten years later, in 1936. However, 1936 coincided with the huge disruption of the collectivization of agriculture and then famine, the beginning of the Stalinist purges, and huge population dislocation. When Stalin saw the disastrous figures, he solved the problem in his own way. He organized the arrest of the outstanding groups of Soviet Russian statisticians and silenced most of them permanently. The information was suppressed—only three years later were two pages of information published, in a format that tried to conceal the major demographic catastrophes in the 1930s.

That information was what we had to go on, as far as the most recent census. All the rest we had to dig out from the Soviet press, a little bit like

---

41   A decentennial refers to a period of ten years.

chess problems. Believe me, I have some notion of what happened in the Soviet Union.

At one point, I asked Evgeny Mikhailovich, "We see that there are all kinds of falsifications in Soviet propaganda, and they claim that the American stuff is full of bourgeois propaganda. Is there any truth to that? I mean, if they do this sort of thing, is there a possibility that the American government sometimes distorts things?"

Then he said, "Listen," and proceeded to tell me about the Beilis case.[42] Now, those individuals with high power wanted to convict Beilis. There was an organization called the Black Hundreds, an anti-Semitic organization in Russia, and there was a guy in the so-called Ministry of Justice, Shcheglovitov, who wanted to see Beilis convicted. The Kiev police knew this was totally wrong, and in a Russian Tsarist court of law, Beilis was declared innocent. He was defended by a liberal group of Constitutional Democrats, including Nabokov's father.[43] Evgeny Mikhailovich went on to say, "Now suppose this happened in the Soviet regime, and they wanted to convict the guy. You think there would have been an acquittal?"

So, later, when my government clearance had to go through the Library of Congress, they saw that I had lived at 212 East 12th Street. A few years earlier when I was living in New York City, finding a place to live in New York wasn't easy, although it was a good deal easier then than it is now. There was a place advertised at 212 East 12th Street. It was a rent that I could afford, so I took it. I had no idea who was in the building, but at night, I'd sometimes hear wild arguments going on. I'd yell back through the walls, "For God's sake, shut up. We're trying to sleep!" It was the Commies arguing with the Nazis! I later learned that the building turned out to be the national headquarters for the Communist Party and the national headquarters for the Nazi Party.

The government workers worried that I had interests with the Communists and wondered why I was living in that area. Well, I received

---

42 Menahem Mendel Beilis (1874-7 July 1934) was a Jew living in Kiev in 1913 who was unjustly accused of ritual murder (murdering a boy in order to make *matzo*, unleavened bread, from his blood). The two-year trial provoked an international scandal.

43 In gratitude for what Nabokov's father had done for Beilis, the American Jewish Committee partially subsidized the subsequent passage across the Atlantic of the writer's family.

an interrogatory.[44] "It has been asserted that you are a member of the NAACP, you worked with a known communist (Erwin Piscator), you lived in a building that was the national headquarters of the Communist Party, and while in Washington, DC, you received an invitation to attend a film at the Soviet Embassy. What do you have to say about this, anyway?" I wrote a fifteen-page typed response that eventually made clear to everyone, at least anyone who had any common sense, that I was not a communist. I was as patriotic as the next fellow, if not more so! If it weren't for my great, great grandfather's immigration to Cincinnati, my whole family would not be among the living.

Despite my written defense, it took a while to hear back on whether or not I was cleared. In a way, I really can't complain. The administration at the Library of Congress was very kind to me; I was on salary, although I couldn't work on any classified material. So I had a desk in another part of the library. I came there every morning, and I could do what I wanted. To an academic, this was paradise! After all, I was on government salary, so I didn't have to worry about where the next meal came from, and I could do anything I wanted in the biggest library in the country. Who had such a privilege for a period of three months? It was like a grant. The guy who eventually worked at the desk beside me was a fellow named Shabad, who was a very famous geographer in the Soviet Union and a very interesting guy. Kornei Chukovsky,[45] whom I later met in Russia, had known his mother, and said, "Madame Shabáda, ia Vas liubliu bol'she shokoláda!" (Madame Shabada, I love you more than chocolate!)

Under the tutelage of Evgeny Mikhailovich, my knowledge of Russian history and culture began to expand greatly. I learned a great deal about politics in St. Petersburg in the years before World War I, in the early Soviet years, and, most especially, during the terrible years of World War II,

---

44 An interrogatory is a legal questionnaire that is sent to a person who, by law, is bound to respond truthfully.

45 Kornei Ivanovich Chukovsky (31 March 1882-28 October 1969) was a widely popular critic and writer in the Soviet Union from the early part of the twentieth century onward. In Soviet times he became an extraordinary grandfather figure owing to his universally popular children's rhymed stories. There were very few political or literary movements over fifty years in which he was not personally involved. He also was a reader and admirer of the works by Dr. Seuss.

which the Russians called "The Great Fatherland War." It would have taken a person without a heart to avoid sympathizing with the Nazi-inflicted suffering of the East European population, including both Russians and many other Slavic and non-Slavic nationalities. At the same time, there was no small amount of suffering inflicted by internal Soviet sources.

Learning this perspective came as a considerable shock to a young man who had heard a great deal about World War II from sources in his native Cincinnati. But I had experienced relatively little exposure to the actual sources from the area and personal reminiscences of those who had endured the suffering in their own lives. Of course, there was a great deal of propaganda issuing from many different sides. The ugliness of Nazi propaganda was immediately apparent; the Soviet distortions appeared less so, since our sympathies sometimes tended to blind us. This, I hasten to add, includes no attempt on my part to cover up distortions and contradictions that came from the American side. However, the internal contradictions in the USSR soon became apparent when looking at the facts, and some of the conflicting statements from different periods when propaganda demands would change as, for example, the materials coming out of periods immediately before and after the signing of the Nazi-Soviet Pact of 1939.[46]

Through all of this, the guidance and advice of my boss, himself a product of the old, Russian intellectual tradition, was enormously helpful and instructive. I heard a great deal of personal reminiscence about Petersburg juridical and social experience, the exigencies of emigration in the inter-war period, both in Germany and in France, where there were significant Russian colonies of highly educated and cultivated people.

---

46 The Nazi Soviet pact, or the Molotov-Ribbentrop pact, was a pact signed in 1939. Up until 1939, the Communist regime had been known to be the violent enemies of the fascists, but suddenly in 1939 Stalin and Molotov amazed the world by signing a treaty of alliance with Hitler's Germany (Ribbentrop was the German foreign minister, Molotov was the Soviet foreign minister). It was signed, and from 1939 until 1941, at least on paper, the Soviets were allies of Hitler's Germany, which both amazed and revolted the world, because, after all, communists around the world had been claiming that the Soviet Union was the real bulwark against Nazism and fascism, and here Stalin turned around and made an alliance. That alliance didn't last long, because in 1941 the Nazis invaded the Soviet Union, and all of a sudden the Soviet Union became the allies of the western powers and the United States.

I also heard penetrating discourses on the natures of radically changing societies, which included a nation that had a glorious cultural history, resting at least partly on top of a population that had been widely enslaved up until the emancipation of 1861. The subsequent struggles of Russian politicians that led to the political earthquakes of the twentieth century entered amply into our calculations of demographic trends apparent in the years right after World War II. The narratives connected with these struggles reached our American eyes and imaginations, deeply influencing the way we viewed Russia.

Since the 1950s, Soviet and then post–Soviet Russian sources have become far more open, and we no longer have to rely on calculations made on the basis of widely scattered details put together with the help of historical and more-or-less reliable statistical assumptions. Still, the education obtained by a thorough and wide-ranging examination of the Soviet press and the details of Russian history, supervised by the first-rate mind of a man who had lived in the vortex of those storms, provided a good basis upon which an American youth could work toward an understanding of the many-faceted reality we call Russia.

Harvard

While working with Dr. Kulischer at the Library of Congress was wonderful, when you work for the government, in a certain sense, you become a bureaucrat. If everyone in the US government did as he or she wanted, it would be total chaos. It has to be controlled, as a bureaucrat's work is controlled. That really wasn't my idea of a lifestyle. At that time, the Ford Foundation was offering fellowships to people who wanted to do graduate work in Slavic studies. So I applied for one, and I'm happy to say I got one the first year I applied, which meant that I could go to Harvard in 1954 and pursue a PhD in the Slavic Department.

The Ford Fellowship supported Viv and me, and in that same year our first child was born. So I had the responsibility for a baby child. I couldn't live on nothing. But I'm happy to say that for the first year the Fellowship supported us. It wasn't like Rockefeller, but we could eat and clothe ourselves. The second year, they turned me down for the Fellowship. But happily, I had some friends at Harvard, and they worked things out so that I got a TA-ship.[47] As a matter of fact, students were only supposed to get three-fifths of the theoretical total salary for a TA, but I said, "Look, I've got to support a wife and child." So they let me have four-fifths, and that was pretty much enough to keep us going; although, to be honest, my father supplemented our meager income.

While I was studying at Harvard, I encountered two very different kinds of academic experience. On the one side was the enormous self-confidence of the old-fashioned New England intellectual upper classes, something rather new to me, with my traditional Midwestern upbringing and background. At its extreme ends, it sometimes seemed to be an expression of boundless arrogance and condescension toward ordinary people and events. This later was to make itself felt in specialists who came to immediate post-Soviet Russia without the slightest background in Russian history yet ignorantly had ready-made solutions for all of Russia's economic and political problems. They were somewhat reminiscent of the Russian students described in *The Brothers Karamazov* who, according to Dostoevsky, impressed their German university teachers with extremely audacious views combined with absolute ignorance; but, give them a blank sheet of paper, and the very next morning they would come up with a chart of the stars!

Despite the boundless arrogance of many students, on the other side was the chance to hear and absorb at least some of the ideas presented by teachers who worked at the highest levels of human understanding. Among such people in the Slavic Department of Harvard University, and perhaps the most famous and influential, was Roman Osipovich Jakobson, a philologist whose work and personality will probably be remembered well into the twenty-first century. A product of the famous Russian Formalist[48] interpretation of language and literature, so roundly cursed by official Soviet philology, he gave a passionately projected version of Russian language structure and style that made

---

47 A TA-ship was a paid appointment in the form of a Teaching Assistant Fellowship.

48 The formalists got into violent arguments with those who took a sociological approach to literature—an approach that argued that what literature had to say was also important and perhaps more important than its form. But the formalists introduced some very original ideas about literary form and, consequently, were taken seriously. Eventually they made their way to the United States and came to be known as the New Critics. New Criticism became the American version of what Russian formalism was.

students reach deeply into the words of everyone from the greatest Russian writers to their nemesis, Comrade Stalin himself. The speeches of Stalin had more in common with Church Slavonic[49] than any good Marxist would care to admit.

Jakobson did all of this teaching using impeccable English syntax and grammar, pronounced with the phonetics of a Hollywood actor representing a Russian accent thick enough to cut with a knife! His French likewise was superb. Mazon[50] claimed that the *Igor Tale* was a forgery of the eighteenth century, and Jakobson proved beyond all possible linguistic doubt that this was an authentic document, and, by God, Mazon was going to read it! Then he went so far as to publish his findings in French so that Mazon would have no possible excuse not to read them. Needless to say, the effect on future Russian language teachers was absolutely unforgettable.

In contrast, and often in opposition to Jakobson, was a scion of an old Florentine family name, Renato Poggioli. A brilliant Italian Slavic scholar, he had fled Mussolini's Fascists and ended up at Harvard's Slavic and Comparative Literature Departments. Renato Poggioli became an immigrant to the United States and a member of the American Army during World War II. After he would listen to my report, Poggioli would say, "Very well, Mr. Weil-a," making my Jewish last name the most Italian it would ever be. "Is a brilliant report-a, but you have missed the point-a." He was priceless. To this day, I see his face and hear him saying, "You have missed the point-a." His pronunciation of Russian names (try "Goliadkin," from Dostoevsky's

---

49 Church Slavonic was the literary form of the Common Slavic language used in the tenth century. Cyril and Methodius, two monks in the Byzantine Empire, were commissioned to make a written version of the language. Accordingly, they translated the Greek Christian documents, e.g., the New Testament, the lives of the saints, the order of the religious service—in short, all the things that were necessary for Christianity, into the Slavic language. To accomplish this task, they used the Glagolitic alphabet; however, followers of Cyril and Methodius went on to develop a different alphabet, which they named in honor of Saint Cyril.

50 André Mazon (7 September 1881-13 July 1967) was a French scholar who was a great expert in Church Slavonic. He claimed that the Russian epic, supposedly from the twelfth century, was actually not written in the twelfth century, but rather was a product of the eighteenth century by someone who was trying to imitate it. This claim greatly upset Roman Jakobson, who was convinced (I think on good evidence) that it dated back to the twelfth century. So Jakobson and Mazon got into a tremendous controversy.

The Double, with a five-syllable, Italian lilt, translated as "naked," and pronounced as if it were "knocked"!) was enough to cause a phonetic riot, but his analysis of literature was superb and deeply moving. He was about as far from the ideas of Formalism as it was possible to be and very much in the classical tradition of Italian intellectuals. Yet his understanding of Pushkin's poetry and the prose of Dostoevsky and Tolstoy brought the American reader very close to the intents and the moral powers of those magnificent writers. It would be hard to exaggerate his effect on future American interpreters of Russian literature.

Somewhere in between the two of these two professors was Mikhail Mikhailovich Karpovich. He had worked in the Washington Embassy of Kerensky's[51] Provisional Government and then had decided to "wait a few months" until the Bolshevik business would run its course. Those few months turned into a lifetime career at Harvard University. He also became a kind of patriarch of Russian émigré intellectuals living in the United States. His New Hampshire farm became a kind of summer resort for such people, a place vividly described in Nabokov's delightful novel *Pnin*—one of the least acidulous of the creations by that remarkable author. Karpovich was the voice of good manners and quiet reason. In his widely heeded presentation of Russian intellectual history, he insisted on the place of rationality and understanding in the development of Russian thought. Karpovich brought calm and common sense to a department in which the sound of harsh polemic was often heard.

Karpovich had the effect of bringing his students to a rather sympathetic understanding of the culture they would teach in the future. It was Karpovich, who once told me, "Well, I know that you're enthusiastic about Dostoevsky. Now you know, some people charge that the Devushkin in *Poor Folk* is like Bashmachkin in Gogol's *Shinel'* (*Overcoat*). Whereas for Devushkin, there's a girl, for Bashmachkin, there's an overcoat. Which would you prefer: an overcoat or a woman." And for the life of me, I didn't know what to say.

---

51 Aleksandr Fyodorovich Kerensky (4 May 1881-11 June 1970) was the man who headed the Provisional Government shortly after the March/April (old/new style calendar) upsurge that forced Tsar Nicholas II to abdicate. Kerensky remained in power until October/November 1917 when the Bolshevik coup d'état forced him to flee to the United States where he lived out his days.

Later on Ralph Matlaw, a fellow grad student, said, "Well, you should have told them it depends on the quality of the goods." That was Karpovich.

At one point, the department wanted to hire Nabokov. He had come in when Karpovich was away for a semester. Nabokov was asked to teach a course on Tolstoy, and he immediately threw out *War and Peace* and brought in *Anna Karenina.* I think Karpovich wanted to invite Nabokov to join the department, but Jakobson was fiercely against it, maybe because he was jealous. Colleagues asked in dismay, "But how can you oppose him? He's a great novelist," to which Jakobson replied, "If this were a zoology department, would you want to hire an elephant?" They never hired Nabokov. I don't think Nabokov ever forgave Jakobson for that.

There was also Chizhevsky at Harvard. Chizhevsky didn't want to speak English, so you had to speak Russian. That was the first time I heard lectures in Russian. He not only talked with a slight Ukrainian accent, but his hand was always over his mouth! I couldn't make heads or tails of the first couple of lectures. Luckily, another guy gave us a sort of summary in English after the lectures. Eventually, I caught on. He believed in vampires, *vampiry*, and he was very Russian.

One evening, he and Jakobson were in a New England country house at night, and he said, "Jakobson! Jakobson! Vampir sidit pod oknom!" (Jakobson! Jakobson! A vampire is sitting under the window!) And Jakobson exclaimed, "Zakroite okno!" (Close the window!)

One day in class, he asked, "Why did they bury Vladimir[52] feet first right away?" I hadn't the foggiest idea. A student replied (brilliantly, I thought): "That was so the devils couldn't get him." Chizhevsky's spooky reply: "Nyet, ne cherty—a vampiry!" (No, not devils—vampires!) I think he actually drew a vampire on the blackboard.

---

52 Vladimir Sviatoslavich was the grand prince of Kiev from 980-1015, who sent emissaries to the Byzantine emperor saying that he wanted to marry the Byzantine emperor's sister (he was looking for dynastic alliance). The Byzantine emperor said he would concede if Vladimir converted to Christianity, which he did. Vladimir subsequently forced the east Slavs in and around Kiev to become Christians, so in that sense he was the founder of the Russian Orthodox Church, and he's revered today as Saint Vladimir. As a matter of fact, according to the *Primary Chronicle*, he had 700 concubines, but evidently in those days you could have that many concubines and still be a saint.

On one of Chizhevsky's exams, the topic of Apocrypha came up. The issue concerned the ancient uprising of the Jews against Roman rule and the famous last stand suicides at the siege of Masada. The heroic leader of the rebels was Bar Kokhba,[53] "Son of a Star," whose name I remembered from a fifth-grade, religious-school class in Cincinnati (circa 1937). So I owed it to my early teachers when I discovered that Chizhevsky thought that showed extensive knowledge! Never put down Sunday school—not even at Harvard!

In the midst of all these classically oriented Russian scholars, I had the temerity, and perhaps the naïve brashness, to undertake writing a dissertation on the life and work of Alexei Maximovich Gorky, a writer whom many regarded as the epitome, or perhaps the worst, of the Soviet literary world. Many of them ignored the stylistic and varied political complications of his career, and they took for granted the vastly over-simplified soubriquet of "the great proletarian writer." Well, you can imagine how happy the faculty members, many of them émigrés, were to hear I was going to write on Gorky. "Why do you want Gorky, that red, that commie?" I said, "No, no. Now wait a minute, you don't quite understand." They said, "Look, it's a free country. If you want to ruin yourself, go ahead. Write about Gorky."

One of the most articulate and eloquent opponents of anything connected with Soviet culture was Vsevolod Setchkarev, another professor at Harvard. He was not only negative about Gorky but also about my beloved Dostoevsky. Setchkarev shared Nabokov's famous distaste for the creator of some of the world's greatest novels. Setchkarev did not go to the extent of Nabokov, flunking students who tried to defend Dostoevsky, but the Harvard professor expressed his dislikes loudly and eloquently.

---

53 Simon bar Kokhba is a famous figure in Jewish history. When the Romans ruled what had been Israel, there were those among the Jews who decided to stage an uprising against the Romans in an effort to become independent. They neither wanted to be a part of the Roman Empire, nor did they want to worship the Roman emperor, and eventually they ensconced themselves in some heights above Jerusalem called Masada in 132 CE. Simon bar Kokhba was their leader and, at least according to legend, a very heroic fighter. Eventually, the Roman armies were too strong for them, and Simon bar Kokhba perished in 135 CE together with those people who had risen up against the Roman emperor.

Nevertheless, the Harvard Slavic Department never tried to prevent me from expressing, as strongly and convincingly as I could, my own approach to these writers. I can only say that many of my professors found my interest in Gorky to be way out in left field, to use a peculiarly appropriate baseball metaphor, yet no one tried to stop me. There were many objections along the way, some of which caused me to write better than I would have otherwise. Of course, there were also intentionally destructive attacks, but that, too, is a part of life that leads to a somewhat different kind of understanding, equally necessary in its own right.[54] The intellectual and cultural atmosphere created by the giants of American academic life in the Harvard Slavic Department had a lasting effect on many young people who later went on to present a picture of Russian culture and of Russia itself to tens of thousands of American students in universities across the entire United States. I think it would be fair to say that the open debate aroused by the pressure cooker of Harvard's New England atmosphere created a kind of intellectual and emotional richness very necessary to a proper understanding of Russia, in particular, and human life, in general.

Brandeis

I was at Harvard for four years (1954–1958). In 1958 I was hired as an assistant professor at Brandeis University in Massachusetts from 1958 through 1965. I was pleased to be a part of Brandeis, which had recently been established as a secular university and was supported by the American Jewish community. It seemed to me an ideal example of what the great Jewish tradition of study and learning could contribute to the best part of the US educational system and would make a great tradition open to an important part of the general population. When I came to Brandeis, the administration said, "Russian? Come on, these kids aren't going to study Russian. Listen, we had someone here that tried to teach Russian, and they gave him hell. We're warning you, give it one year and plan on leaving at the end."

---

54 For those who might be interested, I invite you to read my book titled *Gorky: His Literary Development and Influence on Soviet Intellectual Life*, published by Random House in New York (1966) and in Russian translation in Moscow (1993).

That greeting was what I got from Brandeis. Contrary to the initial warning, a large group of students responded enthusiastically and energetically to my love for the Russian language and its literature. I soon had a wide reputation as an effective teacher and sympathetic encourager of talent and sensitivity. I'm proud to say that no small number of these youngsters went on to have impressive careers in scholarship, politics, and all kinds of creative enterprises. It was especially nice to see that some students overcame an inherited bias they had received from their families against Dostoevsky.

After working as a professor at Brandeis University for several years, perhaps the reader could empathize with my consternation when the University decided to get rid of me, and it hurt like hell. All of the bright memories of six years remembered as sparklingly creative and widely recognized seemed to collapse into dust. The despair produced an unforgettable pain. But, luckily for me, my previous experience and family situation had taught me that life requires action and work, no matter how bleak the circumstances may be. I had been serving as Secretary-Treasurer for the American Association of Teachers of Slavic and East European Languages (AATSEEL), and one of its stalwart leaders, Tom Shaw, let me know about Northwestern University's plans in my field.

Northwestern

When I came to Northwestern to investigate, I met the dean of the College of Liberal Arts, Simeon Leland. He made a very unusual and dramatic impression, judging by his Indiana Hoosier accent and flaming red socks. I later learned that he had once been considered for a high position in the Federal Reserve System, but powerful people feared his colorfully unorthodox ways and decided he could do less harm as a university dean.

Upon our meeting, Leland sensed that I was somewhat skeptical. Then his Hoosier-colored voice poured over me—it was something akin to being caught in a powerful rainstorm. Suddenly the downpour ceased, and he said: "Young man, never turn a man down until you hear what he has to say." That got my undivided attention, and I'm glad, to this day—forty-nine years later—that I took his advice. Of course, it didn't hurt that he also connected my wife, Vivian, with an outstanding professor of philosophy in

Vivian Weil in front of the Illinois Institute of Technology.

Chicago. That connection started her on a track that led to a pioneering, creative, and effective career, eventually as director of the Center for the Study of Ethics in the Professions, at the Illinois Institute of Technology.

Viv has a remarkable mind. Whenever I make a mistake, or whenever I do something that's not quite logical—or whenever I'm just being myself—she's very critical. I get very mad because she's criticizing me, and I get especially mad because, dammit, she's always right! That's what's really insufferable. After I calm down, I realize that, as a matter of fact, she has insight that I don't have. Throughout her schooling, she was always the top scholar. When our kids were born, she was determined that she was not going to let somebody else raise them. As long as they were below school age, she was always going to be with them, for better or for worse.

When the youngest one entered kindergarten, Viv began teaching at Boston University. She taught a course in general literature, music, and art. When it comes to art, boy, she's always the last one out of the museum. The guards would say to her, "Madame, it's time for us to go home!" "Just one more picture!" my wife would say. For her, one more picture means a whole hour because she picks out every single point. "Didn't you see that?" "I didn't see anything!" "Did you see that in the painting? And did you see that?"

Then we came to Chicago; she wasn't entirely happy about the prospect of leaving Boston. That was a traumatic experience, because, you know, I was more or less tossed out of Brandeis. But, when we got to Northwestern, Dean Leland put her in contact with a woman named Ruth Barkan Marcus, who unfortunately died not too long ago. By that time, Ruth had become an international star in cognition and philosophy. Viv approached Ruth and said, "Can I have a job as a TA?" Ruth's reply: "You don't want to be a TA. Look, get your PhD and you'll teach."

Viv said it wouldn't be so easy to combine that with family responsibilities. Ruth replied that it could be worked out and got her into the excellent Philosophy Department at the Chicago campus of the University of Illinois. During graduate school, Viv became close friends with a remarkable woman by the name of Nancy Cartwright, a fellow graduate student. Nancy received a Genius Grant from the MacArthur Foundation. Today, Cartwright lives in Oxford and teaches at another university. She and Viv make quite a remarkable pair.[55]

Viv's doctoral thesis advisor was Irving Thalberg, the son of the famous Hollywood director who was responsible for many of the Marx Brothers films. The son was extraordinarily handsome and could have been a star actor. Instead, he became well educated and a highly gifted teacher and scholar.

Later on, Ruth went to Yale, Irving went somewhere else, and the department sort of broke up. But, when Viv was there, it was probably one of the best philosophy departments in the country. From there, she got a job at Illinois Institute of Technology, where she started the Center for the Study of Ethics and Professions and was a pioneer in the field. People have come to her from all over the world—from Moscow, from London, from Australia—you name it. Her name is really known in that field, and she's a force to be reckoned with.

---

55 Nancy's husband was a very prominent British scholar who was really quite personable and was a close friend of Isaiah Berlin, a twentieth-century Russo-British Jewish social and political theorist, philosopher, and historian of ideas. Berlin came to Northwestern to receive an honorary degree and he heard a little bit about my work. He was obviously interested in Russian studies, so we had him over to dinner at our house. The entire evening I couldn't get a word in edgewise; I was absolutely spellbound. He's a nonstop talker, but he's brilliant. We've had exposure to some wonderful people.

Irwin Weil in full bowtie array.

I accepted the position at Northwestern, which surprised many of my past Harvard friends: "Are you crazy?" they said. "Those blokes don't accept Jews there!" They were reacting to Northwestern's record of genteel anti-Semitism dating back from the 1920s and '30s, when its reputation was as a place for the conventional socially elite. I replied that if such was the case, Northwestern was in for a terrible shock with my Jewish presence and temperament.

I'm happy to say that my friends' apprehensions were totally mistaken. When I went down the Northwestern halls whistling and singing Yiddish tunes, people there expressed friendly interest in what seemed to them charming melodies not previously heard. When students came to me and said they would like to do some work in studying the Yiddish culture of Eastern Europe, I decided to take the bull by the horns and submit the proposed project to the powers that be (or, rather, the powers that were in 1966). To my delight (and the happiness of the students), the reaction of the university could be understood by the reply, "That's exactly what we've been waiting for!" That was the beginning of my course introducing large numbers of students, both Jewish and Christian, to the delights of such wonderful humanistic and penetrating writers as Sholem Aleichem[56] and Yitzkhak Leib Peretz.[57] Over twenty-five years, I had a chance to broaden my own non-specialist knowledge and open a fascinating world to many young students.

At Northwestern, there was no one central ethos to which you felt compelled to respond. There was no such thing as "dressing the way they do at Northwestern." There was no such thing as "thinking the way they do at Northwestern." I mean, it's a mishmash of the best part of the entire American population put together, and showing what you can do with it, whether it's Jewish or Christian, people from the country or the city, black or white—it didn't make any difference. They were all put together, and boy, did I like that. I had the feeling that what we did for them, we could do for the most intelligent part of the American population.

When I first came to Northwestern, there were those who were timorous about studying the Soviet Union, especially if some sympathy could be detected in the teaching. Still, the atmosphere might best be described by an incident that occurred fairly early on: A complaining visitor told the university president that one of his faculty members was a bad person. When the president heard my name, he asked what the problem was. The complainer replied that this man was a "friend of the Soviet Union." And the president's response? "Well, what do you expect? He teaches Soviet literature. Do you want him to hate what he teaches?" That was the end of the story.

For several semesters, I taught a course with eight hundred students. A year or so before I retired, the dean at commencement said, "How many

---

56 Solomon Naumovich Rabinovich (2 March 1859-13 May 1916) was the real name of a writer who called himself Sholem Aleichem. He wrote tales in Yiddish that were marvelously humorous and yet at the same time loving towards the Jewish people. His satires are absolutely irresistible and contributed to his becoming probably the most famous and popular writer in Yiddish. Eventually, he left Kiev and came to New York where he lived out his days. His stories have a humor and understanding that I would say is unique and very powerful.

57 Yitzkhak Leib Peretz (18 May 1852-3 April 1915) was a popular Yiddish writer who knew how to use fantasy and satire to attack hypocrisy and arrogance. He, Sholem Aleichem, and Mendel Mochre Seforim were the big three in Yiddish prose.

Program of Philadelphia Theatre run by Weil's former students.

of you have been in one of Dr. Weil's classes?" Two-thirds of the students raised their hand. For me to see that was something exciting: God, what you could do with those students! Those Northwestern students reacted like gangbusters because if they knew that a professor cared about the subject, they reacted magnificently. What a wonderful experience my life has been at Northwestern from 1966 to the present (wow that's almost fifty years)! I've been so lucky.

Chapter three

Entry into the Soviet Union

The Russian short story begins on page 1,000. A fellow's got to warm up a little.

—*Irwin Weil*

Going to the Soviet Union

In 1960 I was terribly eager to go to the Soviet Union. Up to that time I had been forced to study Russian from afar. In 1948 I had the chance to live in France for two months. While in France, I went to the Soviet Consulate in Paris and requested a visa so I could put into practice my one-year's acquisition of Russian grammar. The Soviet diplomats proceeded to laugh in my face and inquire just what world I thought I was living in. Then, twelve years later, the Committee for International Exchanges at Indiana University sent me to New Hampshire to see Professor Ernest Simmons from Columbia University who wrote an acclaimed biography of Tolstoy.[1] We had a very friendly talk; he was impressed, and the result was that in 1960 I was given the chance to go to the Soviet Union for one month.

Each participant got thirty days in the Soviet Union. I was going with tremendous expectations, but also tremendous fears, because I had read that the Soviet Union was our enemy and that communism was a horrible

---

1   Simmons, E. J. (1960). *Leo Tolstoy*. Boston: Little, Brown and Company.

thing—all kinds of bad things about the Soviet Union. I had no idea how I was going to be greeted or whether people were going to follow me or God knows what.

In those days, there was no direct flight. As I was getting off the plane in Brussels, I realized that a whole bunch of Soviets had just arrived on an Aeroflot[2] flight, and they were running into some place, so I figured I would run after them and see where they were going. They were all running to a place where they could buy something to drink. And what do you think they all bought? Coca-Cola. In those days, there was a tremendous campaign against Coca-Cola in the Soviet Union: "Koka-kolonizatsiia! (Coca-Colonization!) It's a bourgeois drink! It's terrible! It's horrible!" The passengers on the Aeroflot flight said, "Wow, we were expecting something amazing to happen when we drank it." The eagerness with which they drank their first Coca-Cola was incredible. So I went up to some guy and said, "Well, what do you think?" He said, "It's not that bad, but I don't see what all the fuss is about." So that was Coca-Cola.

A Welcome to Remember

When our plane finally arrived in Moscow, you can imagine how excited I was. Some guy came to meet me, and it turned out that he was from Intourist[3] and he started talking with me in English. I said, "No, no, no. I didn't come here to talk in English. I want to talk Russian!" "Nu khorosho. A gde Vash talon?" (Okay. By the way, where is your ticket?) I said, "I'll be very happy to give you my *talon* if you'll tell me what the hell is a *talon*." I didn't realize it was a French word. That was my brilliant beginning in Russia. Then, he said in somewhat of an aggrieved tone, "Vy govorite kak personazh iz Tolstogo." (You speak like a character from Tolstoy.) I replied, "Eto, moi dorogoi tovarishch, ne sluchaino!" (That, my dear comrade, is no mere coincidence!) So we went to the hotel. It was the Ukraina (Ukraine), which was a fairly new hotel, and the hotel employee took my

2 Aeroflot was the official name of the Soviet civilian airline and continues to serve as the name of the airline for the Russian Federation.
3 Intourist, an abbreviation for "Inostrannyi turist," which means foreign tourist, was the organization that received foreign tourists and took care of them when they travelled to the Soviet Union.

passport. That was something I didn't quite expect, although I should have remembered that in all European countries they took your passport at hotels. I said, "Look, you know, I really want to go for a walk down the street. Can I do that without a passport?" They said, "You Americans, come on. Go ahead. No problem."

So I went for a walk; I was dying to talk to somebody. I had studied Russian for twelve years, for God's sake. By this time, it was evening and people were walking about the streets. So I approached a guy; he saw that I wanted to say something. He stopped for a minute, but I was too frightened to say a word. He said, "Ekh, pomeshannyi" (Hey, crazy person!) After he left, I hesitated to speak with anyone for two hours. Finally, I said to myself, "You goddamn coward, the next time you see a young man coming without a girlfriend, you're going to talk to him." So I went up to this young guy and said to him, "Ia-Ia-Ia am-m-merikanets. Eto moi p-pervyi. . . . Vy khotite pogovorit' so mnoi?" (I-I-I am an Am-m-merican. This is my f-f-first. . . . Would you like to talk with me?) He said, "Ei, tovarishchi, amerikanets!" (Hey, comrades, an American!) The next thing I knew, I was surrounded by a giggling bunch of students.

In those years, most Soviet people had not had the chance to meet Americans, so I often found myself surrounded by a crowd of people eager to pepper me with questions. They were as eager to find out about me as I was to learn, firsthand, about them. Initially, what surprised me most was the obvious friendship and good nature that I encountered among the people. I had always taken with more than a grain of salt the American propaganda all around me about the Soviet people. Still, nothing had prepared me for the welcome I felt that summer. They wanted to know everything. One student said, "Peredaite privet kolkhoznikam Ameriki!" (Pass along our greetings to the collective farmers of America!) I said, "U nas netu kolkhozov." (We don't have collective farms.) He was disappointed at our lack of collective farms, but he was adamant that our non-existent agricultural workers accept his enthusiastic and friendly greetings. I did not contradict him further. They wouldn't even let me experience standing in interminable lines. Even when I protested that I didn't want special treatment, they simply picked me up and thrust me to the front of any particular line I headed for.

I later learned that Soviet people often resented the special treatment handed out to foreigners: Why couldn't they receive the same good treatment? But to me personally, they only wanted to show the nature of genuine Russian hospitality. Later on when Americans would ask me, "Wasn't it dangerous there?" I would reply, "Yes: When two different households invited me to come on the same day, I would have to eat two full Russian meals. God forbid that I should pass over any course of the meal!" That over indulgence in good food and drink could send anyone to a dispensary for treating eating disorders!

I started doing things that, if I had acted that way in Chicago, would have gotten me in all sorts of trouble: stopping people on the street for conversations, inviting myself to sit down at a stranger's restaurant table, barging into strangers' conversations, and so forth. People invariably responded in a friendly, hospitable manner. It was bewildering. Before then, I don't think I had ever met that kind of hospitality. I'm not saying that Americans are inhospitable. It's a different style. And, oh boy, did the people I meet conquer me in a hurry.

On one occasion in a restaurant, I heard some guys talking in a foreign language that I'd never heard before. I said, "Pardon me, but could you tell me what language . . ." It was Georgian. I said, "Do you mind if I sit. . ." One of the men replied, "Oh, an American! Sit down right next to us." They praised my grammar. As customers though, they were very dissatisfied. One of them said to the waiter, "Daite zhalobnuiu knigu." (Give me your complaint book.) I said, "What the heck is a zhalobnaia kniga?" He replied, "That's where you write down how you're dissatisfied." The waiter was very upset, but he had to give it to the man. The Georgian customer proceeded to write about how they weren't waited on the way a Georgian should be waited on. These Georgians, they would go even one step further than the Russians in hospitality.

KGB

In the early days, when Eisenhower and Khrushchev signed the agreement for cultural exchange, there would be something like twenty or thirty participants from each side. We would support their people and they would support us. Almost all of the Americans were taking courses in literature, philosophy, or history, and in 1960 at Moscow State University all of us lived in space served by one block of elevators. In the beginning, Russians were very suspicious of the American students, wondering who we were.

On one occasion, I met some guys who were very friendly, and they said, "We want to introduce you to someone from the Ministry of Higher Education." I said, "Sure, that's very nice." And we got to be sort of friends; he would talk with me and I would talk with him, and all of a sudden, he was inviting me to lunch. Pretty soon, I began to wise up a little bit to see who this was. He was one of the guys from the KGB.[4] But, look, what were they going to do to me? Probably the worst thing they could do would be to ship me out of there, and I could live with that. So I wasn't really scared.

After a while, I began to talk to other guys like this and realized that they were pretty shrewd. They were the one set of pragmatists that I met in the Soviet Union. They weren't talking ideology; they weren't talking nonsense. I came to realize that these were the people who had control of the situation in Russia, and if your job consists of controlling the situation, you can't live at a *dacha*[5] in the countryside, or in comfortable circumstances. You have to live among the people you control.

To be sure, there was only one time the KGB tried to intimidate me, and they did it skillfully enough in the beginning that I didn't realize what was up. They said to me, "We know you're sending spies over here on your program." I said, "No, no, you don't understand. These are real scholars. We make them sign assurances that they're only working for themselves, and if we discover later on that they were lying, boy they'll never have a job at another university." They said, "Yeah, yeah, we know that they're spies. We could stop that program tomorrow if we wanted to." I said, "But that would be a shame. It's such a good program!" They said, "Yeah, yeah, we know."

But then it hit me what they were doing. They were trying to intimidate me. So I said, "Well look, it's your country, not mine. I can't tell you

---

4   KGB (*Komitet gosudarstvennoi bezopasnosti*, Committee for State Security) was the last in a series of names describing the Soviet intelligence and police force responsible for maintaining stability and political control.

5   *Dacha* is a house usually located in the country and often used as a vacation home for people from the city.

what to do. But you've got a bunch of people who are coming over here who are treated very well; your people are showing them enormous hospitality. They go back to America and say, 'Russians are wonderful people.' They want to come back. If you stop this program, we still have to give our students practice in speaking Russian. So we'll have to go to the émigrés, and you know how the émigrés feel about the Soviet Union." I continued, "Now look, what do you want? Friends or enemies?" And they said, "Let's talk about something else." Aside from that, they could, under certain circumstances, be helpful. They could often direct me to places where things could get done, whereas if I asked people outside of the KGB, I didn't receive the same kind of help.

Of course, I was dealing with a security police force quite different from earlier Soviet periods when they had gone by different titles—Cheka, NKVD, etc.[6] The days of mass repressions and executions were past. To be sure, there was still some repression and widespread apprehension; Khrushchev had vastly reduced the population of the forced labor camps, so there was a strange kind of balance between a threat in the air and a sense of a possible lightening of the load. The Thaw[7] was a reality in people's minds, as was Aleksandr Solzhenitsyn, novelist, historian, and critic of Soviet totalitarianism.

During my first visit, I was very eager to purchase Russian literary collections that were hard to obtain in the United States. One series I was especially eager to acquire was the twelve- or fifteen-year run of a pre-Revolutionary journal, *Zolotoye Runo* (*The Golden Fleece*). It contained some of the most intriguing literary work and criticism of the early twentieth century. Much of the writing was outside the limits allowed by Soviet rules. When I asked about it in the best Moscow bookstore, they motioned

---

6   Cheka (*Chrezvychainaia komissiia*, Extraordinary Commission) and the NKVD (*Narodnyi komissariat vnutrennikh del*, People's Commissariat for Internal Affairs) were different names for the secret police. The Cheka was the first Soviet organization created to make sure that the regime stayed in power and it did not hesitate to use ruthless means.

7   The "Khrushchev Thaw" refers to the period from the mid-1950s to the early 1960s when the Soviet government lifted certain restrictions and allowed some open criticism in an effort to create a more free society. Originally, *The Thaw* was the title of a novel by Ilya Ehrenburg published in 1954, one year after the death of Stalin.

me toward a man hovering by the side of the room. He asked me if I could really pay, and I told him about the allowance I had from the university library.

Literary Endeavors

The next day, the man to whom I was directed at the bookstore rolled up in a taxi (not easy to get in Moscow in the 1960s). We soon arrived at an apartment district quite different—much better kept—than I had previously seen. He hopped out and went in to get the set of journals owned by his friend. Shortly afterward he came back and told me to follow him back inside to persuade the man to sell the journals. For a reason I can't quite explain—a vague emotion that I felt—I didn't follow him. Eventually he came out with the journals and we set off. After about five minutes, he turned white and said, "The KGB is right behind us." At that, he told the driver to stop the car, and he jumped out.

I simply continued back to the university and made sure that everyone on the floor knew that I had a wonderful literary treasure. The next day, my erstwhile KGB connection called me and said that I evidently had experienced an interesting taxi ride on the previous day. When I asked him what the hell was going on, he replied, "Next time, don't let your friend take you to the neighborhood where they're doing aviation research." Happily, the journals are now resting in an American university library.

The 1960s were days of enormous popularity for Salinger's *Catcher in the Rye*. In 1960 I visited the Soviet Writers' Union in Moscow and there was a guy there who said, "Well, have you got something new for me?" Fortunately, I had brought some books. I said, "Well, I've got some books here that you might enjoy. It's a sensation in the United States that's called *Catcher in the Rye* by a fellow named Salinger. Read it. Tell me what you think of it." He took the book. About two and a half weeks later, I saw him again and he said, "Well, it's a beautiful book, very well written. New York humor." But he added, "It could never be published here. For one thing, we couldn't translate the New York-style humor."

A year later I was surprised to learn that the book was translated into Russian and came out in the Soviet Union. It became enormously popular among Soviet readers. Evidently some adolescent problems are universal, regardless of which economic or social context surrounds them. So I suppose I was the one who brought Salinger into the Soviet Union.[8]

One place I was very eager to visit was the Institute of World Literature. By that time, I was working on a book about the life and works of Maxim Gorky—a writer who played an enormous role in the world of Russian literature as it existed right before the 1917 revolutions and then developed complicated relations with the Soviet regime. Gorky was his pseudonym (literally: "bitter"), and in front of the Institute stood a rather moving statue of the man. Inside were the archives preserved from his life and work. It was also a center of general literary research.

While I was visiting the Institute of World Literature, I was greeted by Nikolai Zhegalov, who turned out to be a very interesting combination of traditionalist Russian ways and the new Soviet system that was supposed to be transcending those backwards customs and replacing them with something much more modern and progressive. I soon came to understand that Zhegalov was interested in me precisely because I came from a family that energetically tried to preserve the best of old-fashioned ways—I was not without sympathy for Russians and their culture, which had undergone such a painful upheaval in relation to their own traditions. It was kind of amazing to watch him slurp tea from the glass through a lump of sugar held by his teeth in the front of his mouth—a genuine relic of the past—while at the same time ardently defending the Soviet approach toward radical change and reform.

I appreciated hearing Zhegalov's Soviet perspective, and he likewise appreciated hearing my American perspective. He was genuinely surprised to learn that Americans in a city called Cincinnati (the heart of what they considered bourgeois barbarism) were actually enthusiastic about a poet named Shakespeare. He grew to love the American folk songs I would sing with him and his friends. Finally, to my surprise, he begged me to bring him a copy of—of all things!—*Little Lord Fauntleroy*,[9] which Zhegalov only touched after carefully washing his hands.

---

8   In Russian *Catcher in the Rye* translates as *Nad propast'iu vo rzhi* (literally, *Over the Abyss in the Rye*).

9   *Little Lord Fauntleroy* is the title of a book about a young man who dresses in very fine-laced clothes and who has a very delicate way of life.

Then I was assigned a woman from Intourist to take me around. She was rather cynical—half amused and half disgusted—at this naïve guy from America who was reacting so nicely to the Soviet Union, the bad sides of which she knew all too well. She sort of patronized me the way an old, experienced person would patronize someone who was almost a baby. The psychology was rather interesting; yet she helped me a great deal and also arranged for a special car that took me to Yasnaya Polyana, Tolstoy's family estate.

My experience at the Tolstoy family estate was very moving. I saw Tolstoy's grave and the birch forest that he planted. He couldn't be buried in Christian ground because he denied the divinity of Christ. He said Christ was a great teacher but wasn't the Son of God, which upset the Russian Orthodox Church. After his passing, the Church denied him a Christian funeral; they wouldn't bury him in sacred ground. On the other hand, he's buried under the magic stick of reconciliation and love, which is kind of nice. There is this little hillock, with dark green stuff over the top of it. The coffin is under that hillock, and then you look out and there's this vast forest of birch trees that Tolstoy planted. The birch trees have white bark and light green leaves, so there's dark green on the grave and light green spreading out all around. It's a wonderful sight.

Trip to Leningrad

During this first visit to the Soviet Union, I was given a chance to go up to Leningrad with friends of my family: Henry David, a high-ranking psychiatrist in the state of Ohio, and his wife, Tema. Henry David was the son of a respected Jewish judge in Germany. The Nazis had organized a severe beating of his father, and—happily—the family managed to emigrate to Cincinnati. Henry had become an American military officer in World War II and had the opportunity to confront the people who had organized the beating of his father. He spoke no Russian, so I went with him and his wife.

En route to Leningrad, the three of us stopped in Novgorod and, wow was that an experience. The Nazis had totally destroyed many churches and it was a city with a church from every century since the ninth. They rebuilt those churches brick by brick. It was astounding, especially considering the atheist ideology of the ruling regime. I saw trees with big nails sticking out of them and asked, "What's going on with those nails in the trees?" I learned that those were the trees on which Germans hung people every day. It was quite the experience. I went to the Kremlin[10] there and heard a talk given by one of the Soviet guides, who obviously didn't know very much about the religious figures painted on the walls of the Kremlin cathedrals. She said, "Now there you see Abraham. He was the first man." Now I swear I didn't say a word. I was not about to ruin her day. But she took one look at my face and said, "That's not right, is it." I said, "No, well as a matter of fact it's not quite correct. Abraham was the first Jew." She said, "Avram byl pervyi evrei! A kto byl pervyi chelovek?" (Abraham was the first Jew! Then who was the first person?) I said, "Vy slyshali pro Adama i Evu?" ("Have you heard about Adam and Eve?") She then answered, "Ooo, da! Adam i Eva!" ("Oh, yes! Adam and Eve!") It was so charming; she really was being very nice, and she knew that she wasn't the deepest scholar of the Bible.

After the tours at the Kremlin cathedrals, a woman came up to me and started talking. I suddenly found myself talking with a very interesting person from Nizhny Novgorod, whose impression of Americans was that they were rich people who liked to come around and shower Soviets with money to show that they were better. I tried to talk to her and said, "Well, you know, we're not all like that. That's really a bit of an overstatement." You could see that there were reservoirs of skepticism inside her. While I was developing a changed perspective of the Soviet Union, I could tell that this woman also was beginning to see the world in a somewhat different way. In any case, she became very interested with what she could learn about America and we corresponded by mail for a while.

Having left Novgorod, we travelled along a road surrounded by farm territory. It suddenly occurred to me that we were in an area of collective

---

10 A "kremlin" in Russian refers to a strong fortress. Many cities in Russia have their own kremlin, however, foreigners typically associate the term with the Moscow kremlin, which houses top leaders, as well as historic cathedrals, a bell tower, and even a plaque dedicated to Dwight D. Eisenhower, who oversaw the American-led invasion of Western Europe in World War II.

farms, the enterprises so widely touted by the Soviet regime. I thought to myself, "Wouldn't it be useful to try a visit?" My glorious experience in farming prior to that time was during World War II. People were needed on the farms, so the Boy Scouts were mobilized. I was one of the Boy Scouts sent out to help a farmer. I had just learned how to drive, so he said, "Drive this truck." I drove the truck into a ditch! That ended my career as a farmer, which lasted about seven minutes. The farmer said, "That kind of help we don't need."

We stopped the car and entered a small village store, identified ourselves as American visitors, and asked about the possibility of visiting one of the famous *kolkhozy*.[11] The man behind the counter said, "Go talk to the chairman in the neighboring house." That man eagerly jumped at the chance to show off his socialist enterprise. He took us into a field near a barn, where a group of women were working with hoes and loading some harvested crops onto a truck. As we watched, a loud clamor erupted. The women began to shout angrily at the driver, who retorted in the Russian way, with not the gentlest profanity in the world. I was impressed by the way the chairman of the *kolkhoz* handled the mini-battle. In soothing, calm tones, he got the driver to improve his language and his tone. At the same time, he convinced the women that complaints would be answered and they would not suffer.

While we were visiting the farm, I saw people working, it seemed to me, fairly efficiently. But from what I've since read and heard about the *kolkhozy*, they tried as hard as they could to avoid work on any place except their own private plot. Consequently, the private plots produced something like seventy- or eighty-percent of the fresh vegetables for the whole country, whereas the income they received from their labor on the general collective farmlands would be comparatively low. The farmers were paid for workdays, but were paid a pittance; however, the fresh fruits

---

11 *Kolkhoz* (plural: *kolkhozy*) is an abbreviation for "kollektivnoie khoziaistvo," which means collective farm. These were the organizations that the peasants worked on after they were driven off their land. They had to sell at government-stated prices and work for government-stated salaries. For the most part, life on the *kolkhoz* was very difficult, although it later improved somewhat after the government allowed workers on the *kolkhoz* (*kolkhozniki*) to sell a small part of their produce at open markets.

and vegetables that they raised on their private plots brought in some badly needed money.

When I had a chance to talk to the chairman, I tried to breech the delicate subject of how the collective farms were set up in the 1930s. He acknowledged that those were very troubled times, requiring a great deal of social repair and administrative tact.

The chairman said, "You know, in the beginning, it was very tough. When we started the *kolkhozy*, a lot of people lost their lives, and a lot of people were exiled." He didn't try to gloss it over. "But we've come to a different stage now. Things are somewhat better today, and you can see that this place is reasonably well organized."

Compared to 1933 or 1934 when the farms were set up, things indeed were better. Those earlier years were terrible: forced grain requisition, leaving the farmers with nothing to plant in the spring, led to starvation. People died of starvation, and others were shipped out to Siberia and dumped in the snow with nothing around them. It was hideous.

At that point in our conversation, we were interrupted by a group of men carrying the largest mushrooms I had ever seen. They wanted to invite American guests to a delicious feast built around fresh mushroom soup. Our response was immediate and hearty. I could easily imagine that mushroom concoction, as my dad would say, going down the hatch. Unfortunately, my dreams were crudely interrupted. Some men came running up shouting that we had to get back on the road immediately. Apparently, the police unit that had been alerted to record our passing had not observed us at the expected time. We were obliged to get back to our journey so that they could make the reported sighting. Thus ended our eager anticipation of good mushroom soup.

Malyshev and Alekseev

After we arrived in Leningrad, I was eager to get to the Institute of Russian Literature, a famous center of research and the location of the Pushkin Archives, including all of his original manuscripts. Roman Jakobson had given me the names of two well-respected literary scholars, Malyshev and Alekseev. I realized that the latter of the two last names was the same as the real last name of Stanislavsky, the founder of the internationally famous Moscow Art Theatre and the Stanislavsky Method so revered (and sometimes cursed) by Broadway actors. It turned out that the Alekseev I met was related to Stanislavsky.

After I arrived at the Institute of Russian Literature, the literary scholars, Malyshev and Alekseev, were curious to talk with a young American who had studied Russian language and literature and had done some work with Roman Jakobson. Jakobson's name and his work carried great weight in the whole world of Russian studies. They eagerly took me to many places in Leningrad. One of my favorite places included the statue of Peter the Great known as the "Bronze Horseman," made famous by one of Pushkin's greatest poems, whose manuscript I saw at their Institute— Pushkin's writing in the lines getting bigger and bigger as his emotions grew stronger. I was impressed by Tsar Peter's thin legs hanging over the sides of the rearing horse, as if in counterpoint to the horse's feelings rising up. The dynamism of Petrine Russia and Pushkin's view of the Tsar's personality made quite an impression. Malyshev and Alekseev's insight into Russia's great literary history was somewhat balanced by their attention to small details. They insisted that I try some of the Leningrad ice cream, one of Russia's very pleasant products. The man at the serving counter asked me how many grams I wanted. What the devil did I know about grams of ice cream?

Jewish Father and Son in Leningrad

After spending the day exploring Leningrad with Malyshev and Alekseev, I spent the evening at the opera. It turned out to be *Il Trovatore*[12]—the Russians called it *Trubador*. As I was watching the opera, I suddenly realized that the guy in the seat next to me was looking at me, so I began to look at him. In Yiddish he says to me, "Are you a Jew?" I said, "Yeah." He said, "*Ich oich.*" (Me too.) And a conversation began. We pretty quickly went to Russian because my Yiddish doesn't amount to a very long conversation. He said, "Well, how are things in America, particularly for Jews?" I said, "Well, there's anti-Semitism, but thank goodness it's not really a problem now. It's a lot less." He said, "I want you to come to my house and

---

12 *Il Trovatore*, literally the *Foundling*, is a famous opera by Giuseppe Verdi.

meet my father." I said, "I would love to, but tomorrow I've got a plane to catch to Moscow." He said, "I'll pick you up at your hotel at 7:00 in the morning, and you come to my house; I'll get you there in time."

So early the following morning, the man I met at the opera came and picked me up and took me to his house. His father took one look at me in a bow tie and American suit and said (in Yiddish), "This is a Jew?" So he goes to the bookcase, takes some books off it, and blows dust off of them. The dust was just flying in every which way. The father said (in Yiddish), "Well, read it to me" (the book was in Yiddish). Well thank God I could read Yiddish. No sooner than I began reading, the father exclaimed, "Did you hear? A Yid! A Yid!"

We had a very nice conversation, entirely in Russian. The father said, "I want to show you my family." I replied, "Well, how nice." So he proceeded to open photo albums, page after page, and I'm a sucker for anyone's pictures. "Oh, very old! Nice cousin you've got there," and those sorts of phrases. I must have gone through two or three albums, every page of every album. Suddenly, the father shut the album and said in Russian, "Molodoi chelovek, ponimaiete li Vy, kazhdyi chelovek, kotorogo Vy videli v snimakh, umer natsistami v voine?" (Young man, do you realize that every person you saw in the photos died at the hands of the Nazis in the war?) Phew! For once in my life, I really didn't know what to say. He saved his family because he worked as a tailor in Leningrad, which was under siege, sewing uniforms for the Red Army. When he explained that to me, I found it hard to hold back the tears. I didn't know what to say. To this day, I still feel that emotional reaction.

After the father showed the album to me, he poured me some tea and preserves and said, "Vy dolzhny imet' varen'ie v Vashem chaie." (You should have jam in your tea.)[13] "Kol Yisrael chaverim." (All Jews care for each other.) It was all I could do to get out of there without bursting out crying. This experience made me realize that although I'd heard a lot about what'd happened to Jews in Europe before, boy, it hit me like a ton of bricks to be confronted with it in that form. We all know that losing someone you love is a very hard thing to take. That kind of loss causes a

---

13 There is a very special kind of jam in Russia called *varen'ie* (commonly transliterated *varenie*) that Russians like to pour into their tea.

deep emotion of grief in anyone's life. It is a terrible thing to experience that loss—not by the natural process of people growing old and eventually dying, but rather their lives getting cut off either in the middle of life or in the beginning of life. The feeling it creates, at least inside me, is a terrible sadness and sympathy for those who have suffered. It arouses emotions that are hard to live through, including sometimes a feeling of terrible rage. "Ooh, if I could only get my hands on those murderers," you know. But that doesn't last very long. I've never thought that vengeance is a particularly admirable quality, although I suppose it's a natural reaction. I didn't seek out such encounters, but they hit me from all directions and were very powerful.

Firsthand Learning Experiences

While in Leningrad, I also had a chance to see a woman who had earlier been my first personal contact with a Soviet citizen. She was Olga Ernestovna Mikhailova, who worked at the internationally famous Hermitage Museum.[14] She had come to the United States to examine artistic glass design. I had the chance to talk with her in Chicago, and she told me about her experiences as a very young woman at the Hermitage during the hideous Nazi blockade—it lasted over 900 days. She had told me to come to Leningrad and visit her and her architect husband, Mikhail Petrovich Sokolov.

When I got to their house in Leningrad, Olga Ernestovna and Mikhail Petrovich told me about the history surrounding the changing of their city's name from St. Petersburg to Petrograd, and then to Leningrad. Mikhail Petrovich had been in the Leningrad trenches fighting Hitler's army. He scorned the traditional tales of heroism—as he put it, the exalted experience of a moment of strong action. The real experience involved sustaining, month after month, year after year, the constant fear and grit required to maintain a fighting army. He showed me the palaces inhabited

---

14 The State Hermitage (*Gosudarstvennyi Ermitazh*) is one of the greatest art museums in the world and was founded by Catherine the Great. It houses a magnificent collection of paintings. During the Soviet era when I first visited it, the expressionist and modern art paintings were kept hidden in storehouses. I had the rare privilege of seeing some of them.

by the Tsarist aristocracy—"They're now all driving taxis in Paris, with which they're more lethal than they ever were in the Tsar's Holy Russian Army. The so-called proletarian politicians are now living like aristocrats in those same palaces." Mikhail Petrovich and Olga Ernestovna (to them, I was always Irvin Sidneevich[15]) gave me a real introduction and complete inundation of the genuine St. Petersburg personality and *stoikost'*, or the ability to stand and survive.

I encountered a number of other people who were young at the time of World War II. Sometimes they tried to convince their parents not to go with the crowd being rounded up by Nazi authorities, but encouraged their parents to try and escape. Some of them, particularly in Eastern Europe, eventually made contact with partisans behind the front lines in the USSR—they were attempting acts of sabotage against the Nazi armies. Some of them managed to survive, and then they managed to get an education for their own entry into life. As a matter of fact, I know a number of people from the West, from France, who went through the same experience as those in Eastern Europe.

There was a woman here in Chicago married to a colleague of mine at Northwestern, whose parents never came back one day during World War II. She and her younger sister had to do something. Luckily, they were taken in by some nuns and were protected. One time the Germans came to give presents to the kids, and she didn't get a present. She was very upset, only to realize later that the nuns were protecting her from the Germans by hiding her. But at the time she was very upset that she didn't get a present. That kind of experience leaves its mark on a person. They go through life with a certain toughness, and a certain paranoia or tendency to paranoia, because everything around them is a potential threat.

Aunt Olga

Eventually I arrived back in Moscow and returned to the States. My Uncle Burt in Cincinnati asked, "I have only one question: Should I defect?" And I said, "Well, Uncle Burt, I think you should wait a couple of years." Burt

---

15 A patronymic is a name derived from the name of a father or ancestor, typically by the addition of a prefix or suffix, e.g., *Ivanovich* (son of Ivan), or as in my case, *Sidneevich* (son of Sidney).

was my father's brother—the youngest of three brothers. He was a free spirit, and he was married to Olga, the only one with a Russian background in the family, and nobody got in Olga's way. Her maiden name was "Rashun." They were in the Jewish encyclopedia from Russia, and I think they were prominent Jewish scholars. She was born in this country and had no real connection with them, except she knew they were her ancestors.

Aunt Olga had strong opinions and a strong arm. Around the 1920s, she became the women's tennis champion in the state of Ohio, and later the women's golf champion. As a matter of fact, she was known nationally as a golf champion. She had a wonderful personality. She was the only Democrat in a family of Republicans, and when the family would get together, she'd argue them to a standstill! Nobody got past Aunt Olga. In the 1930s, she was determined that Hitler was not going to get at least one of the Jewish orphan children, whom she was going to adopt.

So Aunt Olga applied to a Jewish orphan asylum in Germany for a baby girl. She was not going to take a child away from its mother. They found a baby girl. My sister's father-in-law, who had studied medicine in Germany in the 1920s as a young man, knew some German doctors who went to the orphanage and attested to the fact that this child was healthy and normal. I think the little girl must have been somewhere between two and four years old. When Olga went to finalize the adoption, she not only had to fight Nazi bureaucracy in Germany, but to her horror, she had to fight Roosevelt's bureaucracy here in the United States. She was the only one in the family who liked Roosevelt. Oh boy, was that drama. But nobody stopped Aunt Olga.

There was a nurse at the orphanage who showed the child a picture of my aunt, "Das ist die Mama. Das ist die Mama." (That is the mother. That is the mother.) The child managed to get out on the last boat that crossed the ocean before the war, and my aunt was waiting at the dockside. When the girl saw my aunt, she ran up and said, "Ah! Das ist die Mama!" (Ah! That is the mother!) I tell you, the tears came, and my aunt's reaction was heartwarming. By God, she saved that child from a terrible fate. Aunt Olga had that kind of courage.

Back in the United States

After returning to the states, I talked a great deal about my experiences. By and large, people were very sympathetic. I think they thought I was a little crazy. But I think there's something about me, particularly when I've talked publicly, that sort of draws people in. Emotionally they're drawn in, even if they disagree with what I'm saying. So usually the public reactions were very friendly, with one or two fairly violent exceptions. "You think you know something? Where were you when they arrested these people? Where were you when they were sent to camps? Where were you?" I ran into that once or twice, maybe several times. Or it was something like, "Yes, of course, you saw the nicest part of the country. You don't know the horrors that took place." And to a certain extent they were right.

There's some truth to the negative reactions I heard from people to whom I told my experiences. But I've hardly ever gotten into trouble in this country for my relations with people in Russia. Many would say, "He's a nice fellow, he's a young fellow; we like him so let's listen to what he has to say." As to my view of Americans, I soon realized that most Americans didn't have the foggiest idea, heads or tails, of what was really going on over there. They'd read a bunch of propaganda, which, alas, was not entirely untrue. After all, there were indeed some terrible things that happened in Russia. But they saw it in such a grotesquely exaggerated way, and some terrible things happened here in the United States, too, but happily no where near to the extent of Stalinist repressions and mass arrests and executions.

I once had an experience talking to former officers of the US Army, and they had been fed an awful lot of propaganda about our commie enemies and that sort of thing. I said, "You know, I spend a lot of time in the Soviet Union and often I hear terrible things about the United States from the people there. 'Bourgeois reactionary imperialists, racists, unemployment, and public vulgarity.' And I say to them, 'Well, to a certain extent, what you're learning about the United States is true, but if you want to understand the country, you've got to understand both sides. Just as there's a negative side to America, there's also a very positive side, like marvelous universities, good hospitals, wonderful music, free and fair elections, and freedom of speech. These are good things, and one must understand them to get a real picture of the country. At the same time, one must understand the opposite, negative sides: such phenomena as unemployment, racism, and extensive public vulgarity. As in any large collection of human beings, there are two sides of a coin. True understanding requires a balance of vision. Don't ignore the negative sides, but balance it with the good.'"

As I continued to speak to these officers, I explained, "Just as you would like for Russians to see both sides of our country, why don't you keep your mind open to seeing both sides of Russia?" And the officers listened to me. "You know, he's got a point. Let's listen to him," they said. To a certain extent, I received a similar reaction almost wherever I went in this country.

Talking with émigrés was a different story altogether. There once was an attack on me in the *Novoye Russkoye Slovo* (*New Russian Word*).[16] My friends said, "Look, ignore it. Don't respond to it, just ignore it." This negative response wasn't true of all the émigrés. Among the more reasonable émigrés was Professor Herman Ermolaev of Princeton University. While he considered me somewhat naïve, lacking his wartime experience, he also was able to appreciate my own experience in Soviet Russia. Our relations reached an intense moment at a time when Soviet publishers were considering publishing an edition of memoirs by Kornei Chukovsky, with whom I had enjoyed a close personal relationship for nine years. An émigré colleague at Yale (alas, I've forgotten his name) started publicly announcing that the memoirs would contain all kinds of anti-Soviet declarations.

Chukovsky's relatives begged me to get the man to lay off, since his trumpeted (and exaggerated) announcements would inevitably prevent the publication of the volumes. I knew the man at Yale would not listen to me, a well-known enthusiast for international cooperation, so I went to my friend, Professor Ermolaev. I said to him, "Look, Herman. I've always said that if anyone wants to be a big, prominent, anti-communist hero, they should do it at the expense of their own blood. But if they do it at the expense of somebody else's blood, that's totally wrong." And he said, "I

---

16 *Novoye Russkoye Slovo* is the name of a Russian language newspaper in New York run by émigrés who often take a rather conservative line toward American politics.

absolutely agree. We don't agree on everything, but I totally agree." I said, "Now Herman, I want you to go to this guy and tell him to please lay off, because if he keeps talking this way, they're never going to be able to publish what they want to." He said, "Don't you worry. The guy will not say another word." And he didn't—I'm proud to say that.

I came to realize in a very powerful way just how lucky I was to have been born in a country where I could easily express my true convictions and feelings without fear of being assigned to a concentration camp, or—even worse—being killed. To be sure, there was anti-communist hysteria in the United States, which was kind of silly, but at least we weren't killing the accused people, although a small number of them had to leave the country. I began to see how utterly absurd some of the things that were being said in this country about Russia actually were, although, and God knows, there were also some people who really understood. Not everybody who was anti-Soviet was necessarily a knave or a fool. There were things to be criticized and criticized very harshly.

Some years back, in Cincinnati, it turned out that a man whom I had known as a counselor at a summer camp—he was a great favorite of the youngsters—was accused of being a Communist and an active Soviet supporter. There was a great legal hoopla raised against him. He made a public statement along the lines of: "Look, I may have done some foolish things in my salad days,[17] but . . . " and that was the end of the whole affair. To be sure, other people suffered to a much greater extent, but that was a small matter in contrast to the mass surges of public condemnation, arrests, camps, and executions in Stalin's time. Our own excesses are nothing to be proud of, but they can be and were strongly and loudly opposed inside the United States. Of course, this also means that those who had the courage to speak up in the USSR were people of extraordinary valor.

Days at Brandeis University

These early trips to the Soviet Union coincided with my days at Brandeis University, where two eminent figures on the left taught: Irving Howe and

---

17 "Salad days" is an idiom having the meaning of one's best days—the days when one is strongest and most enthusiastic and able to do what one wants to do.

Philip Rahv. Irving was a socialist with a long history of opposition to Stalin. He also was a very sensitive reader of literature, with a traditionally devilish Jewish sense of humor, laced with colorful Yiddish phrases. His humor was particularly sharp when facing arguments, whether they came from his right or his left. I always enjoyed being in his company and watching him satirize arguments from both sides, just like a switch hitter at Cincinnati's baseball park.

Philip Rahv was the well-known editor of the prestigious *Partisan Review*, a highly respected source of sociological literary criticism—the kind that used to drive Nabokov up the wall. Rahv had a rasping voice with central European intonation. Although he was well aware of the repressions in the USSR, he could never quite bring himself to criticize them openly—at least not in my presence. He liked my ability to render in English some of the vitriolic, infernal Soviet Russian-language polemics, and we had a great time rocking with the rhythms of Trotsky's furnace-hot linguistic emissions. Rahv was very much moved by my accounts of the innards of post-Stalinist Moscow, where the metaphor of the Thaw alternated with the periodic angry eruptions of Khrushchev.

In the late 1940s, Brandeis University was proudly founded as a Jewish-sponsored, non-sectarian institution. The sponsoring people from among the members of the American Jewish Community were very eager to establish their reputation as patriotic citizens of the United States. Consequently, when any publicized statements came out about Brandeis questioning the honor or safety of the country, the university administration and its community supporters reacted in a deeply emotional way. Case in point: During the 1962 Cuban missile crisis, with the intended placement of Soviet missiles close to the shores of Florida, a statement by a Brandeis professor created a huge rumpus. The faculty member stated that he wished that Castro had bombarded us with destructive rockets! This stupid, ill-conceived statement, mostly ignored by the community at large, caused no end of hand wringing at Brandeis.

Brandeis invited a scholar named Michael Astour to teach Yiddish and present some of the remarkable literature and poetry in that language. He had been in Poland before the war and was the son of a well-known

Jewish judge in Vilna.[18] He had gone to Paris to study at the university and was brought back to Vilna in 1940 when the Soviets came in. Among the early actions of the Soviet authorities was the arrest of both father and son. After being placed in solitary confinement, the son said to the authorities, "Look, you gotta understand! I can't live without some books at my beck and call. You gotta give me a book!" They said, "Okay, we'll give you a book a week." And what do you think they gave him? They gave him books that they confiscated from people. So he got to read Babel[19] and other books confiscated by the very people who had imprisoned him. He had a wonderful memory; he demonstrated it by telling me stories of Babel by heart.

Eventually the authorities released him from solitary confinement and sent him to a concentration camp in Kazakhstan. The guy who ran the camp soon realized that this was an educated person, a pretty smart fellow, and he said, "Look, you're going to be my bookkeeper, understand? You know what you have to do?" Michael replied, "I must very carefully write down what comes in and carefully write down what goes out." The camp director said, "You idiot! You're going to keep two books: one for the inspectors and one for me. Understand? And God help you if you show anyone my side of your ledgers!" Michael said that that was when he began to understand how the camps were structured.

Eventually Michael married a sweet, little Russian girl, and Khrushchev declared amnesty for anyone who had had Polish citizenship up to a certain year, which Michael had. When he went to get his exit visa, they wouldn't give it to him! His friends said, "Misha,[20] be a reasonable realist—not a stubborn fool!" "I'm not going to give him a bribe! He's bound by law to give it to me, and by God he's going to give it to me! He's not going to

18 Vilna is the Polish form of Vilnius—the capital of Lithuania. It was once a very Polish city and even though it's now the capital city of an independent Lithuania, practically a third of the population speaks Polish. The city has deep ties to Jewish culture.
19 Isaac Emmanuilovich Babel (13 July 1894-27 January 1940) was a famous Jewish Soviet writer who enthusiastically supported the 1917 Revolution, but who became increasingly disillusioned with the results. Eventually, he was arrested, shot, and killed. His tales include a great deal of dialect and mastery of the language and I think still are enormously popular among Russian readers.
20 In Russian, Misha is the diminutive form of Michael.

get any kickback out of the deal." "Misha, give him the rubles!" "No, no. Absolutely not."

Michael (Misha) eventually got out, came to the United States, and he and his wife Masha (the two of them took pride in being a mish-mash) went through the citizenship procedure. Masha was told, "Alright, now write in English: 'I can read and write English.'" She replied, "Okay. 'I can read and . . .'" and the inspector prompted her: "With a *w*." Misha recalled, "That's how it goes in America." Then he said, "Now let me tell you how I became a Soviet citizen. They came to us one night and said, 'You're going to become a Soviet citizen.' I replied, 'No, no! Never! Only by force!' They said, 'Okay,' and pulled out a pistol. 'Come on.' That's how I became a Soviet citizen."

Misha contrasted this experience with the guy saying, "With a *w*." That was Misha. He was an interesting guy. We worked together at Brandeis for a while. Incidentally, he was quite an anti-Zionist. Conversely, I was a Zionist for purely political reasons. When I was a kid, all the pretty girls were Zionists. If the pretty girls were Zionists, I was a Zionist. I was maybe thirteen years old, if that.

Returning to the Soviet Union—1963

I was determined to get back to the Soviet Union, and in 1963, I received a grant to conduct research there for six months. Vivian didn't want to stay in Boston by herself with the kids, so she and the kids decided to live in Florence, Italy. We left by boat from New York and sailed through Genoa and took the train from Genoa to Florence. The experience in Italy was extraordinarily interesting. I learned enough Italian to at least get along. Up until that point in my life, I was almost a total teetotaler,[21] with the exception of Jewish holidays when you have to drink a little bit of wine for the ceremony. But when I saw the Italians drinking wine, it was so good that I lost all my teetotaler-ship. It was really something. The Italians, in their own special way, were charmed by my Yankee Russian accent when I pronounced words in their noble and musical language.

---

21 "Teetotalism" refers to the movement that is against all alcoholic beverages. To practice teetotalism means to abstain completely from alcoholic beverages.

From Florence, I traveled by train to Moscow. Mind you, this was in the winter, so the trip that was supposed to take three days actually took four, owing to heavy snowfall in Czechoslovakia. On the train were some Italian Communists, who were essentially sharing my compartment. They turned out to be delightful guys, people that I really had a good time with. They were tremendously curious about an American going to the Soviet Union. Mind you, I had two typewriters: one with English type and one with Cyrillic. I also had a guitar, box-loads of books, and the normal stuff you take to travel for six months. So I had a whole bunch of stuff in the compartment.

The Italian Communists also had a lot of stuff in their luggage, which later on turned out to be wonderful black market items for the Soviet Union: nylons, sausages, etc. Obviously, they were going to sell at a good profit. They were *good Communists* by God. We had some very interesting discussions. They were particularly upset about the Catholic Church in Italy and felt it had too much power. They loved to talk about the evils of capitalism as it appeared in their Marxist-scourged version. Yet they were very tolerant and accepting of my non-Marxist views—after all, I was their friendly, bourgeois, imperialist reactionary! So the ride to Moscow all worked out very well.

We arrived at the Soviet border, and I must admit, I was a little worried about customs looking at all this junk that I had. What were they going to say? What were they going to do? They got to the Italians first and ripped their stuff to shreds. The nylons were hanging over here, the sausages over there, and I thought, "My God. If that's what they do with Communists, what are they going to do with a stinking bourgeois?" So the Customs officials came to me next. I was literally trembling, and they said, "Do you speak English?" I said, "Yes." They said, "Well come. Our translator's sick today. We need some help." So I agreed.

They led me to a compartment where there were a bunch of British diplomats and asked them some questions, which I, in turn, interpreted for them. They said, "Oh, okay. Thank you. Goodbye." I started to say, "You didn't look . . ." A sophisticated Russian man who had been observing the scene said, "Forget it. Write to the Foreign Ministry later, if you so wish." They didn't want to look at my stuff! I said, "What the hell's going on here?" So I went back and said to the Soviet train conductor, with whom

I had been conversing for several days, "Look, these guys are Communists. How come you tear their stuff apart and leave a confirmed bourgeois alone?" He said, "We know who's going through here. Customs officials knew those guys were a bunch of black marketers. They also knew you were an American scholar who was interested neither in black markets nor in political agitation." So that was that—my first encounter with official Soviet bureaucratese.

Well I got there. Unfortunately, the train was a day late. Other Americans on the exchange who were already at the university didn't know what the hell had happened to me. They had sent someone the day before to meet me at the train station. But the train never showed up, so they didn't know what to do. The Italians said to me, "Look, we'll help you." I said, "That's alright. I speak Russian." They smiled at me, "Okay." Then I managed to get a taxi driver and piled in the huge amount of junk that I was carrying.

When we got to the university, the *starukha*, or old lady, there said, "Dokumenty." (Documents.) I showed her all the documents that I had, which were in English. "Eto ne dokumenty, eto po-angliiski!" (These are not documents. They're in English!) I said, "Nu, eto edinstvennyi . . ." (Well, these are the only . . .) She replied, "Nu, Nu . . . idite v posol'stvo!" (Well, well . . . go to the embassy!) I said, "Posol'stvo? Net, net . . ." (The embassy? No, no . . .) Her foot was almost at my rear end.

Fortunately, at that moment, the Italian Communists came down the hall like the American cavalry to rescue me. They found a guy from inside who got me into my temporary room. While this was going on, the taxi driver came back and said, "Look, you forgot two boxes." I said, "Oh gosh, thank you so much. I'd like to give you something," so I gave him a picture postcard of Boston, which he regarded as a treasure and squirrelled it away. The old lady reacted immediately: "Netu li odna u Vas dlia menia?" (Do you not have one for me?) I replied, "Khorosho, no ne vykidyvaiete menia iz universiteta." (Okay, but don't toss me out of the university.) To which I heard the usual, "Da chto Vy!" (Oh, come on!)

Since I had been delayed by snow, they had to put me in a temporary room. Later, while carrying my luggage down the hall to a permanent room, I encountered an angry woman, a kind of hall guard, who started yelling at me. This woman thought I was stealing the suitcases and guitar.

I said, "Net, net. Vy ne ponimaiete. Ia ne kradu. Eto moi veshchi." (No, no. You don't understand. I'm not stealing. These are my belongings.) She let me go. The next time I came, she came out yelling at me again. After a third time, a Komsomolets[22] came out and said, "Ostav'te ego. Razve Vy ne vidite, chto eto inostranets?" (Leave him alone. Can you really not see that this is a foreigner?) He turned to me and said, "Ne obrashchaite vnimaniia na neë; ona starushka. Ona ne ponimaiet." (Don't pay attention to her; she's an old lady. She doesn't understand.) I said, "Nu, skazhite: kradut li zdes'? Eto sotsializm! Kradut?" (Well, tell me: do people steal here? This is socialism! Do they steal?) He said, "Net, vy amerikantsy nikogda ne kradëte. Eto chërnyie babuny iz Afriki." (No, you Americans never steal. It's those black baboons from Africa.) The black baboons from Africa. Here I was, ready to discuss the issue of racism and the American Civil Rights struggle, and the local Muscovite racism struck me in the face.

Vitya, My Roommate and Advisor

So I eventually moved into my permanent room,[23] and my roommate's name was Vitya. He seemed like a friendly sort, and he kind of liked my Russian. He said, "U menia est' devushka v moëm nomere. Menia netu. Ponimaiete?" (I have a girlfriend in my room. I'm not here. Understand?) "Ponimaiu." (Understand.) Sure enough, ten minutes later a group of Komsomol members knocked on the door: "Vy videli Vitiu?" (Have you seen Vitya?) "Net, ia ego ne videl." (No, I haven't seen him.) After the group left, he came out and said, "Vy nastoiashchii paren'." (You're a true pal.) So from that point on we were friends. I was okay because I had protected him.

Vitya was something of a bubblehead. I think they put him next to me because they figured if he defected with me they wouldn't lose much.

---

22 *Komsomol* is the abbreviation for "Kommunisticheskii soiuz molodëzhi" or the Communist Union of Youth. People like to say it's the Soviet version of the Boy Scouts. It was a youth organization that tried to prepare at least some young people for entrance into the Party and governmental service. It also promoted social activities for young people. A male member was a *Komsomolets* and a female member a *Komsomolka*.

23 Soviet-style dormitories often follow a block design where two rooms share a common entryway and bathroom but roommates have individual rooms separated by a common wall.

But supposedly he was quite a scholar; he had studied German for twelve years. I said, "Sprechen Sie Deutsch?" (Do you speak German?) Later on, I put an English text on his desk; he couldn't tell if it was English or German. Here he had studied German for twelve years. That was Vitya, my erudite roommate.

But Vitya was an awfully nice fellow. He said, "Look, for the first couple of days, don't go anywhere. Just stick with your books. Do your work. I have to write about you, and I'll write, 'He's not a spy. He's a scholar.'" And, by God, he kept his word. He sort of relieved me of heavy oversight. Six months later when I was leaving, he said, "Nikogda ne zabyvaiete. Net ni odnoi strany vo vsëm mire, s kotoroi my bol'she khotim imet' khoroshiie otnosheniia, chem Soiedinënnyie Shtaty. Dazhe esli u nas est' bol'she inzhenerov, chem u vas." (Don't forget. There's not another country in the entire world with which we want to have good relations more than with the United States. Even if we have more engineers than you.) That was Vitya. Bless his soul.

I was assigned an advisor who seemed mild-mannered and friendly. I later learned that he had a wide reputation as a blind conformist to the Communist Party line. He certainly seemed harmless to me. He gave me a suggested readings list, taught me how to use the local telephone, and then disappeared until the end of my stay in Moscow. At that time, without the slightest knowledge of what I had done, he wrote an official evaluation of my work, saying I had fulfilled my plan. Such was my official advisor. My real objective in Moscow was to gather material on M. Gorky, the subject of my PhD dissertation.

The Search for Chukovsky

Back in 1960, I had been working on Gorky to write a PhD dissertation, and I had gotten to the point where I was already doing some writing. While going through stuff at Widener Library,[24] I found a great deal of material that blindly followed a propagandistic line about a writer who was far more complex than such so-called analysis could understand. There was a time in

---

24 The Harry Elkins Widener Memorial Library is the main library at Harvard University where I spent many an hour. It houses a wonderful collection of Russian literature and Slavic materials.

the Soviet Union when Gorky became a sort of a poster boy for the Communists. He was the one big name from before the Revolution who was with them. "Velikii proletarskii pisatel'!" (The great proletarian writer!) In the first place, he wasn't a proletarian; he was from the meshchanstvo.[25] In the second place, it wasn't true that Gorky was always a proponent of one ideological system of thought. There were times in his life when he had all kinds of troubles, and God knows what happened at the end of his life.

But in going through this stuff, I noticed a name in the catalog: Chukovsky—a name that I had never seen before. Since I was rather assiduous in those days, I ordered an old book from the Harvard repository library. The pages were so brittle you could barely touch them. It was a brilliant and sparkly account by a man named Chukovsky and was written in the early twentieth century. In many ways, it predicted accurately some of the turns and twists that would occur in Gorky's eventful twentieth century life. But I thought to myself, "Who the hell was Chukovsky, anyway?"

And so in 1960 when I first went to Moscow, I visited the Soviet Writers' Union and said, "Skazhite, kto byl Kornei Ivanovich Chukovskii?" (Tell me, who was Kornei Ivanovich Chukovsky?) And they said, "Ne byl, a est'. On eshchë zhivët." (Not was, but is. He's still living.) I said, "Come on. He wrote this stuff at the beginning of the century. This is 1960 already. Maybe it's a son, a grandson, maybe an accident of the same name." They said, "No, no, it's him. Would you like to meet him?" I said, "Oh boy, lead me to him."

Meeting Chukovsky

So they put me in a big limousine and sent me out to Peredelkino, which was the first time I'd ever heard the name. A half-hour's tram ride from the center of Moscow, Peredelkino was a specially reserved place with houses for Soviet writers. So I came to the *dacha*, and on the door there was a big sign that said, "Kornei Ivanovich bolen. Kornei Ivanovich zaniat. Shchadite ego vremia." (Kornei Ivanovich is sick. Kornei Ivanovich is busy.

---

25 *Meshchantsvo* is a term for a class that existed in Tsarist times of petty merchants and petty traders. Gorky, for example, was somebody who came out of the *meshchanstvo*. It is somewhat above the peasantry, but somewhat below what we would call the bourgeoisie.

Spare his time.) I'm a timorous sort, but I took my heart in my hands and knocked on the door.

This full-of-energy old man—who was in his late seventies at that point—came to the door. "A Vy kto takoie?" (And who are you?) "Ia Irvin Uail." (I am Irwin Weil.) "Otkuda?" (Where are you from?) I said, "Iz Bostona." (From Boston.) "Iz kakogo universiteta?" (From what university?) This conversation went on for a little while. He said, "Davaite v les. Poguliaem, pogovorim, net?" (Let's go to the forest. A little walk, a little talk, no?) He quoted from *Alice in Wonderland*. So off we tromped into the woods.

While we walked through the woods, Chukovsky said, "Now if you don't mind, tell me in English: Who are you?" I said, "But Mr. Chukovsky, I just told you." He said, "That's alright; tell me again." And I suddenly realized that this was to see if I was a ringer or not—if I really was an American as I said I was. When he heard my Cincinnati English (no *KGB-shnik*[26] talked that way) he said, "Nu khorosho. Pochemu Vy prishli ko mne?" (Okay. Why did you come to me?)

I said, "Well, I'm coming to you because I'm writing about Gorky, and I know that you were very close to Gorky." You see, in the 1920s, Gorky had developed the idea that the revolution should bring about an educated proletariat; proletarians should have the same culture as the aristocracy once had. Incidentally, Mayakovsky[27] thought this was nonsense. Mayakovsky was all for "proletkult," proletarian culture. "We should throw Shakespeare and Plato and Tolstoy over the side of the steamer of history," is what he said. Gorky's take on the matter was, "No, that's totally wrong. We don't want to destroy high culture; we want to distribute it among the whole population!" So Gorky's whole idea was a project called "Mirovaia literatura" [World Literature]. A commission was established to supervise the work of highly cultivated literary specialists. They were going to

26 A *KGB-shnik* was a member of the KGB.
27 Vladimir Vladimirovich Mayakovsky (19 July 1893-14 April 1930) was a poet who was born in Georgia and who very early on was tremendously enthusiastic about the Communist Party and program. I must say that he wrote some very lively poetry, first of all about himself and second, about the things that the regime did. In the 1920s, he became increasingly disillusioned and in 1930 committed suicide. There are rumors going around that he did not really commit suicide, but was executed by the KGB; however, I have no evidence to support such rumors.

Irwin Weil in front of portrait of Gorky at the writer's final and very ornate Moscow house.

translate at a very high level all the best work of world literature into Russian and make it available in inexpensive editions that the proletariat could afford. In so doing, the proletariat would become cultured.

In those days, when Gorky already had a strong reputation, Chukovsky was a young man and had the reputation of someone who really had mastered English. He had become fascinated by the poetry of Walt Whitman. Eventually he published seventeen editions of translated verse of the American poet. Chukovsky's previous wide reputation as a critic and English to Russian translator convinced the organizers of World Literature that he would be the right man to oversee the project. Consequently, I knew that he had worked closely with Gorky. I said, "Look, I know that you were close to Gorky, and I really want to know something about him. I want to know how he died." Now, you understand, this was a very ticklish question because, in 1936, people had been executed on the grounds of working as fascist agents to kill the great proletarian writer. So this was fraught with all kinds of political perturbations and to my amazement, he trusted me. There was something about the way I presented myself that he figured, "I can confide in this guy; he's not going to betray me." If I had repeated what he proceeded to tell me, he'd have been in trouble.

Irwin Weil at the art deco stairway in the Riabushinsky mansion given to
Gorky by Stalin.

Chukovsky began his explanation of Gorky's death. He started, "Ia byl
tam, kogda on umiral" (I was there when he was dying), which surprised
me. He said, "We writers were sitting there, in the house.[28] We knew that
he was dying, that he was in very bad shape. One of us went up to the door,
and suddenly we noticed that the door was locked. So we said, 'Ei, otkroite
dver'!' (Hey, open the door!) And a soldier who was standing there said,
'Tishe, khoziai[29] zdes'!' (Shut up. The boss is here.) Stalin had come to rifle
through the papers. When Stalin left, they unlocked the door."

Now I know for a fact that Gorky had published very famous memoirs
of Lenin that were quite interesting, although already somewhat tenden-
tious. Stalin had wanted Gorky to do his memoirs (that is to say, Stalin's),
and Gorky promised that he would, but either he never did, or Stalin
found something there that he didn't like very much. But in any case, they
never materialized. Once Stalin had gone, the soldier opened the door.
It was only a couple of days later that the so-called information came out

---

28 I thought this was the luxurious Riabushinsky House, which Stalin had made available
to Gorky after his return from Italy in the 1930s; however, I just recently learned that
Gorky didn't die there. He died at a *dacha* in the countryside.

29 The soldier was a fairly crude individual and wanted to emphasize his toughness to the
gathered writers so he deliberately didn't speak the fully educated language, hence
"khoziai" instead of "khoziain."

that Gorky had been assassinated by evil fascist agents. During the purges there was a trial that convicted a man who had murdered Gorky's grown-up invalid son in order to marry his attractive wife. Unlike the other public purge trials, this one was kept secret—it reflected badly on Party members. As Chukovsky put it, the accusation about evil fascist agents was a message to writers that they had better keep their mouths shut, if they knew what was good for them.[30]

A much admired professor by the name of Evgenii Tager, whom I knew at Moscow State University, had come out with a book on Russian literature with a long chapter on Gorky. Sure enough, the book had been published in 1953, which was the year Stalin died, so obviously it had been prepared before then, and stated that "the great proletarian writer was assassinated by the evil fascist agents, etc." A couple of years later, I think it was 1955, the book came out again, and I rushed to that paragraph. It said, "I Gor'kii umer." (And Gorky died.) Period. I said to myself, "This is a signal." I went to the back of the book, and in the appendix they republished for the first time since 1936, the year Gorky died, the doctor's bulletin, which had been published in *Pravda* the day after Gorky died, before the story about the fascist agents had come out. It was a detailed medical description of the last hours of Gorky's life and how he died.

I translated this appendix that detailed Gorky's death and took it to some cardiologists in Chicago. I asked, "Tell me: Is this medically convincing?" And they said, "Medically, it's absolutely correct." So I was pretty sure that this was a signal that the authorities were backing off the story of the murder. Consequently, I wrote in my book that on the basis of newly acquired evidence, I believe that Gorky died a natural death. I'm still convinced of that, although all kinds of speculation have arisen since

---

30 In that first interview, Chukovsky also talked about the Symbolists, and he described their work in a way sure to rivet my attention: He put his arm over his head and brought his hand down to pick his nose. Then he lifted the hand and showed that his finger came up with nothing. "That," he said, "was the way the Symbolists worked." To my amazement, I later learned that Chukovsky had published in a Symbolist publication, the *Zolotoye Runo*, so maybe he was trying to protect himself or maybe he really felt that way. I don't know. But in any case, the *Zolotoye Runo* (*Golden Fleece*, an illustrated journal of art and literature published monthly in Moscow from 1906 to 1909 with the financial backing of manufacturer N. P. Riabushinsky) had published several of his articles.

then. Granted, his death might have been hastened by the pressures that he was under, having to kowtow to Stalin, but I'm pretty sure Gorky died a natural death. I'm certain that that was what Chukovsky meant, although I didn't think I could make such a claim in my book if I only had Chukovsky's word. But it seems to me that Tager's book, plus Chukovsky's word, made a pretty convincing case.

Discussions in Chukovsky's House

Over the next six months I went to Chukovsky's house every Sunday, with one or two exceptions. It was a wonderful time in my life. I met all kinds of intellectuals and saw and heard all kinds of things that wouldn't normally be seen or heard in ordinary Soviet life. There was a unique combination of love for many aspects of Russian life and culture together with a sophisticated skepticism toward certain rigidities of Soviet rules and behavior. The people could bask in the warmth of Russian family and communal life while resenting the barriers that bureaucrats seemed to erect around some of the simplest parts of daily activities. For example, there was the necessity of enduring through three separate lines in a store: first, to find and select the desired item; second, to pay a cashier the determined price; and, finally, to take the payment receipt to show the clerk and take the purchased item. All these steps required enormous time and patience. Just to get into the big public libraries required having special permission to see certain books and materials.

In Chukovsky's house, guests would often take pride in the Russian courage and strength necessary to deal with such daily difficulties, while at the same time express resentment about the difficulties. I would hear such lines as:

> Bystro, nadezhno i bez rabot,
> Vas pokhoronit Aeroflot.

> (Quickly, safely, and effortlessly,
> Aeroflot will bury you.)

Or, to the tune of Chopin's funeral march, "V sel'skom khoziaistve opiat' bol'shoi pod"ëm." (In agriculture there's been another boom.) All of these rhymes were making fun of a certain kind of forced public cheerfulness about realities that were anything but cheerful. The long lines to get travel tickets were frustrating. There were problems in Soviet agriculture that sometimes even led to the necessity of importing large amounts of wheat and grain—all of this in a country known previously as "the bread basket of Europe."

Some guests at Chukovsky's house had a tendency to idealize what life would be like outside their own country. When they would meet me, a visiting, Russian-speaking American professor, they would somehow relate how life must be problem-free for a wealthy American academic person. When I tried to assure them that American professors are not the wealthy paragons created by Russian imaginations, they would reply with some irony: "Yes, you probably have to stand in line to get your car out of a garage!" No pity was to be obtained for such terrible problems!

To a certain extent, Kornei Ivanovich confided in me, although not completely. At times he would open up—I guess when we were in a situation when he knew no one was going to rat on him. Other times, he would be very careful. That's how he survived. Just recently a book came out, a sort of biography of him, from which I learned many new things. For example, his name wasn't really Kornei Chukovsky. It was Nikolai Korneichukov.[31] In any case, I went to his house every Sunday, and it was a wonderful time.

Among other things, Kornei Ivanovich was a very famous children's writer and had started a children's library next to his house with his personal funds. He had gotten books for kids because he wanted to have them grow up with the real stuff, not just the Communist propaganda. He wanted me to spend time with the youngsters, teaching American songs

---

31 Why Chukovksy changed his last name, I can only speculate. Perhaps he wanted a fully Russian sounding name. In any case, he would not have wanted to take the name of his Jewish father who, as a student, got his mother pregnant and then immediately abandoned her. In the memoirs of his daughter, Lydia Chukovskaya, there's a scene in 1915 when a person came to the door and turned out to be the biological father of Kornei Ivanovich. The father and son went to have a conversation, and suddenly there was a lot of yelling and screaming. His biological father came running down the stairs and ran away. Kornei Ivanovich must have given him hell, as he certainly deserved for what he did, making a woman pregnant and then running away.

whenever I came, because I had a guitar. That musical experience was a lot of fun. I got to know some of the kids very well. Unfortunately, when I returned somewhat later, I learned that one of the girls had been murdered, probably by some maniac. I came to realize that this sort of thing happened quite a bit in the Soviet Union, but it was never publicized. After all, there was supposedly no serious nonpolitical crime.

While I was teaching the children music lessons, the young people wanted to know, "What is this rock and roll?" And I explained to them, saying, "Well, you know, in ordinary music, usually the beat is on the first count, although sometimes it's on the last, but in rock and roll, it's on the second beat." They said, "Is that all there is to it?" They really wanted something wild, you know. They were quite disappointed to hear that.

At one point, Kornei Ivanovich let me in on the fact that he had put together a group of people who were translating into Russian some of the stories from the Old Testament and that they wanted to publish them. This was something that wasn't ordinarily done in the Soviet Union, and they were going to call them "Legends of Ancient Times" or something. But they wanted the kids to know the stories.

They were translating the story of the Garden of Eden, and Kornei Ivanovich said:

Kornei Chukovsky pleased with his book.

I bog skazal Adamu, "Gde moë iabloko?" "Ia ne znaiu. Ia nichego ne trogal." I bog skazal, "Net. Vchera bylo raz, dva, tri, chetyre, piat', shest'. . . . Segodnia ia vizhu raz, dva, tri, chetyre, piat'. Net, net! Vy vziali!"

(And God said to Adam, "Where is my apple?" "I don't know. I didn't touch anything." And God said "No. Yesterday there were one, two three, four, five, six. . . . Today I see one, two, three, four, five. No, no! You took one!")

That was Chukovsky's version of the Garden of Eden story from the Old Testament.

To watch Chukovsky translating with that group was really quite an experience because he felt, like most Russians felt at that time, that translation was a very important part of literature. It wasn't something that you just knocked off to get a few bucks. You had to stay as close to the spirit of the original as you possibly could, and they published some wonderful—really wonderful—translations. In the twentieth century alone, there were seventeen full translations of Hamlet, one of which was by Pasternak.[32] And you know what Pasternak did? When he thought Shakespeare had made a mistake, he corrected him. It takes quite a guy to correct Shakespeare. Lozinsky[33] stuck absolutely to Shakespeare, even to the rhymes. It was a remarkable job; his translations are at an extraordinarily high level, much higher than we do now. Although, I must say, the translations of Pevear and Volokhonsky[34] have really impressed me. So Kornei Ivanovich had a lot to say about translation; he called it "vysokoie iskusstvo" (high art).

Chukovsky was the friend of lots of fairly famous people. There was a very popular Soviet comedian named Arkady Raikin, and Chukovsky

---

32 Boris Leonidovich Pasternak (10 February 1890-30 May 1960) was one of the greatest poets of the twentieth century and also highly regarded for his prose and literary translations.

33 Mikhail Leonidovich Lozinsky (20 July 1886-31 January 1955) was a marvelous Russian translator of Shakespeare whose translations come very close to the Shakespearean rhythms and rhymes.

34 Richard Pevear and Larissa Volokhonsky are two remarkable translators who work together: he is American and she is Russian. They've recently completed quite a few translations that have received high praise, although there are some specialists who dislike them. In my opinion, they have produced marvelous translations of Russian classic novels.

would bring him to Peredelkino regularly. One evening Chukovsky hosted a *komsomol'skii kostër* (Komsomol campfire), around which the kids from the whole area gathered. Chukovsky's name was a huge draw for kids. We'd walk down the street and they would said, "Ei, ded Chukovskii!" (Hey, Grandpa Chukovsky!) He'd say, "Ia ne ded! Ia praded! Eto kak budto vy nazyvali genarala maiorom!" (I'm not a grandpa. I'm a great-grandpa. It's as though you called a general a major!) I loved that. I could hardly wait until I got to be a great-grandfather.

One day, Chukovsky wanted me to meet the children so they would know what a real American looked like. So he said, "Look, we're having this *kostër* (campfire). I want you to come. I would like the kids to see what a real American is like. You know, the kids, they read the stuff in the press. It's total nonsense; I want them to see a real American. You come for the kids." It was an honor, of course. "I would love to," I said. So after everyone had gathered around the fire, he said:

> Deti, segodnia u nas est' bol'shoie udovol'stviie. Prisutstvuiet nastoiash-chii amerikanskii professor, kotoryi ispolnit pesni negritianskogo naroda!
>
> (Children, today we have a real treat. With us is a genuine American professor who will perform songs of the Negro people!)

That was the last thing in the world I was expecting. "Pesni negritianskogo naroda!" (Songs of the Negro people!) So, well, okay. Uh, "Go down, Moses . . ." So I sang what I thought were Negro spirituals. It was okay. I don't think I made an impression or anything, but they listened.

Afterward, this guy came up to me, and I noticed behind his back, Chukovsky and his grandson, Mitya, were heaving with intentionally suppressed guffaws. I wondered what was going on. The guy came up, and in a terribly sweet voice said, "A Vy nastoiashchii amerikanskii professor?" (Are you a genuine American professor?) I said, "Da." (Yes.) "U Vas pasport est'?" (Do you have a passport?) I said, "Da chto Vy, chto Vy." (Don't be ridiculous.) So, later on, when we went back to the *dacha* for supper, again, Chukovsky and Mitya were laughing, and I said, "Nu, v chëm delo?" (Hey, what's the deal?), to which Chukovsky replied, "Moi milyi professor, k Vam prishël samyi izvestnyi shpik vo vsëm raione! On poluchil zarplatu za Vas." (My dear professor, the most famous spy in the whole region came to you! He was paid to talk with you.) It was sort of a lesson in reality. Things like that were constantly happening with Kornei Ivanovich, and I must say that in those five or six months, going out there every Sunday, he showed me the real Russia.

I began to understand the difference between Russia and the Soviet Union. That was a real lesson to me. Very often, groups of writers would come and they'd have discussions, but when the conversation got too heated, Chukovsky would immediately change the subject. One time, somehow or another, Trotsky's name came up, and I was sitting there. He said, "Gospoda, pogovorite o chëm drugom." (Gentlemen, talk about something different.) After all, who knew who was there and what might be reported? As a matter of fact, it was reported that some British guy was hanging around Chukovsky, and that British guy turned out to be me.

Here's how it happened. One time, Chukovsky said to me, "What do you do for birthdays?" I replied, "Well, we sing Happy Birthday," (I taught him the song) "and there's a cake with lit candles that you blow out and you eat ice cream." Then I said, "What's the Russian word for *rope*?" He said, "Verëvka." "Well," I said, "we get a big rope and two people hold it in the air while kids run underneath to the sound of music. When the music stops, the rope comes down and catches a person. Then you ask the person caught, 'Would you prefer a diamond or a ruby?' If a diamond, the person goes to one side, and if a ruby, the person goes to the other. When all the children have been caught and there are two teams, they use the rope and have a tug-of-war." Chukovsky said, "O'kei, davaite verëvku!" (Okay, give me a rope!) And they acted this out right there. He said, "What do they do in England for birthdays?" I said, "Look, I was born in Ohio. I don't know what they do in England. I only know what they do in America." He said, "Well, that's okay." That's why word got around that there was this British guy who was hanging around Kornei Ivanovich. So there were many kinds of things like that. I must say, he became like a second father to me. For at least twenty years afterwards, I would have a dream where I was looking for Kornei Ivanovich; I saw him in my dreams. He penetrated very deeply into my personality and my subconscious.

Later on, when my wife and kids were there, the kids came out to see Chukovsky. He had them playing a game where they threw pinecones at a target. When one of the kids hit the target with a pinecone, he said, "Were you trained by the Israeli Army?" (Chukovsky knew Zhabotinsky from childhood. Zhabotinsky was an extraordinarily talented Jewish fellow who became one of the extreme Zionists. He was the mentor of Menachem Begin,[35] and in many ways, the psychological mentor of Benjamin Netanyahu.[36] He leaned very much on the conservative side of the Zionists, and yet had considerable sympathy for the Arabs. As a matter of fact, I think he was friendlier toward the Arabs than many others, but he had a very extreme character. He also was very talented linguistically. The most famous poet in Hebrew in the twentieth century was a man named Hayim Nahman Bialik,[37] and Zhabotinsky translated his poetry from Hebrew into Russian, and they're beautiful translations. So, Zhabotinsky played some role in Chukovsky's life, and he was very friendly toward Israel.) "Were you trained by the Israeli army?" Chukovsky would ask.

Bialik

The guy who was the big specialist on Gorky in the Soviet Union was Boris Bialik. When I heard the name "Bialik," my ears went up. The name of Bialik, the poet, is very well known by anyone who loves modern Hebrew poetry. He was also admired by Gorky, who later received permission from Soviet authorities for Bialik to travel to Palestine (present-day

---

35 Menachem Begin (16 August 1913-9 March 1992) was a Jewish man who was born in what was part of the Russian Empire. Early on he became an enthusiastic Zionist and somewhat of an extremist in the realm of Zionist politics. He was arrested by the Soviets and put in a forced labor camp, which he later wrote about with surprisingly good feelings towards the Russians. He then emigrated to Israel and eventually became the head of a right wing party and the Prime Minister of Israel.

36 Benjamin Netanyahu (21 October 1949-) currently serves as the Prime Minister of Israel. He spent quite a few years in the United States and speaks English like an American. Like Menachem Begin, he is very much a part of the right wing in Israeli politics.

37 Hayim Nahman Bialik (9 January 1873-4 July 1934) was the greatest poet of the Hebrew language of the late nineteenth and early twentieth centuries. One of his well-known poems concerns the infamous Kishinev pogrom, which describes the murder of many Jews at that time.

Israel) and, on occasion, to the United States. On one occasion, I approached Boris Bialik and asked him about Gorky, but Bialik said, "Get away from me! Get away from me, you bourgeois reactionary." He used all the Soviet curse words on me. I said, "But Boris Aronovich, Vy menia ne znaiete!" (You don't know me!) But he kept on saying that I should stay away from him, so I became a bit of a snob. "If he doesn't want to see me, I don't want to see him either!" I told myself.

Six years went by, and my book on Gorky came out. I returned to the Soviet Union and shortly after arriving I met with Vasily Ivanovich Kuleshov, who was the head of Soviet Literature at Moscow State University. Kuleshov said, "Oh, Mr. Weil, it's nice to see you!" I replied, "It's nice to see you too." He complemented me, "I heard you wrote a book. That was a wonderful book!" I said, "Razve Vasilii Ivanovich, Vy chitaiete po-angliiski?" (Really Vasily Ivanovich, you read in English?) He answered, "Net, net, net. Ia ne chital. Mne skazal o nei. Mezhdu prochim, Bialiku nravitsia Vasha kniga." (No. No. No. I didn't read it. Someone told me about it. Incidentally, Bialik likes your book.) I asked, "Chto? Bialik? Na samom dele?" (What? Bialik? Really?) And sure enough, Kuleshov opened up the *Literaturka*[38] and, "I think I quote almost verbatim what Bialik had written: "Professor Uail, konechno, eto burzhuaznyi uchёnyi, no chto-to khorosho est." (Professor Weil, of course, is a bourgeois academic, but has something worthwhile.) And then he went on to say, "Konechno, on govorit mnogo, s kotorym my ne soglasny. No vsё-taki, eto solidnoie." (Of course, he says a lot with which we don't agree, but all the same it's respectable.) I couldn't have asked for a better review. I said, "What the hell happened to Bialik? How did this come about?" Kuleshov responded, "Well, I don't know, but you should call him up."

So I called Bialik, and he answered, "O, Mister Uail! Kak eto prii-atno! Da my dolzhny vstretit'sia." (Oh, Mr. Weil! How nice! Yes, we

---

38 *Literaturka* was a sort of slang abbreviation for *Literaturnaia gazeta*, which by Soviet standards, was a somewhat sophisticated periodical published three times a week that specialized in literary criticism.

should get together.) I thought to myself, "Huh? What the . . . what is going on?"

So we arranged to meet at the Institute of World Literature. Keep in mind that when I saw Bialik in 1960, he only had one tooth in his mouth. He looked a little bit like I imagine Raskolnikov, the protagonist in Dostoevsky's *Crime and Punishment*. I swear you could almost see the axe under the really ragged coat that he had on. He looked a mess, a total physical mess. In contrast to our previous meeting, on this occasion at the Institute of World Literature, Bialik came bounding down the stairs, a guy in a three-piece suit, a potbelly, and a mouth full of teeth, and gleaming with health.

I said, "Boris Aronovich, nu znaiete, chto u Vas est' ochen' izvestnaia familiia?" (Boris Aronovich, well you know that you have a very famous last name?) He said, "Da, on byl moi diadia." (Yes, he was my uncle.) This man was the nephew of Hayim Nahman Bialik, the greatest twentieth-century poet in the Hebrew language. Well, my head was spinning, as you might imagine. So we got to talking; he was very nice.[39]

I was confused as to why Bialik acted differently toward me now. Well, I said to a Soviet friend, "I don't understand. How come six years ago he called me all those names and now he's my best pal? What's going on here?" My friend explained, "Well, you should understand, he could be pretty unpleasant when he wrote, and he really upset one of the big Bolsheviks back in the 1930s, who told him, 'Khorosho, my isportim tebe krov.'" (Okay, we'll spoil your blood.)

Bialik was put in what was called a *shtrafnoi batal'on* (punishment battalion). Their job was to show where the enemy mines were. Can you imagine how? By walking over them. To show where the enemy machine guns were, they walked into them without carrying any weapons. When the people who were behind saw where the resistance was coming from, they sent mortar fire in. The mortality rate was ninety-eight percent, yet he survived. Maybe because he was nasty enough, I don't know. Bialik survived, and when I first saw him, he was in trouble. He knew that if I got close to him, I'd get in trouble. So maybe

---

39 When Boris Bialik came to the United States in the late 1970s, I served as his interpreter. We hit it off famously!

by cussing me out he protected me. I had no way of knowing that at the time. I just took for granted what he told me. Again, this was quite a lesson in Soviet reality.

After that experience, we became good friends. I saw Bialik quite often; he was a lively, bright fellow. Of course, he had to follow the Party line and that was that. I said, "You know, I wish I could have seen what Gorky looked like," to which he replied, "U nego bylo litso starogo rabochego!" (He had the face of an old worker!) That was Gorky.

Additional Thoughts about Gorky

I desperately wanted to get up to Nizhny Novgorod. By that time, the city was named Gorky. I wanted to see the *Dom Kashirina* (House of Kashirin) that Gorky described so beautifully in his memoirs. So I went to my KGB person and said, "Look, can you get me permission to go to Nizhny Novgorod?" He said, "No, don't you know it's closed?"[40] I said, "I know it's a closed city, but look, surround me with soldiers." He said, "I'll give it a try." I don't know whether my KGB person did or not, but he later told me that the authorities had rejected my request. He said, "I'll tell you what we'll do. We'll show you a documentary film on Gorky at the first Writer's Conference." Well, that would be interesting, I thought.

I watched the film, which proved typical of Soviet propaganda films. It wasn't very interesting, although it did show Gorky breaking down in tears, which is something he often did, I was told. In the film, Gorky said, "The Party is not taking away any rights from you. It's taking away only one right, and that's the right to write badly," in response to which, Babel, the famous Soviet short-story writer said, "They've taken away the right to write badly. Consequently I am practicing the genre of silence." So, you know, just the fact that he broke down in tears at that point maybe shows you something of the kind of pressures he was working under. That's only speculation on my part; I really don't know. But, clearly, in those last years, Gorky had a rough time.

Incidentally, in 2013, I finally had a chance to see the House of Kashirin. Colleagues from the University of Nizhny Novgorod invited me

---

40 A closed city refers to certain cities in the Soviet Union that were absolutely forbidden territory for foreigners.

to deliver a lecture, and I must say that their hospitality and the city itself on the banks of the Volga River were very impressive. The home just reeked of the book that Gorky wrote. When Gumilev[41] was arrested and condemned to death in 1921 (Gumilev had refused to inform on his friends), Gorky interceded with Lenin on behalf of the poet. Lenin agreed and Gorky informed the relatives of Gumilev. Then, either accidently or on purpose, Lenin's reprieve disappeared. You can imagine the emotional reaction. It was then that Gorky decided, with Lenin's urging, to emigrate—first to Berlin, then, via Prague, to Italy.

Gorky earlier had been a close friend of Khodasevich, a talented poet who liked Gorky in spite of their political disagreements. When Gorky returned to the Soviet Union in the late 1920s, Khodasevich, still in emigration, remained objective about his friend's work. After Gorky's death in 1936, the poet wrote an extremely sensitive appraisal of his friend's fascinating life and work. His memoirs of Gorky are the most sensitive appreciation that I think I've ever read about the man—clearly written by someone who knew Gorky well. Khodasevich describes coming into the house in what was still Petrograd at that point, and he saw that Gorky was sort of talking away in a room where people were sitting. Khodasevich later said of what he heard: "It was the most wonderful set of stories. It was about his childhood. It was utterly fascinating, and I noticed that, one by one, people in the audience were walking out."

I wondered how could people be walking out of this wonderful stuff. These stories eventually became the material for what I think was Gorky's best work, the first two parts of his autobiography—*Childhood* and *Among People*. Khodasevich said, "Later on, I learned that Gorky was constantly telling these stories and these people were hearing them for the fifth or sixth time." Apparently, this was how Gorky polished them. His memoirs about his childhood were utterly marvelous. They included the character of *babushka* (grandmother), the character of

---

41 Nikolay Stepanovich Gumilev (15 April 1886-25 August 1921) was a fine poet at the beginning of the twentieth century who was friendly with some of the people who were against the Revolution and communists in the early days of the Soviet Union.

dedushka (grandfather), and his mother who never liked him because she thought he was responsible for his father's death.[42]

Tolstoy once said: "We talk about the Russian people; Gorky knows them." In other places, Tolstoy criticized Gorky pretty heavily, but he said, "Don't publish what I say," because publicly he wanted to be seen as a friend of Gorky. Being a critic would have put him on the side of the nasty reactionaries, and he didn't want that. But, in truth, Gorky later wrote some pretty bad and heavy prose.

---

42 His mother had eloped with his father because her brothers in the house wanted the inheritance entirely for themselves. They didn't want to share with an outsider brother-in-law, who was temperamentally totally different from their crude hostility toward the world. Suffice it to say, they would have given hell to the newly married couple. So they went down to Astrakhan, down the Volga, and Gorky was about two or three years old when he contracted cholera. His father was absolutely fearless; most people would have stayed away from Gorky at that point. Instead, his father tended to him, caught cholera himself, and died, although Gorky survived. So the mother always held Gorky responsible for the death of his father, and she was rather cold toward him.

Chapter Four

Social and Political Reform in the Soviet Union

> *Years ago, I was riding home at midnight in a friend's car.*
> *We were near the Moscow River, where it's very dark.*
> *Suddenly some young-looking fellows started waving their*
> *hands. My friend sped away. I asked, "Who were those*
> *guys, anyway?" And he said, "Well, if we would have*
> *stopped, they would have beaten and robbed us." "Really?"*
> *I said. "Well, where are the police?" And he said, "They are*
> *the police."*
>
> —Irwin Weil

Evtushenko

In 1960 I went into one of the bookstores on Kuznetsky Most[1] that was especially favored by writers and artists. There you could often find books unavailable elsewhere. The girl behind the counter was impressed; here was an American who knew Russian. She said, "Do you like poetry?" To which I replied, "Oh yes." She looked to the right, and then to the left, to make sure nobody was watching, and faster than I could follow her hand, she went to the counter and said, "Here, read this." I asked, "What is

---

1   Kuznetsky Most is a well-known street in Moscow that has a magnificent bookstore. That's where writers went when they wanted to find material to help them with their own novels.

it?" She said, "Read it. You'll see." It was Evtushenko.[2] Clearly the poetry contained a fresh voice, articulated in a manner that seemed in some way to depart from the official cant. That exchange in the bookstore marked the beginning of my acquaintance with Evtushenko.

Later on I was at the Russian Research Center at Harvard—a well-known place for research and knowledge about the USSR—and Richard Pipes, who later became President Reagan's chief advisor on Russia, was there. Pipes said, "I'd like to invite you to dinner." He explained that a Soviet poet was coming to dinner that evening—his name was Evtushenko. I expressed how much I would really like to meet him. So, I went to the dinner, and Evtushenko came in roaring drunk. Professor Vsevolod Setchkarev was there, a real appreciator of poetry. He seemed to Evtushenko a homosexual (although Setchkarev was happily married to a woman), so the brash, young, Soviet poet went after the Harvard émigré, saying, "Nu, po krainei mere ia liubliu zhenshchin!" (Well, at least I love women!) Setchkarev crushed him with the reply, "Gospodi! Muzhchin, zhenshchin . . . Eto ne vazhno! My govorim o poezii!" (Lord! Men, women . . . It's not important! We're talking about poetry!) The air went out of Evtushenko like a punctured balloon. This showed the weak side of Evtushenko who was, nevertheless, an interesting and sometimes courageous poet.

Not Discussing Politics

When I was in the Soviet Union, I usually avoided public discussions of politics because I knew it was hopeless and because I didn't want to get others into trouble by forcing them to take a certain position. Sometimes at the entrance of our part of the dormitory, I was introduced as an example of what American philologists were like, I was expected to reply to questions not only with correct grammar—but in rhyme. You can

2   Evgeny Aleksandrovich Evtushenko (18 July 1932-) is a Soviet-era poet. I met him when he was a very young man. To be sure, he wasn't what I would call an outstanding poet, but there was a freshness about his lines that was tremendously attractive and he became enormously popular among the Russian population, particularly among the young people. He used that popularity in some cases to express mild opposition towards the regime and got himself into some trouble, but he survived it. He was always coming up with something that would shock and amaze you.

imagine what happened then. It was always in good fun. But one day, they managed to seduce me into talking about politics and we got into an argument.

The people around me burst out laughing and said, "You're a little bit more to the left than some of the people they send over here, aren't you?" I said, "That's terrible! This was supposed to be an argument; it was nothing more than a goddamn provocation!" With my nose in the air, I went down the hall, snubbing them for doing such a terrible thing. Well, a couple of minutes later, there was a knock at the door: "Mr. Weil, are you mad?" I said, "Well, that wasn't a nice thing to do, you know." "Come on," they said, "let's smoke the peace pipe." "Well, okay," I replied. So we smoked a peace pipe, figuratively speaking.

They said, "Tell us: Is American television as bad as we hear it is?" I said, "Worse." They said, "You wait until you see ours." Well, word got around. The next night there was a party, and this guy came up to me and said (and remember this was still reasonably close to World War II), "Now the trouble with you Americans is . . ." I said, "Okay, what's the trouble? I've heard this a thousand times. What's the trouble with us Americans?" He said, "You're too soft; you're too liberal. You've got a lot to learn from the Germans." And believe me, he wasn't talking about Goethe and Schiller. I said, "Yeah, the Nazis came into this country and killed twenty million people. We've got a hell of a lot to learn from the Germans."

Well, that ended the conversation right there. The next day word got around about the interchange. I said to myself, "These guys call themselves socialists, but boy they could be the worst Nazis you've ever seen in your life. When the change comes, I sure hope it comes gradually."

Although a generation later when change did come, it didn't exactly come gradually (at least from the point of view of political administration at the time). One of the first things I saw was a swastika printed in a newspaper for sale on the street. In the early days of the post-Soviet regime, there were all sorts of Nazi-type newspapers on the streets employing the word *zhidy*[3] in them. I was not exactly happy with these things, and would

---

3   *Zhidy* is the plural form of the word *zhid*—a very offensive Russian word when you're talking about a Jew. The polite word for Jew in Russian is evrei (connected with *ivrit,*

say to my friends, "How can you put these things on the streets? Don't you understand? The Germans . . ."

They would respond to my unhappiness by saying, "Look, look, look. These guys are extremes. You have extremes in your society too. Don't worry; we'll prevent them from coming to power." These were my friends, and I had a lot of faith in them, really. Some of them were courageous in a way that I often ask myself, "If I had been in that situation, would I have been equally courageous?" I'm not so sure. But these were courageous people, and I took their word seriously.

I remembered from my childhood back in the 1930s hearing some Germans talking about Hitler who, at the time, was coming to power. (Remember that Cincinnati was a very German city.) People were incredulous and would say, "Look, the German people are a highly educated people. They are fine people; they would never fall for a clown like Hitler." And you know the upshot of that. Then I began to tremble, comparing those words with what I heard from my Soviet friends. But, I'll admit, thus far I don't think they've turned into Nazis. The current international political polemics involving Russia are much more arguments about national interests than they are about totalitarianism. It's a mistake to turn those age-old arguments into a demonization of political leaders.

I had a student, this was back at Northwestern in the 1970s or '80s, who was translating Dostoevsky, and said, "I've come across a word that I can't find in the dictionary. Could you help?" I replied, "What is it?" She said, "*Zhid*." I said, "Oh, that means 'kike.'"[4] She said, "What's that?" Her

---

the Hebrew word for Hebrew). In Polish the word *zhid* is perfectly normal.

4   The word "kike" is an insult; it's like saying "nigger" to a black person. A kike or a "*sheemee*" is the n-word for Jews. The source of the term "kike" is uncertain, but the *Encyclopedia of Swearing* claims that the most reasonable and likely origin of the term is the one proposed by Leo Rosten, according to whom: "The word kike was born on Ellis Island when there were Jewish immigrants who were also illiterate (or could not use Latin alphabet letters). When asked to sign the entry forms with the customary "X," the Jewish immigrants would refuse, because they associated an X with the cross of Christianity. Instead, they drew a circle as the signature on the entry forms. The Yiddish word for "circle" is *kikel*, and for "little circle," *kikeleh*. Before long the immigration inspectors were calling anyone who signed with an "O" in place of an "X" a kikel or kikeleh or kikee or, finally and succinctly, kike." Quoted in Rosten, Leo. (2001). *The New Joys of Yiddish*. New York: Crown Publishers.

reply surprised me because in my childhood no one I know would have had any hesitation in recognizing the vocabulary of anti-Semitism. She had never heard the word. I would like to think that her ignorance of the word indicates a change of generational attitudes.

Once in Cincinnati, a guy said to me, "You're trying to *Jew* me down?" And, boy, did that get me mad. The idea was that I was pulling some kind of financial deal over him that would be to his disadvantage. Later, a friend of mine said, "You want to *Jew* me down." I responded with, "No, I want to *Episcopalian* you down."

Khrushchev

In November 1963 Kennedy was assassinated, and the following year Khrushchev fell. I remember Khrushchev going to the US Embassy to sign the mourning book for Kennedy. One thing to remember about Khrushchev was that he ended the concentration camps. For many people, that caused them to overlook many of the obnoxious things he did. After all, Krushchev was responsible for the Thaw and the Stalin speech, or so-called "secret speech," whose text appeared two weeks later in the *New York Times*.

The revelation of some of Stalin's murderous crimes was quite shocking for anyone who grew up in the first four decades of Soviet power. There were many things that Krushchev did that endeared him to at least a certain part of the population. Now granted, I was dealing mostly with people who were fairly well educated. The guys in the Party were kind of fed up with Khrushchev when they deposed him. They'd had enough of his malarkey, as they saw it. But what he did in terms of the Thaw and the end of the camps was something that was not forgotten.

It's true that Khrushchev was seen kind of as a bumpkin. Take, for example, what he did at the United Nations. It was sort of comical in a way, banging his shoe on the table during a UN General Assembly and getting angry that he couldn't go to Disneyland.[5] He said something that was translated as "We will bury you." That was not exactly the language of

---

5   While for security reasons Khrushchev was not permitted to visit Disneyland, he did get to Hollywood, where his attraction to American female beauties mightily irritated Mrs. Khrushchev.

diplomacy, and later he admitted that mass burial of hundreds of millions of Americans was not in the cards, even in the minds of the most convinced of Marxists!

There were times that Khrushchev made writers furious, such as calling them in and excoriating them in very nasty language. Also, in Russia, there was a famous exposition of modern art, very unpopular with the Soviet regime, which a bulldozer crushed. I told a colleague of mine, "You see? Russia's way ahead. You've never thought of a bulldozer for art criticism!" You know, there would have been some Russians who said, "That goddamn modern art! They deserve to have it bulldozed!"

There were people who felt that way. Sort of like a Komsomol boy who escorted me to the Hermitage in Leningrad and proceeded to make very clear that modern art was unacceptable. This kid was on the Party line all the way. I asked him, "When you have full communism, what are you going to have?" He answered, "Well, everybody's going to have a necktie, everybody's going to have an automobile, and everybody's going to have a refrigerator." I questioned, "Well just like America, huh?" He started, "No, no, no. You don't understand." I said, "Well, explain it to me." Just then, the bus pulled up and we got on. He said, "I'll tell you later."

He was embarrassed to have other Soviets hear him talking this way to an American. We sort of went our separate ways, so I never heard his explanation. But what struck me was that all this Party line stuff that he was feeding me seemed like real enthusiasm, and yet, as soon as other people could overhear him, he was embarrassed to continue. He knew very well it wasn't popular among people. They were likely thinking, "The bastard's been co-opted by those jerks who are oppressing us." That's why he suddenly said, "I'll tell you later."

Kennedy

Kennedy's popularity amongst Russians really surprised me. This was after the Cuban missile crisis. I was somewhat skeptical of Kennedy. If I said anything critical about him, my Soviet friends would say, "You can't talk that way!" I'd say, "What do you mean I can't talk that way? I come from a free country." They said, "Criticize him at home, but don't criticize him in Moscow."

I was at Brandeis when Kennedy died, and as soon as letters could get through, within two weeks I got three letters of condolence from my Soviet friends, one of them quoting a poem by Mandelstam that never had been published in his lifetime. "Chelovek umiraiet. Pesok ostyvaiet sogretyi, i vcherashneie solntse na chërnykh nosilkakh nesut." (A man dies, the heated-up sand cools down, and yesterday's sun is carried on a black stretcher.)

Later on, a Soviet delegation comprised of a bunch of intellectuals who were being herded by a woman who was obviously overseer came to my office. I had that quotation on a blackboard in my office and they said, "What a sad thing for a person like you. Who wrote that, anyway?" I said, "Well, that's Mandelstam."[6] The woman replied, "Etot Mandel'shtein. On nash?" (This Mandelstein [*sic*]. Is he ours?) And I said, "Da, on Vash." (Yes, he's yours.) Other members of the delegation said to her, "Dura, molchi!" (Fool, be quiet!)

Judge Not

Some people were fearless, others principled in their actions and comments. There were those like Solzhenitsyn[7] who was absolutely fearless and would always say exactly what he thought, and he suffered for it. There were people who were totally principled and, by the way, some of them untouched by the authorities.

---

6   Osip Emilyevich Mandelstam (15 January 1891-27 December 1938) was one of the greatest poets of the twentieth century. He came from a classical background and much of his poetry reflects his classical roots. The language is very heavy and powerful; when you read it you almost feel like you're under the weight of the words. Unfortunately in the repressive times of the 1930s, he made a politically critical remark that found its way to the NKVD. Under tragic circumstances he died in a forced labor camp.

7   Aleksandr Isayevich Solzhenitsyn (11 December 1918-3 August 2008) became a very famous writer around the middle of the twentieth century, particularly after the publication of his book describing a typical day of an inmate of one of the forced labor camps: *One Day in the Life of Ivan Denisovich*. Khrushchev, for reasons of his own, saw to it that the book became popular and the result was that Solzhenitsyn became a kind of celebrity of modern literature. Eventually he left the Soviet Union and lived for a time in Vermont. After the collapse of the Soviet Union, he returned to Russia where he lived out his days. He was a very courageous, impulsive, and somewhat imperious man, demanding that people see the world exactly as he saw it.

For example, there was a woman who played Mozart beautifully, and one evening on Soviet radio she played Mozart. The studio got a phone call from Stalin: He wanted a recording. Well, there was no recording, so they brought her back in the studio and made a recording and sent it to him. Then he sent her a letter of thanks with some money in it. She replied, "Dear Comrade Stalin, Thank you so much for your kind attention to my playing and for the money. I've donated the money to the church, to assuage the suffering of people you've oppressed. Sincerely, yours." When her friends heard about her reply, they said, "My God, woman! You've committed suicide!" And nothing happened. Nothing happened. The night that Stalin died, that record was on his phonograph. So, you know, you could never tell.

And there were people like Bulgakov.[8] He wrote to Stalin at one point and said, "Look, they won't let me publish anymore. I'm going to starve to death. I know I'm supposed to say that I've now studied communism and I understand it better. But I can tell you I never liked it before, I don't like it now, and I'll never like it in the future. So I ask of you one of two things: Either let me go to Paris, where you let Zamyatin[9] go, or give me a job to direct plays at the Moscow Art Theatre. I'll direct any play you say." So Stalin gave him a job at the Moscow Art Theatre—much against the will of Stanislavsky, by the way. It ended up a total war between Bulgakov and Stanislavsky.

You never knew what was going to happen. So there were some people who really were totally pure, but it took a kind of courage. I'm not sure I would have had that kind of courage if I had been in that situation. I'd like

---

8   Mikhail Afanasyevich Bulgakov (15 May 1891-10 March 1940) was the author of *Master and Margarita*, which I consider to be one of the greatest novels of the twentieth century. He lived his life in a sort of quiet opposition. *Master and Margarita* is a wild satire of the Soviet Union and there was a chance that it would be published there, but at the last moment, it was turned down. Bulgakov became enormously popular among the intelligentsia of the Soviet Union.

9   Evgeny Ivanovich Zamyatin (1 February 1884-10 March 1937) was the author of a famous book titled *We*, a satire on the Bolshevik Revolution, which served as the precursor for Orwell's *1984*. Zamyatin was allowed by Stalin to leave the Soviet Union and ended his days in Paris. He also was a fine poet.

to be able to say I'd have had it, but I've never been tested under such circumstances.

There were others who would make compromises and betray associates if they felt like they had to. It depended on the person, depended on their will, depended on their beliefs. You couldn't be entirely sure. Well, take the example of Ilya Ehrenburg. He wrote a novel, *Julio Jurenito*, which contained some mild criticism of a system that produced workers with the impressive energy of ants, but "who ever heard of an ant Shakespeare?" When he was pressed by Soviet authorities at the beginning of the Cold War, he produced a foolish travesty of a book about his trip to the United States. In the late 1950s, the title of his book, *The Thaw*, marked the beginning of changes in the USSR that led to a mild loosening of some governmental restrictions. He was a survivor who knew how to remain objective and knew exactly to what degree he could safely take criticism. It's easy to criticize him, but it's not so easy to say honestly what you would do in his situation. Maybe somebody who was really courageous would be in a position to blame him.

There are people who are total hypocrites, there are people who break under pressure—and maybe I'm one of them, for all I know—and then there are people who say what they think. They did it with Solzhenitsyn, they said, "We'll shoot." And he replied, "Go ahead and kill me." Of course the authorities knew that such a murder would have reverberations throughout the world. Solzhenitsyn certainly counted on this knowledge, but he had the rare kind of courage to react bravely when a gun was literally at his head. If somebody put a pistol to my head and said, "Shoot," who knows what I would do? So you can't generalize.

But take Pasternak. *Doctor Zhivago*[10] was not published until he thought it was possible. Much earlier, in the 1930s, Stalin had called and said to Pasternak, "Well, you're a poet, I know. What do you think of

10 On 23 November 1958, Pasternak was announced as the winner of the Nobel Prize, but accepting it would entail traveling to Stockholm. Nikita Khrushchev, then General Secretary for the Communist Party of the Soviet Union, granted Pasternak permission to travel abroad and encouraged him to live out his days comfortably in England where Pasternak's sister was living. However, he explained that if he went abroad, he would be refused reentry to the Soviet Union–a condition that Pasternak could not bear to accept. Two days later, he declined the award.

Kornei Chukovsky (left) with Boris Pasternak (right) on the day the poet's Nobel Prize was announced.

Mandelstam?" And Pasternak replied, "Well you know, Iosif Vissarionovich,[11] we poets are very jealous, and it's hard for us to praise a fellow poet." To which Stalin replied, "Well, I think it's enough that you don't think much of his poetry." And he hung up. Then, much later, came *Doctor Zhivago*, and it was almost published by a Soviet publisher, but at the last minute, they turned it down. So, Pasternak sent it to Feltrinelli, who was a Communist publisher in Italy, and he said to him, "Hold it for a year, and if I can't get it published here, you go ahead and publish it, and even if I denounce you for doing it, go ahead and publish it, no matter what." Well a year went by, Feltrinelli published it, and Pasternak publicly said, "How dare you publish it without my permission!" knowing full well that it would be published. What can you say about that? I mean, Pasternak is not a Solzhenitsyn, but certainly you can't blame him for what he did.

Ovcharenko

In the 1970s, I brought a number of people from the Soviet Union to Northwestern. There was a well-placed man in the Soviet administration

---

11 Stalin's first name and patronymic was Iosif Vissarionovich. Incidentally, his real last name was Dzhugashvili, which he later changed to Stalin, literally "Man of Steel."

Irwin Weil in 1978 at St. Basil's Cathedral near the Kremlin on Red Square.

by the name of Ovcharenko. Although he was hard to reach in the beginning, after about ten years he became a constant visitor to the United States, much to the jealousy of his colleagues. He also was quite hospitable in Moscow. Some of my friends both in Moscow and in Illinois razzed me a great deal for maintaining relations with him, but I felt that such relations made it possible for many USA-USSR exchanges to take place. It was a good thing for both sides to have a close look at each other. The fruits of many of these exchanges have become evident in the last twenty-five years.

Although our exchanges over the years were positive overall, Ovcharenko could write some god-awful stuff. As a matter of fact, one time he wrote some nasty things about me. But through Ovcharenko I was able to get things done that I couldn't have otherwise. On one occasion I had the opportunity to talk with Nadezhda Mandelstam, the poet's widow. Her husband, Osip Mandelstam, was one of the most powerful poets of the twentieth century. He made a critical remark about Stalin and it got reported. After his eventual arrest, he perished in one of the Soviet concentration campus under terrible conditions. His widow had no patience with those who wanted relations involving the Soviet authorities.

Nadezhda was not one who was going to compromise with anything that the Soviets said: "Why are you giving in to those monsters? Don't you know what you're doing?" While I understood and sympathized with the hardships she had heroically endured, I think her attacks on our exchanges were misdirected.

Chukovsky's daughter, Lydia, whose husband suffered hideously under the Soviets, was very angry at me: "Why do you deal with those people? Don't you know who they are? Don't you know what they are?" I tried to say, "But, but . . ." "Nikakikh no!" (No buts!) When the vote came to expel Pasternak, everybody in the Union of Soviet Writers voted to expel him except Lydia, who voted to keep him. Lydia didn't censor what she said publicly! "They murdered my husband, those bastards." She wouldn't have anything to do with them. Chukovsky would say, "Lydia, Lydia, calm down." Those were the types of reactions I would receive. But if I didn't deal with these people, the exchanges that I was seeking would not have taken place. These were the kinds of exchanges that gave people an opportunity to see another way of life, and provided a way of making a country somewhat better.

Many people in the Soviet Union would agree with the émigrés that I had no business dealing with the government. Even Chukovsky himself sometimes got angry with me. One time he called me a *poddonik*, which is not a very nice thing to be called (literally "one from the bottom"— perhaps "scum" might be a good translation). But, my God, how was I going to get anything done if I didn't deal with the people who were in power?

It was a very complicated and a very shaded business. The newspaper *Novoye Russkoye Slovo* attacked me because I urged our national professional organization, the American Association of Teachers of Slavic and East European Languages (AATSEEL), to join cooperative teaching ventures with the International Association of Teachers of Russian Language and Literature (MAPRYAL). Some colleagues, mainly émigrés, saw this as high treason. Again, I sympathized with their previous suffering, but I think they disastrously underestimated our strength in forwarding our own programs. It was the Soviets who feared incursions from abroad—it was we who confidently sought exposure, both in the

United States and the USSR. We were by no means helpless babes in the international woods. That was precisely why the Soviets were so concerned about our presence.

One of the activities of MAPRYAL involved awarding a medal with the image of Pushkin to celebrate the work of individuals who had accomplished outstanding work in the field of Russian language and literature. Happily, I received the Pushkin Medal. The ceremony took place in the old Soviet Embassy not far from the White House. Anatoly Dobrynin, Soviet Ambassador to the United States for twenty-six consecutive years, presented the medal to me. He had established a remarkable reputation as a diplomat who knew how to ease some of the tensions between the United States and the Soviet Union without, at the same time, endangering his position at home in Moscow with a government that didn't always look favorably on such activities. He was one of the wiliest politicians I think I have ever met.

During the ceremony, he turned to one of his assistants and said, "Let's have a little Pushkin." The poor guy, who was a native Armenian, picked up the book and started, with a heavy non-Russian accent, stumbling through Pushkin's sublime Russian lines. I intervened by grabbing the book (I had met the chap earlier and we were casual friends) and I

Irwin Weil receiving the Pushkin Medal from longtime Soviet Ambassador Anatoly Dobrynin.

Ilya Tolstoy standing beside Irwin Weil.

proceeded to read the lines in my best Russian poetic manner. Dobrynin said, "Bravo, professor, you read Russian better than I do. I've been in this country too long!" That was vintage Dobrynin.

On a separate occasion while attending a Russian language and literature conference held in Washington, DC, participants were unexpectedly taken aback, more accurately, nearly swept off their chairs, when Leo Tolstoy walked briskly into the room. How was that possible? He was already dead for over seventy years! The person turned out to be Ilya Tolstoy, one of the writer's grandsons. Not only was his beard the same, but the nose, the cheeks, the brow were all the same as Leo Tolstoy's, according to the famous photograph taken when Gorky met his literary idol. The grandson was a professor in the Philology Department at Moscow State University and, judging by his behavior, a decent and kind man. It turned out to be very easy to have a conversation with him, and our encounter ended with him impulsively kissing me on the cheek. I like to say that for a whole month I refrained from washing my face! I keep two photos on my office wall: Leo Tolstoy together with Gorky, and Ilya Tolstoy together with yours truly. I suppose you can imagine the series of fantasies that go through my head when I look at those two photos.

Marina Rafailovna Kaul and Rosalia Semyonovna Ginzburg

Marina Rafailovna Kaul is another example of the fearless type. We met through her mother-in-law, Rosalia Semyonovna Ginzburg, who was a remarkable woman and a wonderful specialist in English. She was the one who criticized me for talking like an American: "Can't you say *cahn't*?" She would say, "You and your goddamned electoral college system!" To which I would reply, "No ia rodilsia v Amerike!" (But I was born in America!) "Erunda! Liudi ne rozhdaiutsia v Amerike." (Nonsense! People aren't born in America.) She was wonderful; Viv absolutely adored her. She said to Viv, "Are you a witch? I've fallen in love with you!"

Rosalia Semyonovna was a loyal Bolshevik, a loyal Communist, but she was of the absolutely pure type. She would have no truck with those people who were oppressing others. Her husband, Fyodor Arkhiptsev, was a member of the Academy of Sciences. He made a visit one time to Chicago to one of our colleagues, and I was there in the evening, and we got to talking. He was very friendly and said, "Look, you should come to my place when you come to Moscow." When I came, I met him and his wife, who was Rosalia Semyonovna.

Rosalia Semyonovna immediately glommed onto me. Well, first of all, I was Jewish. She would never admit to being Jewish or having any longing toward being Jewish. She said, "By the way, do you eat pork?" She was technically assimilated. But the fact that I was Jewish was something she recognized, and we immediately became best friends, even when she shook her fist at me: "Your goddamned electoral system!"

She would make absolutely denunciatory or completely supportive statements; you could either agree or disagree, but that was okay with her. She had a wonderful personality, and, by the way, she did ask me questions about the English language I couldn't answer. She had never been out of the Soviet Union, but her knowledge of English was absolutely superb. Rosalia Semyonovna compiled a very famous dictionary, which had to be published under somebody else's name for reasons that I'm not sure of. It may have had something to do with her being Jewish. I don't really know.

But she was an absolutely fearless Communist. She had a picture of Lenin on her wall, and by God, it was a nice picture of Lenin! She said, "By the way, when you come next time, could you possibly stop in London? My grandson needs a special kind of ping-pong paddle that's only made in London." I got the paddle. Her son is now a capitalist in the United States. Oh, there were so many wonderful things about her. One time I managed to rent a car and I went to her place. I came two hours late because I didn't know how to make a left turn in Moscow. She said to me, "Kakoi idiot Vam dal pravo vesti mashinu v Moskve?" (What idiot gave you the right to drive a car in Moscow?)

I met Marina Rafailovna through Rosalia Semyonovna and Fyodor Arkhiptsev, and we had many, many social events together. Later in the 1970s and '80s, when some Jews were beginning to emigrate successfully from Russia to Israel and the United States (often through Italy), it was quite difficult for them to leave, but occasionally, one or another person would get out. There was a woman, who for some time had worked in the Institute of Foreign Languages where Marina also worked and had succeeded in getting a visa and permission to leave. So a public meeting was organized in which everybody was supposed to denounce her, and one person after another got up and yelled about what a traitor she was and how she was betraying this and that and the other thing. You could feel the mob psychology. Marina got up and said, "Well I would like to thank her for what she's done for us over the past years and wish her the very best for her future life." Can you imagine how that went over with the government? Marina was on half salary for the next two years, and thank God they didn't touch her physically. Marina was quiet but absolutely determined to do exactly what she was going to do, and nobody was going to tell her otherwise. She absolutely refused to be cowed. Her home was always open, no matter what the neighbors might say.

Being Cautious

In spite of protests from émigrés, I reached out to people when visiting the Soviet Union. By doing so, I don't think I ever put close friendships in jeopardy, partly because the KGB was watching me pretty closely. They knew that what I knew about rockets was zero. The way they put it was, "Vy nepartiinyi demokrat." (You're a non-party Democrat.) They were pragmatic enough by that time to recognize that I really wasn't trying to do them any harm. One time I got into trouble for singing the Soviet National Anthem. Why on earth would anyone on the Soviet side criticize me for doing such a thing? Well it turned out that the anthem was no longer to be sung with words; it was only to be played with music. My KGB friend asked incredulously, "Didn't you know that?" I said, "No, I didn't." All I knew was that it was a nice song, and I liked it. They said, "You were singing about Stalin!" I said, "I didn't know any lines that referred to Stalin." As it turned out, the second verse referenced Stalin.[12] I only knew the first verse.

On one visit to the Soviet Union, I stopped over in Germany, at Viv's request, to order some plates and silverware that she specifically wanted. A German friend of ours took me to the place that had the plates, but they didn't have the silverware. So I ordered the plates; they packed them up, and I paid for them. I went on to Moscow, called home, and said, "Look, Viv, I got the plates you wanted but they didn't have the silverware. We'll have to do it some other time." She agreed and I forgot about it.

Well, two or three weeks later when I was returning, one of my colleagues, obviously co-opted by the KGB, said, "Look, I've got a present for you." I said, "Oh, gee, that's nice, but what is it?" He said, "Open it up and you'll see." Usually it's either candy, or pictures, or something like that. I got on the plane and opened it, and what the hell do you think it was? It was silverware. Even then I didn't quite catch on. Then I remembered! The KGB was listening. Somebody had told them, "Look, get him silverware." "Are you crazy?" "Never mind. Give him silverware!"

Now maybe it was a signal to let me know they were listening, or maybe they were really trying to be nice. After all, I'd said that my wife wanted silverware, so they gave me silverware. It was pretty low-grade silverware, by the way. We eventually gave it to my daughter. That was the one time I had sort of a signal that somebody was listening in on

---

12 The passage referring to Stalin went as follows:
   "Through tempests the sun of freedom shone to us,
   And the great Lenin illuminated our path,
   We were raised by Stalin to be true to the people,
   To labor and heroic deeds he inspired us!"

me. In retrospect, I should have said, "I couldn't quite get the Mercedes . . ."

In 1966 and 1969, my family came with me to the Soviet Union. The first time, the Ministry of Education and my KGB contact arranged for an apartment in the professorial part attached to the dormitory on the campus of Moscow State University. The second time, they put us up in a Ministry of Education-reserved apartment located near the Academy of Sciences where Varshavsky Prospekt joins up with Leningradsky Prospekt. When my family came back to the United States, they said, "Boy, that's one hell of a country." They were with me, and they were treated well. People were curious to see my family and took an instant liking to Viv. That seems to be a constant thread throughout our marriage. People just naturally gravitate to her, no matter who they are, much more so than to me. She just draws them in.

When it came to correspondence, I was very guarded. One universal rule was no names, absolutely no names. By the way, in my address book, I had all the names of my friends. That never left my coat. By God, if I was

Irwin and Vivian in New York, 2014.

in the shower, I knew where it was. One day, my friendly KGB agent said, "How would you like to see the ring around Moscow?" "Oh boy, I would love it." He said, "Look, tomorrow I'll meet you early in the morning and we'll take a trip to Vladimir, Suzdal, you know." We went, and, by God, I had some of what they called *medovukha*.[13] It goes down easily and pleasantly, but it packs a terrible wallop. I drank a little bit too much of it and fell asleep. Wonderful stuff, you know. I came back that night, and what do you think? Stuff in my luggage had been misplaced. I could tell they'd been through my luggage. The reason he took me out there was so he could look through my stuff. But they didn't get the book, the address book, because that was in my pocket. That was an absolute rule. It always stayed with me, and I would never name names. You could torture me all you like. I'd tell you anything you wanted to know, but I wouldn't give you any names.

American Association of Teachers of Slavic and East European Languages (AATSEEL)

In the mid-1960s, a very nice German professor, Dr. Anatole Alitan invited me, as a representative of AATSEEL, to come to a suburb of Frankfurt and discuss the formation of an international professional association that would be parallel to the English-speaking Union and the Alliance Française. I accepted the invitation with enthusiasm. I have to confess that it took some time for me to feel natural in the country that had gone through a Nazi administration with all its attendant horrors and murderous actions toward Jews. I did come to realize that one has to react to individuals, not to notions of groups. A Jew, of all people, must understand that. It certainly helped that the Germans I met were sensitive and cordial individuals. The only problem I had was with a drunken American soldier!

At a later meeting in Paris, I met Viktor Vinogradov, a close friend of my Harvard professor, the famous Roman Jakobson. Vinogradov chaired the meeting in which representatives of Russian language teachers from

---

13   *Medovukha* was a rather dangerous alcoholic beverage. It was the kind of drink that went down smoothly, but the reaction of the body was very powerful. It put me out for a while.

quite a few countries gathered to work out the creation of an international association for our profession. Vinogradov skillfully managed to maintain a friendly and working tone throughout our time together and deserved his high international reputation. Because Vinogradov was able to listen carefully and react sensibly, he was just the kind of person people wanted to listen to and work with.

A few months later I met Vitaly Kostomarov, a favored protégé of Vinogradov and destined to be the president of the international association. He turned out to be an intelligent and witty colleague, with a marvelous appreciation of American and British humor. He clearly recognized our position in the United States; we were prepared to embrace the Russian language and the magnificent Russian literary canon with full-fledged enthusiasm—no political strings attached. My colleagues and I were not interested in affecting the politics of Russia; however, we certainly hoped to enhance mutual understanding and appreciation of each other's history and culture. Kostomarov fully sympathized with our views and aspirations. I had the feeling, and I think that my American colleagues with me shared the same feeling, that this experience was a very good thing. The connections, particularly with Kostomarov, were very pleasant. It was something I was very enthusiastic about.

During the 1960s, I was Secretary-Treasurer of AATSEEL and came back to the United States with the hope that all of our American colleagues could work together with the newly formed international organization in order to encourage Russian language instruction and improved relations between our countries. I brought back an agreement stating that we would become a part of this international organization. I think there was something about Soviet law that really irritated the émigrés. When the vote concerning the acceptance of the agreement took place in AATSEEL, eighty percent voted yes, but twenty percent voted a very bitter no, and soon there was such a din put up by the émigrés that I said to myself, "Look, I don't want to spend the rest of my life fighting the émigrés," because many of them were my very good friends. I suggested instead that we form a separate organization that would cooperate with AATSEEL, but AATSEEL would not officially be a member of the international organization."

American Council of Teachers of Russian (ACTR)

That marked the beginning of ACTR. When I headed it up, it sort of limped along. However, the organization grew in a vigorous way and became a remarkable force for good in the field when Dan Davidson came along.

My early involvement with ACTR largely consisted of attending congresses that took place in various Eastern European countries. In my presentations, I often talked about Russian-American humor, to which participants responded enthusiastically. So, for me, it was always a very pleasant experience, although I was well aware of the bitterness of many of the people from Eastern Europe over being forced to study Russian. In East Germany—East Berlin, in particular—I sensed how upset the people were about how they couldn't get across the wall and about how the Russians were pushing them around. In East Berlin, when people walking by would see my badge connected with the teaching of Russian, they would give me hostile looks. When they then noticed the large letters "USA," a smile would break out. I was happy for the smile, but sad for the denigration of a beautiful language and culture.

Most of the time, Russians were extremely happy that foreigners were in their country and studying their language. How sensitive they were to the bitterness among the Eastern Europeans, I'm really not sure. I suspect that those feelings were pretty well concealed from them; they didn't want to hear that. What they got from us was tremendous enthusiasm, because we loved the Russian language; we loved Russian culture. So it turned into many happy experiences for me.

Changes in Soviet Politics

In Brezhnev's day, one often heard the word *zastoi*,[14] the Russian word for stagnation. I heard that term all over the place. Is it possible to read anything about nothing that has happened? That's what people would ask

---

14 *Zastoi* was the Russian word for "stagnation." It was the word that was used for Brezhnev's regime that seemed to go simply nowhere. It was a time when important political changes were anticipated but almost never realized.

me rhetorically and quite openly. However, after the Prague Spring,[15] people in the Soviet Union understood that progress required change, which scared the hell out of authorities in Moscow because they knew very well it might spread to you-know-where. As one acquaintance put it, "The car went over the street and onto the sidewalk." Many of my friends put it to me this way, "We thought that if we took very tiny steps, there'd be continual progress. It would be slow, almost unremarkable, but it would be there."

During the 1968 meeting of MAPRYAL in Moscow, the Czechs and the big delegations from all the Eastern European countries were there, and all of a sudden delegates burst into spontaneous dance around the place where the Czechs were eating. They kept on dancing around, and they made it clear that it was a demonstration about how they felt about the invasion. They felt it was a terrible mistake. On the other hand, the KGB agents were defending the invasion like crazy.

Some members of the Soviet delegation were honestly enthusiastic, probably the more naïve of them. I can still remember some of them with their wonderful ideas about how they were going to make everybody learn Russian; it reminded me a little bit of what someone might call living in a dream world. However, a large number of the members were extremely bitter about the Russians. You couldn't say anything good about the Russians when you were talking to them privately. If you would ask them how they reconcile their profession with their personal feelings, they would say, "S volkami zhit', po-volch'i vyt'." (Live with wolves, howl like wolves.) They were very cynical. I heard that over and over. This was a survival tactic and their way of having a halfway-decent life. But privately, they would express a great deal of resentment at how the language was being stuffed down their throats. I would get quite an earful, and I could certainly understand the source of their feelings. At the same time, it galled me to see them vent their feelings on a bunch of Russian women

---

15 The Prague Spring (1968) was a time of revival in Czechoslovakia. Two Communist leaders, Alexander Dubček and Ludvík Svoboda, instituted some fundamental political reforms. The Soviets soon mounted a crushing invasion, thereby frustrating many hopes inside and outside the USSR. Decades later, Gorbachev looked back on those events as premature harbingers of his reforms.

teachers who were quite innocently trying to get across some of the beauties of their language. I would try, not always successfully, to get them to
lay off!

Cold War Rhetoric

When I came to Northwestern in 1966, there were still tiny remnants of
the Communist Party in Chicago. Knowing what a helpful fellow I was,
members of the Communist Party would always come to me when they
wanted help. What they wanted was a room to celebrate the Great October
Revolution. I said, "Look, it's a free country. You want to celebrate? Okay."
So I got them a room on the Chicago campus of Northwestern University,
and there was always a big Soviet delegation in attendance. The American
Communists would speak in an enormously hostile way about every
action of the American government and many aspects of bourgeois
society. In whispered tones the Soviets would say to me, "What's he talking
about? Things are very nice here—we're having a great time."

Around this time, Angela Davis, a black woman who in many ways
was sympathetic to the Communists, was being prosecuted, perhaps
unfairly. She may have been involved with something I don't know about,
but she was being prosecuted in California, and the Soviet diplomats went
around with great big buttons saying, "Free Angela Davis! Free Angela
Davis!" And what do you think? She was acquitted, and, boy, were the
Soviet diplomats disappointed. A verdict of guilty would have provided
the diplomats ample propaganda possibilities to use in criticizing the
American way of life. I've never forgotten that.

I once got into a discussion with a Soviet diplomat, and he was not at
all happy about Western influences. He said, "I challenge you, Mr. Weil!
Tell me one good thing we've gotten from the West! Everything we've
gotten from the West has been to our disadvantage, and you can't find
any!" I said, "Now wait a minute, comrade. Aren't we being a little bit
hasty here? What about Marx and Engels?" He said, "That's just what I'm
talking about! You stuck us with them, you bastards!" That nearly knocked
me over.

In the mid-1970s, there was considerably less fear in the USSR toward
Americans than there had been earlier. Instead, people responded friendly

toward someone coming from the United States, much more so than now—now that they really know us. I mean, in those days, it was all rumors about how free the United States was. Sometimes I'd try to say, "You know, look, we have problems too." "You don't know what problems are. You're a little Lord Fauntleroy[16] in lace pants." Now they have a much more realistic picture.

In the Soviet days, up to about the mid-1980s, people were always taking a risk by being with me, particularly by inviting me into their homes. Doing so took a great deal of courage. That I understood pretty quickly when I got there. I only learned much, much later that several of the people who were close to me were interrogated by the police, who wanted to know what I was up to, what they did with me, and so on. Luckily, I don't think they suffered from it in the sense of being arrested or physically harmed in any way, but they were interrogated.

If I were talking to a crowd, they wouldn't risk saying openly what they thought, because God knows how many informers were in that crowd. But individually, that was a different story. Typical was this kind of crack: An American living in the Soviet Union was having trouble getting to sleep, and he asked if they had sleeping medicine in the Soviet Union. They said, "Look, you're not in Chicago now, darling. Out here, this will do the trick in ten minutes." They gave him the book on dialectical materialism and said, "Guaranteed, ten minutes." There were all kinds of wise cracks like that.

There were two troubles from the point of view of the government trying to have well-indoctrinated people. In the first place, there was the difference between what people said and what they saw. I was told that up to the age of about eleven or twelve what they saw impressed them very much, but when the juices began to flow in their bodies, they suddenly realized that what they saw with their own eyes, and what they were hearing with their own ears—this ideology—was totally opposite from what they thought. There had to be something wrong with it. They didn't

---

16   Cedric Errol is a poor American boy who finds out that he is the sole heir to a wealthy British earldom and thus becomes Lord Fauntleroy.

know exactly what was wrong with it, but something had to be wrong with it. The result was confusion and a great deal of cynicism.

Try to push something down someone's throat and sooner or later there's a reaction against it. Attempts at indoctrinating people in the Soviet Union were so overwrought that even the most insensitive person got sick and tired of it all. People heard the same thing day after day after day. As a matter of fact, some people in this country, particularly in those years, had a similar experience; they became totally cynical because they realized they were being manipulated. I saw that all over the place, a very deep kind of cynicism. For example, there was this guy whose apartment was taken away from him. Before being put into a much worse apartment, he pulled the bushes outside his apartment up by the roots in protest. "If that's the way you're going to treat me, I'm going to tear everything apart." All these things were reactions to the kind of pressures that were put on the people, partly ideologically and partly psychologically. People reacted to those pressures in a very negative way.

However, visitors to the Soviet Union learned quickly to avoid making a snide remark in any way, shape, or form about Soviet reality because people from the Soviet Union were deeply convinced that every American looked down their noses at them. People living in the Soviet Union were terribly cynical about what was being told to them about their government. But when it came to what they identified with in their own lives— their families, their own ambitions—that was a different story. Largely owing to this deep sense that Americans looked down on them, the slightest hint, even if it wasn't intended that way, could produce a very hot reaction. I saw how American tourists sometimes would do very stupid things and I saw the reaction, which was a very strong one.

I can remember a lot of people who talked endlessly about peace. "We want peace!" The obsessive way Soviet propaganda used it was pretty obnoxious, but you could tell that, as far as the Russian people were concerned, it was deeply personal. They really believed it, particularly if they or somebody close to them had been hurt during the war. But there was so much cynicism that, more often than not, when you got into a situation where you talked one-on-one, and people were confident that you wouldn't be stupid and quote them to somebody or report them, then they would open up, and, boy, they would talk. Then you felt a bitterness that was about as deep as anything I've ever encountered in my life.

Prejudices and Privileges

Official propaganda projected a spirit of egalitarianism, but the people's prejudices against black people flew in the face of this image. I finally got so fed up with it that I challenged them on it. I said, "What's this business against the blacks? Why are you so against them? You're supposed to be socialists." "Yeah, but they bring debauched women into the dormitories." I said, "Well wait a minute. Don't you bring debauched women into the dormitories?" "Well, of course! How can you live without that?" Literally, that's what they said. I said, "Well if you can bring debauched women into the dormitories, why can't the blacks bring them?" They answered, "Oh, well that's different." I asked, "Why is it different?" "Well, they're black." I swear that is literally what they said. Somebody told me that when he got married, he made a "misalliance" because he married somebody beneath him. He didn't specify whether the "misalliance" was of an intellectual or material nature, but simply said that black people weren't of "our class."

Listening to people preaching socialist equality would drive me nuts, because .I saw that it was the total opposite. For example, the way they would react to people who didn't have a university education, the way they would react to a simple worker, or the way they would react to somebody who was just outside what they thought was their caste. One time while in Moscow, I went with a group of friends from the university to a restaurant. At the restaurant, the waitress was behaving very rudely. I said something in English. She said, "Why are you talking to me in English?" I said, "Because when I talk to you in Russian, you're nasty. When I talk to you in English, you're polite." I continued, "Talk politely in Russian and the whole world will speak Russian." Everybody at the table burst into applause and said, "Let's go next door and do it again." The resentment that working people felt often stemmed from being snubbed—not just the hypocrisy of the ideology, but the fact that they were snubbed by people who considered themselves higher class.

At the same time, I often ran into a kind of self-righteousness. Many people didn't like self-righteousness in Americans, but boy, they had plenty themselves. Paraphrasing Dostoevsky in *The Brothers Karamazov*: "Americans have wonderful mechanics and they can make me another face," says Dmitry Karamazov. "The problem is the soul." There is the question. Often they're too polite to say it directly, but underneath, many Russians' reactions to people who are not Russian is: "They have no soul. We're the only ones with a soul. We're the ones who do everything right." In fact, they often do lots of things that are wrong. That attitude can be terribly annoying at times, but I sort of account for it and let it go past me. But I'm sure that many people would bristle at it.

When it came to alcoholism, there were scenes that made me shudder. I saw young women at the university dead drunk to the point that they could barely walk. I saw people diving into snow banks because they couldn't stand on their legs. I saw people urging eleven- or twelve-year-olds to drink, so they could make them alcoholics when they were very young. I'm not entirely sure what was driving this sort of attitude. An easy answer would be that their lives were so embittered that this was their one out, but I don't think that. I'm sure that has something to do with it, but I don't think that explains it. I'm reminded of the line in the *Primary Chronicle*:[17] "Rusi est' veseliie pit': ne mozhem bez togo byt'." (Russians find pleasure in drink: without it we cannot be.) The statement refers to the tenth century when representatives from Kiev were seeking a new religion. When they came to the Moslems, they were impressed with their knowledge of algebra and Aristotle, but when they discovered the Moslem ban on alcoholic drinks, that stopped them in their tracks, or so the *Primary Chronicle* stated it!

In terms of people's attitude towards the Party, there was some ambiguity. I ran into a lot of people who resented terribly the advantages that Party members had, and they would say the nastiest things about them. On the other hand, I ran into some people who admired members of the Party, because they had the guts and the discipline to go through what it took to do that, and, after all, there were some people in the Party who were genuinely what we would call *socialists*: they were genuinely concerned about the welfare of the people. So sometimes it was

---

17 The *Primary Chronicle* is a history of Kievan Rus from about 850-1110 with year-by-year entries recounting the early history of the Eastern Slavs.

contempt—but not always. There was a certain echelon that allowed the possibility that somebody in the Party might genuinely be one who wanted to help the people, who genuinely might not be a hypocrite.

Party members had privileges not afforded the average citizen. For example, they had special hospitals and special stores that nobody else could go in. There were the *Beriozki*[18] that you could go in if you had *valiuta* (foreign currency), but there were also special stores that only Party members could go in. They could often get food other people couldn't get and would often get transportation that other people couldn't get. They had special telephone lines. There were all kinds of things that were privileges of the *nomenklatura*,[19] as they called it. One time I was standing in front of a *Beriozka*, and a woman tried to get in, and she was rather nastily kicked out. She turned to me and said, "What's going on?" I informed her that, "These stores are only for people who have *valiuta*." She said, "Chto takoie valiuta?" (What is foreign currency?) I said, "Well you know, dollars, francs, marks." She said, "Really? Who needs it?" and walked off.

In terms of work ethic, what I saw was huge numbers of people really soldiering on the job. The very cynical slogan, "They pretend to pay us and we pretend to work"—characterized this type of work ethic. They were drinking or they were conversing or they were doing only God knows what, but they were doing anything but working. I wasn't the only one who saw them. When Andropov[20] came to power, he decided to go arrest everybody that was at the movies in the daytime. I asked my KGB man, "Well, did you get the guys in the movies?" He said, "What are you talking about?" He was totally cynical about that.

---

18 *Beriozki* were restricted entry stores that catered to people (not only diplomats) who had managed to obtain foreign hard currency.

19 The *nomenklatura* were people in the Soviet regime who had power and privileges that the common people did not enjoy.

20 Yuri Vladimirovich Andropov (15 June 1914-9 February 1984) served as the head of the KGB and, for a short time after the death of Brezhnev, served as the General Secretary of the Soviet Union. What most people didn't know was that two or three months after becoming the leader of the Soviet Union, Andropov had to be hooked up to a dialysis machine that, interestingly, was supplied by the United States. He remained on dialysis until his death and, as such, had little influence on affairs of state, even though he was the titular head of the regime.

Favorable Aspects

Prejudices and privileges aside, what always got me was that almost every-body I met—and this wasn't just intellectuals, this was waitresses, people who I met in the park, taxi drivers—were almost immediately ready to be hospitable. This reaction from so many people was partly because they knew I was an American, and, at least in those days, it was popular to be one (although now I don't know if that's still the case). Perhaps these people treated me so kindly because I was a human being, and I wasn't looking down on them; they just opened their hearts to me in ways that would have been unthinkable in a country like France or England. It's not that French or English people are necessarily unfriendly, at least in my experience, but this warmth, opening up to somebody who they felt was on their wavelength was, to me, overwhelmingly powerful. In Soviet times, officially atheist times, within five minutes of a conversation, they'd say, "Vy veruiushchii?" (Are you a believer?) "What, huh, what? Me?" That's unthinkable in an American conversation. If they want to talk about something deeply emotional, they will talk about it without the slightest embarrassment, and they expect you to do the same. They don't shove anyone off with a surface formality. With them, going right to the heart of the matter is important.

I have yet to meet a hostile response, particularly now, when I go up to somebody and start to talk to them. These days, people might be a bit busier than they were in those days because they really have to work. But there's an openness about them that just gets to me. It's the reason why I'm sort of obsessed with Russians. For example, when they tell you to come to their house, they mean it. When they want to know how you feel about something, they really want to know. When I would go to a movie over there, they would say to me, "What did you like about it?" And all of a sudden, you're talking about something that's very deep and very important to them. The same thing's true of music, art, cooking. There's a humanity there that is completely open. It was especially noteworthy in Soviet times because it contrasted so strongly with the harsh agenda. Nowadays, I suppose it may be slightly more under control, but I still experience it. It can be with a taxi driver; it can be with a pedestrian; it can be with a person who's sitting on a park bench. That's the reaction

I always get. Their welcoming reactions may have something to do with me or may have something to do with the fact that I'm American, but I think it has something to do with the Russian makeup.

News

In the 1970s and '80s, sometimes it was possible to get access to Western news outlets at one of the big hotels or the Lenin Library. I think special permission was required to read something like the *New York Times*. I still remember: One time we were driving a car and had, without thinking, put a copy of the *New York Times* on the back seat, and pretty soon there was a group of people crowded around the back seat trying to read it through the window. That being said, remember that the Soviet government blocked the Western stations a lot, but they couldn't block them completely because if they blocked them completely, they also blocked their own navigational signals.

My friends became absolute experts at finding exactly the right channel. Everybody knew that if the BBC said it, then it's true. If the Americans said it, you didn't know if it was true or not, but the American music was terrific. They loved rock music. So they listened to BBC for news, the Voice of America for jazz and rock, and the Voice of Israel because they wanted to hear good Russian. To my amazement, they would say things like, "I think the Dow Jones went down twenty points yesterday. What do you think happened?" Stuff they were supposed to know nothing about, they were absolutely up to speed on, because they got it through the radio.

Comparatively speaking, if you exclude Americans who were specialists or were particularly educated in matters pertaining to the Soviet Union, I would say ninety percent of Americans hadn't the foggiest idea of what was going on in the Soviet Union. Everything's important that happens in the United States; everybody knows that. A lot of Americans were like that, and are like that even today, although less so. Whereas, in Russia, because it was forbidden, there was a whole class of people—again, mind you, these were the people I dealt with; whether they were typical was another story—but the people I dealt with, oh boy, they strained every muscle to know what was going on in the United States.

Russians' level of understanding of what was happening in the United States was a different story. Some people had the idea of the United States as this place where there were no problems whatsoever. Others had sort of a distorted Commie idea of what was happening. I wouldn't say their sense of the whole system was very accurate. Yet when it came to small details, like what was happening with the Dow Jones, I was amazed at how much they knew. I was in the Soviet Union when the rioting took place after the death of Martin Luther King, Jr. To tell you the truth, it kind of worried me because I didn't know what was happening in Chicago, and my Russian friends were very accurate in telling me where the rioting actually took place. They said, "Don't worry; it didn't happen where you live in Chicago."

Shostakovich

The excitement on the Northwestern University campus was electric when we heard in the winter of 1973 that Dmitri Dmitriyevich Shostakovich had accepted Arrand Parsons' invitation to receive an honorary degree at our June commencement. Shostakovich also agreed to meet with groups of students and faculty, as well as with local composers. Carlo Maria Giulini, previously the Chicago Symphony's principal guest conductor, wanted the composer to conduct one of his symphonies with the famed orchestra, but after a stroke and a heart attack, Shostakovich was not physically strong enough to accept such an invitation.

When Shostakovich had come to New York in March 1949 to one of those so-called "Peace Conferences" that were sponsored by people very much on the left, banner headlines in the *New York Times* had trumpeted the news of his statement (and later silly articles attributed to him) that he supported the ideological condemnation of music by his friend and colleague Sergei Prokofiev. Shostakovich himself could not possibly have forgotten how the leather-booted associate of Stalin, Andrei Zhdanov, publicly displayed a score by Shostakovich, called it "junk," tore it to shreds, and then stomped the pieces into the floorboards; this humiliating event took place while hundreds of assembled members of the Soviet Composers' Union applauded thunderously, and Shostakovich sat glumly, with folded arms.

Irwin Weil (right) was privileged to assist and support Shostakovich during his stay in Evanston.

Dmitri Shostakovich at Northwestern University. Irwin Weil as translator behind the composer.

The music department asked me if I would serve as Shostakovich's guide and interpreter. Naturally, I was very excited about this opportunity and agreed to do it. We were at the train station when Shostakovich arrived, and, to my surprise, he was very easy to talk to. He was very curious about what was going on in the United States and what happened in regards to Watergate. We talked for quite a long time about that. It turned out that the guy who was chauffeuring us in the university car was not going to be around the next day because he was getting married. Shostakovich said, "Well, then you have to give him time off!" He made a point of congratulating the young man on his upcoming marriage. I was very much impressed by that. When I tried to turn the tables and talk to him about what was going on in the Soviet Union, he was less eager to talk. He was obviously concerned. There were people from the Soviet Union traveling with him, and from that point of view, he was clearly frightened.

By the time of Shostakovich's visit to Northwestern, I had been going to the USSR almost annually for thirteen years, teaching and doing research at the Moscow and Leningrad universities and at the Soviet Academy of Sciences. I spent a great deal of time with Soviet intellectuals in literature and in music, as well as with people in many different walks of life. Shostakovich's name and work, as well as his political position and troubles relating to the regime, were widely known and discussed.

What I did not know until the time of the Evanston visit was another personal link with Shostakovich and his family. For nine years during the 1960s, I maintained close relations with Kornei Chukovsky, an extraordinary Russian critic and children's writer, a kind of unofficial dean of the Moscow Writers' Settlement in the lovely Moscow suburb of Peredelkino. Chukovsky used his wide popularity to offer quiet protection to many courageous figures, including Boris Pasternak and Aleksandr Solzhenitsyn. Chukovsky's grandson, Zhenya, was courting a beautiful young Russian woman, whose lively and intelligent presence added a great deal of zest to our typically Russian discussions. I only learned later in Evanston, in 1973, that the lovely young woman by that time married to Zhenya Chukovsky was Galina Dmitriyevna Shostakovich, the daughter of Dmitri Shostakovich! In retrospect, I suspect that Galina and Zhenya were probably scared and didn't want to have any contact with bourgeois types, and they saw me as a bourgeois type. They couldn't know that I would keep my mouth shut. Chukovsky guessed it, almost immediately, that he could trust me, but Zhenya and Galina weren't that sure; they weren't taking any chances, even if we were, it seemed to me, on very good terms. In any case, the heritage of the composer's genius was destined to mix with that of the writer's genius—all in one family growing before my very eyes.

You can perhaps imagine how emotionally charged the events were around that June commencement. Shostakovich came to the Chicago area in a whirl and swirl of publicity. Large numbers of people wanted to meet with him, and there were numerous receptions and interviews, one of them still on tape at WFMT.[21] The interest was overwhelmingly friendly, perhaps best typified by a touchingly earnest young man who cried out from a large group, "Ia liubliu Vashu nebesnuiu muzyku" (I love your heavenly music), with the "u" sounds so blatantly turned into American diphthongs that Dmitri Dmitriyevich and his wife exploded into good-natured laughter.

---

21 WMFT is a prestigious, nationally syndicated classical radio station located in Chicago.

(from left to right) Irwin Weil, Dmitri Shostakovich, and Alex Dunkel at a
radio interview held at WFMT.

Dmitri Shostakovich receives an honorary doctorate of fine arts from
Northwestern University. From left, Roscoe Miller, chancellor of
Northwestern University, Shostakovich, and Professor Weil.

Normally, when honorary degrees are conferred at June commence-
ments, there is polite, desultory applause: Graduating seniors and their
families and friends have other, more pressing concerns than recognizing
elderly scholars. However, in Shostakovich's case, thousands of people
stood up, with cheers roaring like a storm, and with sustained applause
led by the music students. Dmitri Dmitriyevich was deeply touched, and I
felt great pride for my American contemporaries as they recognized a
truly creative personality.

At another point in the ceremony, the Northwestern University Orchestra played some of Shostakovich's music. It was wonderful to watch his reactions to the performance up close. He started with moving his fingers, almost imperceptibly but perfectly reflecting the time of the music. Then it spread to his arms and legs, in spite of the fact that they were crippled by disease at that time, and finally his whole body became a registry of the musical beat. It was a gigantic human reflection of musical rhythm. Yet, for those sitting five or six feet from him, it was not at all noticeable. His reactions were intense and deep, yet, at the same time, quiet and private. Several of the students in the orchestra clearly signaled their greetings to him; they made wonderfully clear their delight in his musical and physical presence.

Unfortunately, there were also some less than sensitive reactions to his presence. Certain critics evidently felt it was their job to be ideological watch dogs, something like reverse mirror images of their Soviet counterparts. They peppered him with hostile questions: Who was behind his trip? What kinds of political machinations were involved? What purpose could there possibly be in Soviet music? One of these so-called critics even had the gall to ask Shostakovich, in a nastily hostile tone, "What the hell do you know about twentieth-century music?" Shostakovich handled such moments with great dignity and with very simple answers. He said he had gladly accepted a friendly invitation, and he could only judge twentieth-century music from what he had heard, but was pleased to have the chance to learn more about contemporary American music.

Dmitri Dmitriyevich expressed a lively interest in American life and politics. He asked many questions about the presidential election campaign, which had taken place about eight months earlier, and he was intrigued to find out the basis of many American intellectuals' antipathy toward Richard Nixon. It was easy to hear in his questions the then-typical Soviet-educated approach to American conservatives: Russian thinking people—smarting under a repressive regime—saw in American conservatives a counter force against Communists. Nixon could often be counted on to say exactly what the Soviet intellectuals would have liked to have said, if they dared. There were exceptional people, like Solzhenitsyn and Sakharov, who spoke their opinions openly, but they were rare.

Shostakovich was willing, in very private conversation, at least to hint at his angry views about the Soviet regime, but he almost always stopped before expressing these opinions openly. He was in many ways a very frightened man, both for himself and for his family. It was not hard to understand the basis of his fright.

Shostakovich did follow through on his desire to learn more about contemporary American music. At his request, we invited Easley Blackwood from the University of Chicago, Alan Stout from Northwestern University, and John Downey from the University of Wisconsin to our house to meet Shostakovich. We listened to recordings of their musical compositions, and I was deeply impressed by the insight and accuracy of Dmitri Dmitriyevich's reactions. As I had noticed in the performance at Northwestern, I saw the subtle, barely perceptible movements of Shostakovich's body in time with the music.

After listening to Blackwood's music, Dmitri Dmitriyevich said how pleasant it was to hear the harmony so well worked out in the piece. He noted what he considered to be a major defect in the work of many modern composers, namely, that they didn't seem concerned with seeking solutions to the harmonic problems in their work. Blackwood responded in his characteristically breezy and direct style: "Well, Mr. Shostakovich, I've been teaching harmony for eighteen years. I always make my students master everything, all the way to the augmented sixth chords!"

After the piece by Alan Stout, there was a long pause. Dmitri Dmitriyevich finally said, "What a terribly tragic piece of music! What a heavy weight it carries!" Stout explained that he had composed the piece while his father was dying, and he had finished it within a day of his death. Dmitri Dmitriyevich had the most compassionate look on his face, yet at the same time he was not in the least embarrassed. There was strong emotion in how he spoke, without the slightest excess, which could have led to sentimentality.

After we had heard Downey's *Symphonic Modules,* Downey asked Shostakovich if they weren't perhaps too long. Dmitri Dmitriyevich replied that, on the contrary, they were too short and really needed musical expansion; he thought listeners would like to hear more. In every case, Shostakovich managed to catch the essential quality, or musical center, of the sounds he had just heard. Shostakovich demonstrated generous musical understanding at a very profound level.

Almost immediately after Shostakovich's return to Moscow, he did something that upset many of his admirers, both inside and outside of the USSR. He agreed to sign a Soviet government–sponsored statement attacking the ideas and actions of Andrei Sakharov,[22] one of the most decent scientific and political figures of late Soviet history. This action led Kornei Chukovsky's courageous daughter, Lydia Chukovskaya, to turn her withering polemical blast against the composer (as she had done earlier to the Nobel Prize–winning writer, Mikhail Sholokhov).[23] She wrote that Shostakovich's joining the anti-Sakharov campaign disproved the aphorism that Pushkin, in his drama *Mozart and Salieri*, had put into the mouth of the dying Mozart: "Genii i zlodeistvo—dve veshchi nesovmestnyie." [Genius and evil doing—two things that cannot coexist.]

I must confess that I found myself tempted to join in her condemnation of Shostakovich. God knows she had earned the right to make such judgments after her enormous courage under the most intense kinds of pressures. I had also not forgotten Shostakovich's courageous moments. These certainly included his actions around composing and performing the Thirteenth Symphony,[24] a choral symphony devoted to poems by

22 Andrey Dmitrievich Sakharov (21 May 1921-14 December 1989) was a famous physicist who was responsible for the Soviets getting the hydrogen bomb. He also believed that the American and Soviet social and political systems would grow closer. Eventually, he was exiled to the city, which then was called Gorky (now Nizhny Novgorod) and kept under surveillance until 1986 when Gorbachev granted him and his wife permission to return to Moscow.

23 Mikhail Aleksandrovich Sholokhov (24 May 1905-21 February 1984) comes from a Cossack background. He was a famous writer who won the Nobel Prize with his novel *Quiet Flows the Don* (in Russian, *Tikhii Don*)—a novel devoted mostly to the Cossack culture, which was very anti-Soviet. Surprisingly, there are parts of the novel that got past the Soviet censor. It became very popular in the Soviet Union. Sholokhov later became something of an alcoholic and in a rather sad way took up the extreme right wing of the Soviet Union, applauding the government when they would arrest other writers and send them to hard labor.

24 Symphony No. 13 in B-flat minor (Op. 113, subtitled *Babi Yar*) by Shostakovich came to be known as a choral symphony. The first choral movement tried to deal with a hideous event that took place during the Nazi invasion of the Soviet Union. Evtushenko memorialized the event in verse and Shostakovich set Evtushenko's text to music.

Evtushenko, including the famous *Babi Yar*.[25] (Chicago audiences had the pleasure of hearing it in a beautiful performance under Sir Georg Solti in 1995.) But that was hard to put in the balance against Shostakovich's callow denunciation of Sakharov.

Even worse, Shostakovich's latest action almost seemed like a payoff to the Soviet government in return for the permission to make the trip to the United States and to receive the honorary degree. However, I was stopped in this line of reasoning by an eminent scientist who had himself suffered greatly under Soviet repression. He reminded me of the many earlier times Shostakovich had been forced to play the fox, to run in many different directions to escape the pursuing hounds of the government. Every time, he had survived to compose and to fight another day, and his work lived on as testimony to his courage. He was not one to risk his life and the lives of his family, as some others did, and to deliver them to the mercy of those who had no mercy. But his work stands as a living monument to a man with a deep sense of honor and dignity, a rollicking sense of humor, and a knowledge of history gained through personal experience and considerable suffering. If he sometimes appeared weak, he redeemed himself mightily. It was a real privilege to be associated with him briefly while he was in the Chicago area, and to see up close the effects of his creativity and personality in both the Soviet and post-Soviet periods.

I later visited Shostakovich at his home a couple of times before he died in 1975 and got to be on close terms with his family. The whole experience was exciting. I tell everybody, "I meet a genius every 46 years, so I'm due at 92."

Prokofiev

About three or four months after Shostakovich was at Northwestern, Lina, the first wife of Sergei Prokofiev came to visit. She looked remarkably well

---

25 *Babi Yar* was a slightly elevated place located outside Kiev. There were places where the ground was two or three feet lower because the plough had gone by and piled up earth beside the furrow. It was on these parts that stood above the furrows that Nazis forced 60,000 Jews plus some Gypsies and Communist officials to march so they could be shot down by machine gun fire. Many of them were shot and killed; others were shot and simply wounded and buried alive. Eyewitnesses saw the ground quivering above the dying people for at least twenty-four hours.

Lina Prokofieva et al. (left to right) Alan Stout (composer at North-western University), Irwin Weil, Lina Prokofieva (Sergei Prokofiev's first wife), students at Northwestern University.

for somebody who had endured what she had. It was hard to believe she was in her seventies. When Prokofiev came to Chicago in 1921, he met Lina, who was half French and half Spanish. As a matter of fact, one of the characters in his opera *Love for Three Oranges* is named Lina. They fell in love and got married in Chicago. The opera premiered in Chicago and did very well, but New York critics absolutely tore it to shreds.

Later on, Prokofiev went to Hollywood and really wasn't appreciated there the way he should have been, or how he felt he should have been. So he made up his mind to return to Russia in 1936, which was a terrible year because of the purges. Stalin took one look at Profokiev's wife and sent her to a forced labor camp because she was a foreigner, and then he married Prokofiev to a Jewish woman named Mira Mendelssohn. As a way of proving his patriotism, Prokofiev teamed up with Eisenstein and wrote the film score for Eisenstein's movie *Aleksandr Nevsky*, showing a Russian victory over seemingly Germanic soldiers (actually Livonian Knights), and later a cantata for *Aleksandr Nevsky*, which debuted in Moscow in May 1939. That was all well and good until September 1939 when Stalin signed a pact with Hitler, and then it couldn't be played any more because it portrayed the invaders as German. So I like to say that Prokofiev had no luck! He came back at the wrong time, which prevented his music from being played, and in 1953 he died on the same day as Stalin. Lina spent four years in a forced labor camp before eventually getting out.

Nabokov

Another figure in the world of famous artistic creators was Vladimir Nabokov, whose remarkable and provocative temperament I first met as a graduate student at the University of Chicago. While at Northwestern, I published an article in the university's *TriQuarterly*[26] journal, in which I said that we owe Nabokov greatly for what he did for Russian literature in this country, if only he would control his temper. Later on, he wrote a rejoinder and said, "Well, for Mr. Weil, for whom niceness is a good thing in a critic, so much for Mr. Weil."

When my book on Gorky came out, I wrote him a letter saying, "Dear Mr. Nabokov, I've just published this book. I know that you're probably not very fond of Gorky as a writer, but I'd be grateful if you'd read my book and tell me what you think of it. By the way, I think I know somebody who knew your father. Evgeny Mikhailovich Kulischer says he knew your father; do you remember him? He was my first boss. Sincerely, with great respect," signed my name.

Later, I received a reply from Nabokov: "Dear Mr. Weil," (remember, I'd talked about his temper), "thank you for your courtesy in sending me your book, with which I totally disagree." He said, "As for Dr. Kulischer, yes I do remember him. My father used to say, 'If Evgeny Mikhailovich says something, it's true.' Sincerely, yours."

In 1974, I went to Moscow, and some of my old friends at Moscow State University met me. They knew what I'd love to do, because I'm something of a ham, so they said, "How would you like to talk to a group of Soviet undergraduates about Pushkin in America?" I said, "Yeah, sure, I'd

---

26 The *TriQuarterly*, published by Northwestern University, is a review containing literary criticism.

be glad to talk about that, but one thing you've got to remember." I told them about the polemics between Edmund Wilson and Nabokov.

Edmund Wilson was a very highly respected American critic; he was someone who always did something you didn't expect but was very interesting. At one point he even tried to study Russian, but he was already at a fairly advanced age, so he didn't learn it too well. When Nabokov first came to this country, Edmund Wilson was a great supporter of his, and they were friends for many years. As a matter of fact, in reference to Wilson, Nabokov would sometimes use Wilson's commonly known nickname "Bunny."

When Nabokov's translation of *Eugene Onegin* came out, Wilson was bitterly critical because he felt that it just didn't render Pushkin well. Wilson's reaction infuriated Nabokov, so where there had been friendship before, there suddenly came about a tremendous polemic that went back and forth. Sometimes I felt that poor old Pushkin got lost in the shuffle.

I said to my Moscow colleagues, "Look, if you're going to talk about Pushkin in America, I must say something about this famous translation of Nabokov's *Eugene Onegin*, but I know that Nabokov is forbidden here, and I don't want to get you guys in trouble." They said, "No, that's alright, you can talk about it any way you want. Don't worry; we won't get in trouble."

Well I took them at their word. There were 400 Soviet undergraduate students there, and they gave me two hours. Well I talked for about forty-five minutes, and at the end of the time I said, "Look, I want to hear from you. This is my real chance to know what you guys think, and I want you to tell me what think about all these issues." Well there were four students who asked me questions about Nabokov that were obviously based on detailed reading of the stuff that was totally forbidden in the Soviet Union, which really surprised me. So when I got back to the States, I wrote a letter to Vera Nabokova, telling her what had happened. I got a letter back, saying, "Yours is the third such letter I have received." So, obviously, he was already well known among the Soviet intelligentsia who read him in *samizdat*.[27] Today, Nabokov's a big shot in Russia. So that was my encounter with Nabokov.

---

27 *Samizdat* represents a body of works that the Soviet government did not want published. Consequently, people would go to their typewriters and literally type out whole novels using many sheets of carbon paper. These samizdat copies were then

Afanasyev

Sometime between 1985 and 1988, I met Yuri Nikolayevich Afanasyev, who founded Russian State University for the Humanities (RGGU) as a non-Soviet university. He was able to do it because he had clout with Yeltsin,[28] who was rising at the time. There were thousands of faculty applications, and Marina Rafailovna was one of those who was chosen. She invited me to come to her class, and when I came, I did what I always did in the Soviet Union. On the one hand, I never said anything I didn't believe, but on the other hand, I did not want to be responsible for getting those kids into trouble. If so, my conscience would have bothered me for the rest of my life. So I would try to phrase what I said in a way that was still constant with my beliefs but that wouldn't get them into trouble. But the students could see me avoiding issues. "Come on, man, out with it! What's going on here?" I had never experienced that in a Soviet university before. The first thing I knew, there was a real give-and-take discussion going on, the same way we have discussions at Northwestern University.

I realized Afanasyev had done something miraculous, and Marina was there. That was when we really became close allies. In the 1990s, after the collapse of the Soviet Union, she said, "You and I are going to start an American Studies Center here." I said, "No Marina, ia ne rossiiskii grazhdanin!" (But Marina, I'm not a Russian citizen!) She said, "We're going to do it."

And when Marina said that, the only possible answer was yes. The first thing we had to do was to raise some money. We raised $10,000 that was given to Russian State University for the Humanities as seed money for the American Studies Center. It was such a successful fundraiser that all I had to do was show my face in the hallway at Northwestern, and

---

circulated secretly among people who wanted to read the forbidden literature. Many people believed that the Soviet government turned a blind eye, perceiving *samizdat* as a kind of safety valve for social discontent.

28 Boris Nikolayevich Yeltsin (1 February 1931-23 April 2007) was a politician who succeeded Gorbachev and tried to institute a series of progressive economic reforms. Unfortunately for Yeltsin they did not work out well. At the end of his life he became something of an alcoholic. He eventually voluntarily resigned and was responsible for the elevation of Vladimir Putin, the current President of the Russian Federation.

Irwin Weil receiving an honorary degree from Efim Pivovar, Rector of
Moscow State University for the Humanities.

everyone would disappear. I could empty a hallway faster than anybody
you've ever seen. "He's at it again!" (Phew!)

Change

During the Gorbachev years, there was a lot of chaos. It's a wonderful
thing when the controls are removed. Some very good things happen, and
some equally very bad things happen. In spite of the downsides to
increased freedom, Russians were doing things they never could have
done before. The press was as open as I'd ever seen it in Russia. I wished it
had been completely open, but in contrast with Soviet times, my God,
it was a huge change. Maybe it's just because I'm from Cincinnati, but I felt
a sort of optimism about the days of Gorbachev.

In Gorbachev's time, I began to see healthy social elements in the
country that had been largely lacking before. While these people faced
tremendous opposition, all kinds of cynicism, and economic manipulation
of the kind that would make you want to vomit sometimes, I thought that
there was a realistic chance that they could come through to at least a better
society than they had before.

Although I had always believed that change was bound to come about
in the USSR, I was taken by considerable surprise by the events leading up

to 1991 and the fall of the Soviet Union. Many people in the United States used the metaphor of window dressing to describe what was going on. My own experience told me that boiling forces previously kept in check had at last burst forth through the surface. There was a kind of euphoria among many of my friends. Travel abroad was made much easier, all kinds of new economic enterprises were springing up, people were more openly (sometimes violently) expressing their dissident opinions, and artistic life was set free of many onerous controls.

While change brought out the best and worst in people, I couldn't help but believe that the positives that I saw in the Russian people, and in their culture as a whole, would alleviate the negatives. Perhaps it's just my American Midwestern optimism, but I think that there's at least a realistic possibility that Russian society will mobilize its better sides and progress toward a future that offers opportunities for the great talent that exists in that huge country. Utopia is, of course, an artist's dream. But a decent society—even with all the faults humanity is heir to—can come about in this world.

Needless to say, such experiences have created a very specific American view of Russian reality, one that I have never forgotten. I have been able to teach the Russian language and Russian literature for well over fifty years, the last forty-nine of which have been spent at Northwestern University. Since that remarkable first visit, fifty-five years have passed; I have been in the USSR (later the Russian Federation) over one hundred times. I have literally talked with many hundreds of people, going out of my way to corner anyone who would talk with me—sometimes begging them not to talk too fast for American ears educated about Russian declensions of ever-changing nouns and conjugations of tricky, sneaky verbs. At certain glorious linguistic times, they would even mistake me for one of their own, expressing skepticism that I was born not on Volga's banks, but rather on those of the Ohio. Through all of this, my baseball hopes have never ceased from resting on the Cincinnati Reds. Some things are eternal!

Chapter Five

Letters from the USSR

Tues. Sept. 6, 1960
Belmont, Mass.

Dear Mom and Dad,

How long a time it has been, and what has happened in between! Let me try to catch you up on what has been happening to me, and I'll skip the practical details of the moment in this letter. The latter can wait until a second letter this week. We will see each other later in October, but I'll see what I can do to capture some of the details, which you missed.

Forgive me for not writing more from Russia; the reason I wrote so little and so skimpily is somewhat complicated. I had very little time since I ran myself ragged from seven in the morning until midnight, seven days a week; of course, I was stimulated, and the running around that I did helped me see things I would not have seen otherwise. My letters must have sounded episodic and perhaps unconnected—this was partly because I was not sure who was reading them (actually, I now have the feeling that my letters were probably <u>not</u> read by any Soviet officials). My letters were also that way because I literally felt like I was swimming in the middle of an ocean of new impressions, so different from what I had known before that it was impossible to contain them in an organized framework. The psychology of a person in a completely new environment, using a different language all the time, is a very strange thing. By the time I met Henry David, English sounded like a foreign language to my ears. I began to forget all sorts of little things which I knew perfectly well in English; e.g., I couldn't think of the English word for Brussels sprouts, I forgot legions of names and places, etc., etc.

I had no trouble whatsoever in talking to people. When Russians would learn that a Russian-speaking American was in the area, they would flock to see me, speak with me, and ply me with questions about the United States. For the most part, I tried to avoid attracting crowds because I was there to learn, not to play propagandist and orator. When crowds did gather around me, however, I answered their questions patiently for hours on end—I always felt that these were friendly occasions; never once (aside from two drunks) did I encounter the least trace of hostile feelings from Russians. On the contrary, when they saw I was an American seriously interested in Russian literature, they treated me like a king; nothing was too much for an American guest. I never minced words, and I always made it plain from the beginning that I am not a Communist and that I do not believe in Marxism or Leninism. At the same time, I tried to make it clear that most Americans do not care what the Russians believe, as long as they don't try to force it on anyone else.

I also had no trouble at all seeing the people I wanted to see and getting to the libraries, archives, and institutions where I wanted to work. I had anticipated that only firm insistence on what I wanted to do would bring small results. When I went in to my first man, the head of the foreign commission of the Soviet Writers' Union, he was very surprised by my insistent manner. Very calmly he told me not to get excited since he personally would see to it that I visited all the people I wanted to see. After I gave him the list, he sat down to the telephone, just like an American businessman, and called for appointments with my men. Sure enough, as the days went by, I saw the people on my list. Whenever I simply knocked unannounced at the door of an office or institute I wanted to visit, the welcome mat was laid at my feet. As you probably know, the Russians are an extremely hospitable people, and they certainly showered me with kindness.

The kindly feelings also came out in numerous little ways—no one would let me stand in line; they always insisted that I go right up front, and when I would protest, they would simply carry me up front ahead of everyone else.

Most of my days were spent working in various institutes and libraries, talking with people who shared common interests with me. At night, to try and preserve a balance in contrast to the intellectuals I was dealing with, I went to the park benches, ice cream parlors, etc., stopping people and talking with them. I think I talked to a very large selection of different kinds of people who live in cities. I did talk to a few people from the countryside, but only to a very few. I know so little about farming in any case that I really have no way to judge the background of what they told me. I was invited into six or seven houses and apartments, and I saw many different kinds of houses and families.

I expected to find that the most serious problem in the Soviet Union is a lack of freedom, particularly a lack of freedom to speak openly in criticizing Soviet life. This turned out to be less serious than I had anticipated. There are still many traces of the old fears, but the country is much, much freer than it was in the days before 1954. In the USSR, one does not say "before Stalin's death"; one says "before 1954," as if the very word "Stalin" has a kind of magically evil quality about it. There was much more controversy of opinion, and in a much more spirited and gay way than I would ever have expected. In this respect, their newspapers do not represent them very well. The more intellectual among Soviet people tend to be rather contemptuous of their own newspapers, and many openly expressed the wish and the hope that foreign newspapers will soon be sold on the streets. One can read foreign newspapers in the libraries and institutes, but they are not sold on the streets.

So far as I can judge, their most serious problems in style of life (aside from material shortages, which they are working hard and fast to overcome) are alcoholism and petty bureaucracy. I ran into these problems in many forms, and I discussed them with many different Russians, not one of which tried to deny the seriousness of the situation. They are trying to fight these things in many different ways, but they are obviously not going to solve them overnight.

When an American is speaking with a Russian, he has to be very careful how he phrases his statement of anything, which might be wrong with Soviet life. Anything which smacks of smugness, of the idea that the American way of life must naturally be better and richer than the Soviet way of life, is deeply and bitterly resented, in spite of the fact that almost all Russians know very well that the United States is an extremely rich country and that most Americans live comparatively richly and comfortably. On the other hand, if they see that an American approaches them with an open mind, ready to praise and blame as the occasion may turn out but eager to understand and to learn, they themselves will turn to what they think is wrong with their country in a fairly open way. I am afraid that I saw some American tourists there with completely closed minds, complaining bitterly at every step and absolutely convinced that anything Russian must be bad; I need hardly emphasize that these people are not exactly our best ambassadors.

Don't misunderstand me—I am not trying to claim that the USSR is as free as the United States; there are still many, many tragic aftermaths of the terrorist dictatorship and the wars in Russia. On the other hand, most people there think of these things as "aftermaths," as irritations, which are gradually being removed as life becomes better and more pleasant. Barring a major international catastrophe, they may well be right. Of course I would not want to live permanently in Soviet Russia; I far prefer my own native land with its comforts and its freedoms. On the other hand, most Russians would not jump at the opportunity to move to the United States; they too prefer where they have been born and brought up. But above and beyond men's natural preferences for what they know best, the United States and the USSR are swiftly moving closer and closer together. Industrial and urban life in the twentieth century have much more powerful methods of bringing people together than competing ideologies have to keep them apart.

That should give you some idea of my most general impressions about the trip. Let me then turn to some specifics which you might find interesting or amusing.

The trip over was fast, pleasant, and smooth. The idea of a night lasting only four hours, sunset at twelve o'clock and sunrise at four o'clock by the same set watch, is in itself as fantastic as the idea of jet travel. The service and the food were fine. I landed at the Brussels airport and had an hour stopover. I met my first Russians at the airport cafe; they were Soviet tourists who had just left Russia for the first time in their lives. They rushed breathlessly into the cafe, with a wild look in their eyes, faces glowing like little schoolboys who were about to pull a naughty trick. They then proceeded to order Coca Colas for everyone in the party. Some of them sipped it slowly, carefully, like a potentially explosive drink. Others downed the glassful in one gulp, like it was a slug of vodka. I asked one of the latter how he liked it. He eyed me askance for a few seconds, gulped, and said, "Well, I never really know how I like anything that I drink." When I laughed at his evasiveness, he added, "No, really, I have been drinking beer for ten years, but I don't know if I like it or not." I was amused at his diplomacy!

Love, Irwin

Wed. Sept. 7, 1960
Belmont, Mass.

Dear Mom and Dad,

When I got on the Soviet jet at the Brussels airport, I finally felt that at last I was in Soviet territory. My travelling companion was a Soviet diplomat who is the assistant to the head of the Soviet UN delegation. This man has lived in New York for three years, and he is a mighty shrewd cookie. We had a long, interesting chat, but the thing that impressed me most was my first blunder. I did not feel I had to be so much on my guard with this man since he was very sophisticated; I picked up a copy of *Pravda* from the plane, and my eye happened to catch one of the countless propaganda stupidities in the paper. Without even thinking very much, I read out loud one of their howlers in a satiric tone of voice. He looked at me, laughed, and said, "Watch out, my friend, you won't get very far in the Soviet Union that way." I suddenly realized that I had made a rather serious blunder, and my realization stood me in good stead for the rest of the trip. The Soviet patriotic sensibilities are always active on the surface, and you have to be very, very careful that what you say does not irritate these sensibilities.

Another instance in which I made the same blunder, quite unintentionally this time, was in a shoe repair shop while waiting in line. The shop had the radio on, and I heard the closest thing in Russia to a soap opera, complete with the resume of the previous day's plot and violin music to bridge into the story. I smiled, without even thinking about it, because it so reminded me of our sentimental radio stories. A lady asked me why I was smiling, and I said, "It just reminds me so of New York!" She answered in a huff that I was wrong—it did not remind me of New York; New York reminded me of Moscow! In other words, she interpreted my words as meaning that the Soviets had copied New York and were inferior to the American product. A soldier who was standing beside her felt the same way because he said, "That's telling him, young lady!" These incidents are typical of how easily a Westerner can give offense to the Russians without half trying. Of course I tried to use these incidents as lessons, blunders to be avoided a second time. As I said before, I could make remarks that were very critical of the USSR, but I had to be very careful how they were phrased and at what point in the conversation they were introduced. What they resent most is the implied attitude that somehow everything non-Soviet must be better. Of course, this only means that they themselves half believe that many things American are better, but they are trying to catch up, and they do not like to be reminded of their own attitudes.

When we landed at the Moscow International Airport, my first view of the country was a forest of beautiful and gigantic birch trees. The Russians are very fond of birch trees, and they made an appropriate welcome. They are much taller them the American variety in New England, but they do not lose any of their natural grace from their great height. Again and again, the Russians referred to these trees as a national symbol—"women's slender fingers," they are popularly called.

My only feeling of fear in the USSR was when we landed. The stewardess did not think the situation through very well because she left the plane without telling the foreigners what to do. We sat and sat while nothing happened until finally I went to the door to inquire. A border guard was standing there, just waiting to inspect our documents. He was very quiet and solemn looking, but he let us through after a careful examination of passports. In the waiting room, a young receptionist, a member of "Intourist" (the Soviet tourist agency), met me with a face appropriate for a funeral. In sepulchral tones, he greeted me and solemnly motioned me on. After one look at his face, I expected to be conducted straight to prison for torture, brainwashing, etc. It later turned out that he was a young student who was awed to meet an American professor, and he was acting in what he considered a most formal, respectful, academic manner. We later had an animated chat about the teaching of foreign languages in the USSR and the United States. Their customs check was perfunctory—they didn't even look at my grips. I was whisked by limousine to the Hotel Ukraina (the telegram botched the spelling), where they assigned me a room and left me to my own devices. After going to the room and eating, I wanted to take an evening stroll, so, still feeling a bit nervous, I went over to the desk and asked the girl for the return of my passport. She said she was sorry, but I couldn't get it back until the next day since it was needed for processing. I explained to her that I wanted to walk, but I was leery of going out without my passport. She laughed at me in a kindly way and said there was nothing to fear, that no one carried his passport for a walk. Her laugh suddenly made me relax and feel that I was acting like an old lady, and my fear immediately left me. I walked out away from the hotel, across the Moscow River, and up several boulevards. I tried to make some phone calls from numbers that I got from the United States, but everybody was away on vacation.

Moscow turned out to have a much less heavy atmosphere than I had expected. There are plenty of architectural monstrosities, but no one curses them more violently than the Russians, particularly the Russian architects. They were evidently forced on the people by Stalin; at least, the new ones going up have lost the absurd ginger bread. In spite of the monstrosities, however, the city as a whole is attractive. They are rebuilding it section by section, and the whole thing has a lot of the hustle and bustle of New York. Great buildings are going up – stores, offices, and apartments. There are still plenty of the old, dilapidated houses left, but they are gradually being erased by the new buildings. Housing is very tight; a separate apartment per family is by no means the established norm yet, but they are building fast. Consequently, one walks often from impressive facade to dilapidated, old housing and back again. The dilapidated places are kept clean and neat, and the people who live in them seem to behave themselves without any violence or unseemly behavior. I had no hesitation walking alone late at night through the poorest looking section of Moscow, and I gather that Russians also have no hesitation in doing so. The people on the street are extremely friendly, and they will knock themselves out to give you proper directions to get somewhere, even chasing you if you set out in the wrong direction.

On my walk the first night, I was anxious to find an intelligent-looking group to talk with. I finally settled on a group of youngsters, about college age, seated on benches in front of what turned out to be the apartment buildings where their families lived. Some of them were indeed students, and others were working in factories. All of them were interested in technology and engineering. The ones working were intending to take college entrance examinations. The Russian government now forces high school graduates to work for two years before applying for college entrance. The reason advanced for this is to give the youngsters a taste of life and work so they can choose their specialties more intelligently. Perhaps this is a part of the real reason, but another part is the shortage of labor right now in the USSR after their huge wartime losses in population.

In any event, I went up to the fellows and said, "Hey, young people, would you like to talk with me, an American?" They shouted with delight, and we became friends in five minutes. We talked from about ten o'clock until one in the morning, and we talked about almost everything. Of course they were surprised to meet an American who could speak Russian the way I do, and they wanted to know everything they could about American life. I, on the other hand, was equally eager to feel them out, but I wanted to be sure to avoid the blunders I knew an American must inevitably make until he knew Russian everyday customs better than I did. Consequently, I let them lead the conversation, which they were more than eager to do anyway. What impressed me most about them and about almost all the other Russian youth that I met were their seriousness of purpose and their knowledge about a wide range of subjects. They knew and loved literature, not only Russian, but also European and American. I can assure you that they were not bluffing because I asked them detailed questions about writers, Russian and American, whom I know very well myself. Of course, their attitudes were somewhat naïve since they are very young men who still have much to learn about life experience. But the proved fact of their interest and their knowledge was deeply impressive. I had this experience over and over again, and it above all else makes me optimistic about the future of Russia. These people are the ones who will furnish their leadership of the future, and they are serious, friendly people, not the generation that their fathers and grandfathers were. Their expectations for improvements in the future are also enormous.

I must admit that American youth suffers by comparison with the Russian youth whom I met. There is a range of knowledge, seriousness of purpose, and aliveness to the expression of beauty, which simply does not exist on such a mass scale in this country. If you compare our best to their best, I think we equal them and perhaps go them one better—the best products of a free education are impressive in any man's league. But if you compare the mass of our youth to the mass of theirs, I fear that we would get an answer not very flattering to ourselves. We have somehow let the dynamism of our own lives run down at the very time that the Russian dynamism is on the upswing. I felt there, more than ever before, the importance of the work I am now doing in the United States. They are beating their brains out to catch up with and surpass America in the field of technology. Believe me, we would do well to catch up with and surpass Russia in the field of education of youth, in both the narrow sense of specialized education and the broad sense of making people who are seriously competent in fields which go beyond their own narrow specialization. There are Russian equivalents of rock n roll, bobby soxers, and all that goes with the sicker aspects of American adolescents, but they are far, far less common in Russia than they are in the United States. You find no slick pornography or mailed smut in the USSR. Of course they do have their own vulgar propaganda organs, but even those boring sheets of howlers are less unhealthy than the products of our pornography mills and mass circulation publishers. The whole subject of sex is much less agitated in the USSR than it is in the United States, particularly among young people.

The next day, a Sunday morning and my first day in Moscow, I went to the Moscow Institute of World Literature, which is also the location of the Gorky Archives and the Gorky Museum. I trust you understand by now why I concentrate so much on Gorky; in addition to being a key Russian figure before and after the Revolution, he is the subject of my own research, my most important work at the moment. The museum was impressive, with a nice bronze statue of Gorky in front. He stands brooding, looking into the sidewalk from behind a row of trees. His back seems turned almost purposefully on the row of new apartment buildings that rise behind him, next to the museum in his name. The people inside the museum were delighted to meet an American interested in their man, and we spent about six hours talking and going through the materials in the museum. By this time, one of the people from the archives was called, and she made a special trip on Sunday to meet me and assure me that they would be happy to have me in the archives and talking with their people just as long as I would care to be there. They also asked me to send them any possible information about Gorky from the United States, including any American work being done on him. Of course I promised to help them, and they will send me all their new information and material as it comes out.

Later on that week, while I happened to be passing through the museum part of the building, they asked me to meet an excursion of high school kids from the middle of Siberia who were seeing the museum. Of course the museum people wanted to impress the high school kids and their Siberian friends with the importance of a museum which could attract the interest of an American professor. It was fun and interesting for me to meet the kids, since this was my first contact with any group of students in Russia. Since I was there in August, it was not so easy to meet groups of students. They were a fresh and wide-eyed lot, as interested as all Soviet people in the United States and much impressed that there are Americans who know their language and their culture well. We had a very nice chat for about an hour, at the end of which they gave me one of their school pins and I gave them a picture postcard of Boston, which made them ooh and ahh.

In the course of the next two weeks, I had long, long sessions of interviews and work at the Institute of World Literature and the Lenin Library, both in Moscow. I met some extremely interesting people at both places, many of them highly erudite and well read, knowing material that I did not imagine a Soviet scholar would have read. I am talking not only about material in their special fields but general philosophical and psychological material, most of it opposed to Marxist doctrine. I talked with them for six and eight hours at a stretch, and in some cases, I feel that I got to know them very well. Of course we had multitudes of disagreements, but in every case, I felt I could talk with them in such a way that both of us understood what the other was saying and why he thought the way he did. Again, many of them are extremely friendly to the United States and to American culture. I have the strong impression, from these people and from others, that the regime will find it very difficult to make the Russian people feel unfriendly toward the United States. On the other hand, we gave the regime ample material to work with in our handling of the Powers[1] plane incident.

---

1   Francis Gary Powers was an American pilot of a U-2 spy plane—an intelligence gathering plane that flew at unprecedented altitudes, which Americans believed exceeded the range of Soviet rockets. The Soviets, however, developed a rocket capable of reaching such altitudes and on 1 May 1960 shot down Powers' U-2 plane. Powers managed to survive using his parachute, was arrested, tried, put in prison, and then exchanged for a person from the Soviet Union being held in the United States.

I could write volumes about the actual work that I did in Moscow, but I am afraid that much of it would be a list of boring details for you. Therefore, instead of doing that (I'll keep you posted on my work as it goes along), I'll try to give you some of the human sidelights. I had interviews with a series of people not directly connected with my main subject of Gorky. One of them was a "Soviet Millionaire," a highly successful children's writer and one of the finest critics the Russians have today. He is a man, incidentally, who knows the English language extremely well, in spite of the fact that he has never lived in an English-speaking environment. He has lived through every conceivable kind of human tragedy and has suffered deeply in the last thirty years; repeatedly, he was on the edge of death. His experience has taught him a great deal and has left him with greatness and wisdom. It was delightful to talk with him and be with him. In the future, I'll tell you some of the things I learned from him. You may remember that I wrote you the compliment, which Khrushchev paid him when they received prizes together: Khrushchev pointed at him publicly and said, "There is a man whom I cannot abide!" When my man confusedly asked him why, Khrushchev replied," Because when I come home tired from a day's work, my grandchildren won't let me rest until I read them your stories and poetry!" This man took me through the writers' colony of Peredelkino, where Pasternak lived, and showed me many, many things about that charming and fascinating place. I had dinner with his family, and he asked me to sing him some Shakespearean songs, which I did. I have the feeling we formed a good relationship. He has most of the latest American poetry and literature, but I shall find some good things to send him.

He has also set up a wonderful children's center in Peredelkino, and he showed me with great pride the library; again, I promised to send him some English language material. His librarian, a young fellow about twenty years old, is the best young poet I met in Russia.

I went over to the Soviet Writers' Union and had a very interesting set of conversations with the head of the foreign section and his assistant. They were invaluable to me in Moscow and sent me straight to most of the people I wanted to see. The head of the foreign section is also a translator of American literature, and he fell with delight on the paperbacks I had brought with me. It was wonderful to hear him explain the rules of baseball, as if he had learned the game from Aunt Lee herself.

These people also arranged an interview for me with the editorial staff of the magazine *Youth*, a magazine of literature and literary criticism. I met a group of young writers together with their editors. I tried to ask them questions about the process of literature and literary criticism, but my questions did not really elicit much useful information or even interesting reactions. These writers, at least, are very <u>un</u>interested in abstract problems of literary creation. When they started asking me questions, however, things got started in a grand way. They, of course, were extremely interested about details of life in the United States and about details of my own life. As we got going, they began to reveal themselves and relate what I had said to details of their own lives and work. Although some of them still talked a little like the stereotype of a Soviet writer, banal clichés all in place, there was also a palpable freshness of spirit about them, a kind of tightly controlled sense of humor and irony which I usually associate with a writer. There may be a fresh talent or two among them which will flourish in the future as they gain more experience and practice. Again, one could sense an extensive feeling of friendliness toward things American. They were highly impressed by the details of American life that I dropped very casually among them. Because I did not talk about these details as great things but only as incidental details of my own life, they were very much impressed by them and unafraid to say so.

I went into the "Children's World," the FAO Schwartz of Russia, paradise for kids. It was easy to find especially Russian toys for Alice but very difficult to find anything different for Marty. Evidently, girls of the world play differently, but boys of the world all play in the same way. While there, I took a look at musical instruments, just for kicks. Guitars, accordions, etc. were very cheap, but they were also not made very well. I started to monkey around with a Russian guitar, but it was hard because the number of strings is different, so the finger positions are entirely different. I did make out enough to interest a fellow behind the counter, and he later favored me in return with a concert of Russian folk music on the accordion. He was terrific, and he soon had all the store help around him dancing to his accordion. One old woman, probably recently a peasant, danced right up the stairs while holding onto a bag of waste material which was as tall as she was. I finally clapped, said "Bravo!" and walked out of the store, or there would not have been much selling done there on that day.

I saw the opera *Prince Igor* at the famous Bolshoi Theatre in Moscow. Unfortunately, the leading Russian company was not there, so I had to see a young Siberian Opera company that was on tour. I enjoyed the performance, although the singing and acting was extremely spotty: some wonderful voices and some lousy. It was the first time I have seen or heard the whole thing, which is based on one of the most famous Russian epic poems, the story of Prince Igor, who goes off to fight the invading nomad hordes and takes one hell of a beating. The opera, written in the nineteenth century, is full of the Christian religion, and the Russians obviously had a wonderful time acting out the old religious roles. There was a cathedral built on stage with a religious picture painted on the outside gate in the old-fashioned Russian church style. Every time one of the opera characters came out of the cathedral, he ceremoniously crossed himself and obviously had a whale of a time doing it.

Behind me there sat two school teachers from the far north, in Moscow on vacation, and we had a good chat during intermission. I think they were disappointed at my lukewarm reaction to the performance, but they were pleased to see how much I liked the opera itself, as Borodin wrote it.

I saw a Russian performance of Shakespeare's *Merry Wives of Windsor* (Remember my junior year in walnut Hills?), and I invited myself backstage to meet the director of the piece. He was a genial chap who had worked in New York last year, and I also had the satisfaction of meeting the director of the famous Italian Teatro Piccolo. We conversed in French, since the Italian did not speak Russian. Zavadsky, director of the theatre, is a lucky guy who gets all the material support he needs and is now working in a new theatre especially built for him. His troupe is obviously very vigorous and popular, and he puts on plays of superior quality for the most part. I was amazed at how closely they came to the atmosphere of Shakespeare in the original English, in spite of the fact that it was played in Russian; perhaps this is only a restatement of the well-known fact that Shakespeare is the most universal of all writers regardless of time or place. Zavadsky had added some parts to the Shakespearean text in an attempt to bring the play closer to the lives of his audience. Ordinarily, I do not like people who tamper with Shakespeare, but I must admit that the atmosphere of the performance was so congenial that I overlooked his additions. They had an imitation of an Elizabethan English fair in the foyer of the theatre during intermission, complete with jugglers, sword swallowers, etc. Masked girls went around with sacks, and everybody pulled his "fortune" out of the sacks: printed couplets from the works of Shakespeare. The whole evening was most enjoyable. I had some more conversations with Zavadsky and later saw another play at his theatre, a Soviet comedy *Without a Moral.*

Buying books was a delight in the USSR—the stores are well kept and well run (unlike most other Soviet stores), and the books are amazingly cheap. The Russians obviously love books and love to read; the stores are always jammed, and the public is always reading. Literature is very popular, and they especially go for translations of foreign literature, including American literature. An edition of a single book does not last more than a few days in the Russian bookstores, and they print many of them in hundreds of thousands of copies, even millions of copies. Every Russian house or apartment, however dilapidated or crowded, has a large collection of books. The people in the bookstores are extremely interested in talking with foreigners, and I never got out of one without a long, long description of life in the United States.

While standing in line outside the best restaurant in Moscow, a place run in the Georgian style (Georgia is a republic in the Caucasus Mountains, down in the south of Russia above Turkey; Stalin was a Georgian), I heard some interesting-looking people speaking in a language I had never heard before. I asked a Russian what they were speaking, and he replied, "Georgian." I finally got up the nerve to approach the guy and ask him if I could join him and his family for supper since he was the first real-live Georgian I had ever met. He was delighted, and I had one of the most pleasant evenings in the USSR with him, his niece, and her friend. He is an architect from Tbilisi, the famous capital city of Georgia, and he was on a business trip to Moscow. His niece and her friend were studying at an institute for candy factories, and they were getting experience at a factory in Moscow before returning to their native city to practice. He insisted that we have a banquet in the old-fashioned Georgian style, complete with toasts drunk in wonderful Caucasian wine. He was delighted to hear about life in the United States, and he certainly gave me an earful of life in Georgia. He was a man of swarthy complexion but with bright blue eyes, and his temperament reminded me very much of what I have always read about the Italians. He is passionately fond of art, music, and literature, and we spent a delightful evening. He and his family joined me again on the weekend for an evening, and they were a delight to be with. They kept on trying to picture a gay young fellow like myself as a stern professor, but they finally gave up on the attempt. When the fellow got around to architecture, he was of two minds. He did not like talking badly about Stalin, a fellow Georgian, but he could not stand the kind of architecture that Stalin went in for. He also emphasized how much things have loosened up since the death of Stalin.

When I went over to Henry's hotel to find out about when he would be in, I met a very interesting woman at the telegraph and post office desk of the hotel. I mentioned her briefly in a letter as the descendant of a French soldier who came to Russia with Napoleon's army. She was not a well-educated woman, but she had a most sophisticated outlook on everything that went on around her. I was interested by one incident that took place while I was there. I asked her to use the phone, and she just waved me right on, telling me to feel free to use it as long and as often as I liked. About ten minutes later, a most unpleasant looking guy in a trench coat walked in and nastily told her, "Hand over that phone!" She told him to go to hell, as it was her phone, to be used for official business of the post office only. He again demanded to use the phone, and she answered him back in kind. He then pulled out some kind of wallet, showed it to her, and again demanded the phone. She resisted again, whereupon he really swore. She then said, "Go ahead and use the damn thing, if you want to." After he made the call and left, when there was no one else close by, I asked her who that fellow was. With great disgust she replied, "A detective; I hate those guys, always making it miserable for someone."

Love, Irwin

Thurs. Sept. 8, 1960
Belmont, Mass.

Dear Mom and Dad,

Before I go into the details of meeting Henry and our trip to Leningrad, let me see if I can remember some more details from my first stay in Moscow. They will be somewhat disconnected, more so than the other remarks, but I would like to keep them in my memory.

Intourist is staffed mostly by college-age girls who have studied English and/or French. Their linguistic abilities vary widely, although some of them speak English very well indeed. They are harried beyond belief since their ranks are thin and the summer tourists are many. Most of them, I think, try to do a good job in spite of the fact that the majority of American tourists obviously get under their skins. They are the ones who bear the brunt of the American "I can't stand anything about Russia" approach. A few of the girls simply retreat into a dull and stupid bureaucratic attitude, doing everything mechanically and even taking a kind of sly pleasure in fouling the tourists up and watching them squirm. I was the victim on a few occasions of such an attitude, but luckily, I was not completely dependent upon those lemons. The majority of girls, however, really do try their best to help people. They often get fouled up, but it is not entirely their fault: the system itself is really not set up to serve the interests of tourists who are accustomed to a very different kind of social experience. I personally found that after I would spend five or ten minutes chatting with some of them, showing them that I had some personal interest in what they were doing and what they hoped to do, they treated me as a friend. The pocket book classics of American literature which I had brought along helped greatly. Tips are usually resented, but pocket books are usually welcomed with gratitude; the latter implies respect for the recipient while the former implies condescension, which they cannot stand from a foreigner and which particularly disturbs them when it comes from an American. One girl at the Ukraina was a honey, the sort of girl who would make an ace American secretary. She always had no less than two telephones in her hand at once, sometimes three or four (Sidney Weil take notice), and she never got harried, however much confusion or shouting there might be around her. I gave her a book of Edgar Allen Poe, inscribed, "To Miss Rovanshina, cool as a cucumber when everything around her is in confusion." She accepted it gratefully and then puzzled over the inscription. When I explained it to her she laughed kindly, and ever after that, she had a smile whenever I came by.

On the whole, I avoided guides and translators like the plague. I do not like to use such people in general, and I particularly want to avoid their "services" when looking at things associated with Russian literature, which I love so deeply. The Russians were very happy to leave me to my own devices since this relieved them of one extra headache at a time when translators were going crazy. As a matter of fact, I sometimes lent a translating hand when I happened to be around the Intourist desks in the hotel or in the restaurants, and they seemed grateful for this.

One time when I did want some help, however, occurred while I was working at the Lenin Library, and the work consisted of doing some copying which would have taken many valuable hours of my time. I asked the library people if they would mind my bringing a "translator" in to do some copying for me, and they said they had no objection if Intourist did not mind. I asked my Intourist girls, and they said they had no objection if the translator did not mind. After they called her and she came, I asked her if she would do it for me, and she jumped at the chance of getting away from the awful routine of shepherding Americans around the Moscow museums and sightseeing places.

Tatiana was an interesting girl, and I was glad I had the chance to meet her. She had finished the English Institute, and she will be teaching English in a high school starting next year. She tried very hard to carry out efficiently the tasks I gave her, and she showed a good deal of sense and initiative in the process. She had a peculiar combination of typical Soviet contempt for "bourgeois" things with an obviously deep desire to dress and primp attractively. We never passed a mirror without her giving attention to the basic feminine attributes. She also mixed a sophisticated contempt for the crudities of Soviet propaganda with the typical Russian bristling if there were some suggestion that things American were better than things Soviet. Her father is an old time Communist Party member, and her mother is a would-be singer who suffered an accident which cut off her career. Tatiana is obviously rather bitter about her parents and the fact that they never paid as much attention to her as the child would have liked. She expresses her independence from them in every way she can, but the housing shortage forces her to live with them. She pays her bills, she does the cooking, and she sleeps outside the house whenever the weather is good enough to sleep outside in the garden. Tatiana is determined "never to be made a sucker" in the course of her life, and she very toughly wards off any suggestion of idealistic talk. Yet she refuses to deal in the petty deceptions which most of the Intourist translators willingly use to get short rests from work. I am not sure that she as a future teacher will give the children much love, but she will certainly work hard and intelligently, enough to satisfy her very considerable pride.

Tatiana was upset by an incident of which I involuntarily witnessed a part: she introduced me to an American, a pleasant chap whom she obviously liked, whom she had shepherded about Moscow for several days. The next day, tight-lipped, she asked me if I had read *Pravda* that morning. I said no, and she showed me an article that said that this American had been found taking pictures of military installations RDX (naval ships on the Black Sea), had been searched, and that a belt of secret pictures had been found under his clothes. According to *Pravda*, he had then been kicked out of the country. Tatiana was deeply upset, both at the incident and at the idea that she had been connected with the guy and he had seemed such a nice guy. After she had calmed down a bit, I tried to explain to her that there had also been many, many such spies whom the Russians sent to the United States—she heard this with interest (as did all Russians to whom I told it), but it could not possibly offset her feelings at having been personally in contact with the American chap.

The Lenin Library is a great institution. The service they give could well be a model for American libraries which I have known. One must have a ticket to use the library, and you apply for the ticket when you first come in. The application card asks for the usual information plus your academic degrees and the field of your work. Those with degrees go to different service halls from those without degrees. I went to the professors' hall and was treated royally. The catalogs seemed very complete to me, and I found everything I wanted in my own work, including many,

many items about Gorky that were by no means sympathetic to the Communist approach to this writer. I also ran a spot check on some literature which is not in favor in the USSR, and I found card entries for a large part of it. I gather that the presence (or perhaps return presence) of some of these cards has taken place over the last few years with the general loosening up of the regime. The card catalog can be used by everybody who can enter the library. I doubt that any person whatsoever would get working entrance to the Lenin Library, but I would be surprised if many people with serious scholarly interests would be kept out. I did not have time to look at a more popular library where the average person might take out books, but I doubt that the selection there would be anything like the Lenin Library. In some ways, this is similar to our own distinctions between serious research libraries and popular libraries, although it is probably easier for the common man to get into our research libraries.

The serious Soviet libraries do have copies of the foreign newspapers, which you cannot buy on the streets of Soviet cities. How much papers like the *New York Times* are read in the USSR, I have no idea. I suspect they are read very seldom, most Soviets preferring the English-language newspapers which are more sympathetic to the USSR, i.e., the Communist newspapers. The Russians were always impressed when I told them that I receive *Pravda* in Boston every day and that the FBI never bothers me about it. Many Russian students told me that they would like to be able to buy the *New York Times* on the streets of Leningrad and Moscow. Some of them claimed that such a move is now under discussion, and they expressed the hope that they could get the paper easily in a few years. From what they told me, I gather that it is not too easy to read the *New York Times* regularly, even in the library. Again and again, I tried to emphasize to them what an asset it would be for them and for their government to be able to read the opposition press regularly. I tried to emphasize to them that it would be a symptom of Soviet strength; their present attitude implies weakness because it seems to imply that the Soviet government cannot stand the expression or reading of opposition views. I did not find a single Russian, even a Communist, who disagreed with me on this point.

Before I went to the USSR, I had hoped to meet some Russian children and play with them for a while. As it turned out, this was not so easy. While I had no hesitation in accosting adults on the street or anywhere else, I don't think it's a good idea to do this with children; I would only approach children through their parents, and this I was very seldom able to do because I was not in many places where children and their parents were together (except for the houses I visited, and then the adults, naturally, monopolized the conversation). Through some of my friends, I finally gave away the chewing gum I had and the stamps that Henry left with me; according to the recipients, the presents went over big, both with the parents and with the kids, but I got no firsthand impression of the operation. I was sometimes stopped by kids on the street who wanted to talk with an American, and in a few cases, I had some interesting experiences. The "code" for kids who approach you is to ask what time it is. If your answer shows a foreign accent, they will then address you in English. In my case, they often hesitated: my clothes proclaimed the American, but they could not always place an accent. In a few cases, we talked for some time, and they told me about their studies and ambitions much as American kids would. In every case, the ability to travel to a foreign land sounded like a wistful dream to them, one which they would have for many, many years.

The Russian cops were universally pleasant and courteous to me. Like everybody else, they knocked themselves out to make sure I went in the direction I asked for. They have the habit, a little disconcerting to me, of saluting you every time you walk up to them. One of them said, when he noticed my surprise at first, "It's obligatory, sir; we have to salute everybody." I talked to a cop on the bus, who was very pleased to get some sympathetic attention from an American. He said that the cops crave kinder reactions from the population but that they were resigned to being always in an unpopular occupation. Don't confuse these police, by the way, with the secret political police; they are two very, very different organizations. The only time I saw the regular cops get tough was when dealing with rowdy drunks. Ordinarily, they walk disarmed, so far as I could judge, but I noticed the cop who dealt with the drunks had a sidearm pistol. Evidently, they have stern instructions to deal toughly with the drunks; so far as I could tell, most citizens were happy that "at last" they were doing something about the pesky sots. In Leningrad, I saw more of these problems, and I'll describe them in sequence.

All foreign embassies have Soviet policemen in front, whose unabashed purpose is to keep unauthorized Russians out of the embassies, I saw this with my own eyes when some Russians tried to enter the American Embassy. When I went to register at the embassy, I asked the cop some questions in Russian. He said, "Who are you?" I answered that I was an American. He said, "Says who?" I said that I was shocked that he didn't believe me, but I would be happy to show him my passport. When he indicated, curtly, that he wanted to see it, I started to pull it out from my coat pocket. As soon as he caught one glimpse of the green binding of an American passport, he smiled, saluted me, and waved me in. It was 9:00 a.m., and nobody was in the embassy. I then came out and asked the cop what time they start. He answered nine o'clock. When I indicated that nobody was there yet, he smiled (happy at having caught me) and said with a shrug, "There's American punctuality for you!" I told this in some glee to my good Russian friends in Moscow, and one fellow said, "You should have told him that lack of punctuality is something the Americans in Moscow picked up from the Russians."

I had a very interesting auto trip down to Yasnaya Polyana, the home of Tolstoy. I think I already described to you the wonderful experience this was, to see the grave of Tolstoy in the midst of a huge, seemingly endless birch woods. I met Tolstoy's former secretary, and I met some of the research personnel down there. My driver was an interesting young man who had supported his orphaned brothers and sisters after the war by working as a chauffeur and who was now going to finish his own education. He was the sort of fellow who attends to his job thoroughly and accurately, and I am sure he will make his way successfully in the world. It was a pleasure to be in his pleasant, cheerful company, in spite of the fact that he is not the brightest person in the world.

I had the privilege of using Intourist limousines with drivers for three hours a day, but I did not ordinarily use them unless I was carrying a load of books which would have been hard to manage on the buses. Riding the buses and streetcars, I had a chance to see a not insignificant part of

Russian daily life, with its strains and its tensions. When their buses are crowded, they are like sardine cans. The people line up fairly easily, and there is not too much problem of shoving and rushing unless they sense that you won't get on quickly enough for others to follow—then they turn into shoving maniacs. You must also be sure to get up ahead of your stop if you want to get off at the proper time. Navigating through that mob is an art in itself, although a simple "excuse me" is usually enough to get you through a tiny space between Russian humanity. I heard some of my juiciest Russian ever when a young squirt would try to grab a place from an older woman. That Russian is not grammar-book Russian, I assure you.

When I did use the limousines, I invariably had a good conversation with the cabbie. Most of the ones I met were older fellows, seemingly kindly, who had been driving in Moscow and Leningrad since the late l920s; in other words, they had stuck with the same job for about thirty-plus years. They had almost all come to the cities during the time of collectivization of agriculture, and they missed the countryside in spite of their pride in being auto drivers and auto mechanics. Almost without exception, they had fought and had lost most of their families in the War. Those who lost their families remarried after the war, but they all said, sentimentally and sadly, how much they missed their first families. I gathered from them that the temptation toward drowning one's sorrow in drink was strong but that they managed to resist it. Without exception, they were worried about the possibility of another war and were happy to see Americans who were obviously not warlike.

It was, of course, no exception to meet people who had lost over half their families during World War II. The depth of their experience and suffering during the war is something which will not leave Russia for generations. It is something that sounds like a cliché in the United States, where we know about it but have not shared the experience to the same depth.

For the most part, I kept away from government offices that have part in official exchange business, but I did go to the State Committee for Cultural Exchange on behalf of Henry. I had an interesting talk with an official at the office, a real cool fish with his eyes pointed upward toward promotion and a shrewd outlook on the world situation. He wanted a quick appraisal of my outlook on the American situation, and I could see that he took it in swiftly and with an experienced eye and ear. I then turned the tables on him, and he was happy to admit that there had been forced labor camps in the USSR, but he claimed that the recent changes in the regime have all but eliminated them. He, like the others I met, emphasized the increasing amounts of freedom the Russians are now enjoying. He also agreed to help Henry (and later kept his word without any trouble), but he did not do it easily or pleasantly. He said that the Russian visitors to the United States had been running into a great deal of interference, which was preventing them from seeing most of the people they wanted to see. I told him I was surprised at this—that I myself had received several Soviet individuals and delegations, and that I and my colleagues had done everything in our power to make sure that our guests saw every last detail and person they wanted to see. Moreover, I stood ready to guarantee that any bona fide academic person they would send to Boston would see every last person and thing around Boston University that he wanted to see. Moreover, Henry himself and Governor Meyner in New Jersey had done this for several Soviet people and delegations.

I then asked him for some particulars. He told me of a congress of metallurgists in Chicago. The Soviet people came and were put on a bus for a tour of factories. After the bus started, there was an announcement that the Soviet delegates could not go into all plants on the tour, and they had to wait while the others went in. If this is true, it is disgraceful on our part. I would like to check it and find out if it is actually true.

At a small restaurant in the Ukraina where I went, when a congress of Orientalist specialists monopolized our regular restaurant, I met an interesting bunch of waitresses, one of whom talked with me for a while and gave me some added insight into the problem of alcoholism. Her husband works hard in a factory all day, drinks up his money after work, comes home dead drunk, falls unconscious into bed, and does the same thing on the following day. Their son, as you can imagine, studies poorly in high school, and the woman is at her wit's end. She thought about divorce, but it is expensive, and she was afraid that the housing shortage would force them to end up in the same apartment anyway. I asked her if she still loved her husband, and she replied, "How could anyone love such a thing?

Believe me, we are not the only Moscow family in such a fix." I am sure this sad story is not the only such incident, and it probably throws some light on to the problem of alcoholism. Soviet society does not seem to offer any outlet for those who cannot, for one reason or another, throw themselves into the central movements sponsored by the regime for purposes of the regime. The only escape for such people is alcoholic forgetfulness. It is a sad sight and a sad problem, one which the Soviets are battling fiercely and will have to battle for a long time, I fear.

While I was waiting at Henry's hotel for him to come, I discovered that I had two hours on my hands. Since I had not had much time to do sightseeing in Moscow, spending most of my time doing very necessary work for myself, I decided to visit the Kremlin at last. On the way over, however, I could not quite bring myself to go in that massive place for such a short time, and I went into the Lenin Museum instead. It had the usual garish propaganda effects, complete with dramatic pictures of revolutionaries storming the Petersburg palace gates. One thing that impressed me, however, was the row of aristocratic sensitive faces, photographs of the people who were close to Lenin. Where, I asked myself, does one see such faces today in the land where Lenin's name is magic? The faces have all turned in other directions. I was also impressed by the library of Lenin, who read just about everything he could lay hands on. Where, I asked myself, are the Soviet citizens who have read half as much, making allowances for the unusual intellectual endowments of Lenin? Of course the Soviets love to read, but they don't read the kind of philosophical material that Lenin read. When I broached this subject to some Russian friends, they told me they often had exactly the same reaction when they saw the same photos and book lists.

Oh, I almost forgot to tell you about my introduction to the famous Moscow subway. The fellows I met the first night in Moscow would sometimes call me on the phone in the hotel and ask me to join them. I soon discovered that they were hesitant to come into the hotel, mainly used for foreigners, but they had no hesitation in meeting me outside the hotel. I heard the claim later that the reason they did not come into the hotel was not the reason I suspected. According to this claim, they had no fear of being seen with foreigners, but they did fear being taken for dealers in second-hand American merchandise, a black market operation that some Russians engage in right around the hotel. I have no idea which was the proper explanation for their reluctance to enter the hotel, so I can only report the facts. In any event, I readily accepted their invitation to join them, and we fell to talking as usual. All of a sudden, they asked me if I had seen the subway. I had not, so I asked them if they would take me. They enthusiastically set out with me under their wings, and they explained the history of every Moscow square we crossed en route to the stop. As you undoubtedly know, the subway is perfectly neat and clean, with statues, pictures, and decorations galore, as if it were a kind of museum. Each station is decorated in a different historical motif, and they really went all the way to make it beautiful, according to their idea of beauty. It was impressive and sad, all at the same time. The young fellows were tremendously enthusiastic and proud, and I did not have the heart to spoil it for them by giving what I would consider an objective reaction. I admired what I honestly thought deserved admiration and was silent about the rest.

In my opinion, what really deserves admiration is the organization of the subway itself. It is really very convenient to go from one direction to another, whether the change is in the central line of traffic flow or whether the change is lateral in relation to the central traffic flow. It is beautifully done so that there is no problem of moving "cross town." As for the artwork, some of the mosaics were, in my opinion, rather tastefully done. The rest, alas, is all in typical Soviet heroic style, without a single original idea to its credit. As mass appeal art it is passable, and I suppose you have to judge it in that category. Still, it would have been nice if that expenditure of money and effort could have led to an original movement of sculpture and art. The Russians are capable of it, I am sure. On the whole, however, the subway was to me a very impressive achievement, and I could honestly, without hypocrisy, respond to the tremendous pride of the young people in their country's achievement.

The first evening that Henry and Tema were there, we walked around Red Square together, and we got some feeling for the immenseness and grandeur of the Kremlin palace and the outside parade grounds. We found out that it was impossible to get into the famous mausoleum where Lenin and Stalin are kept because the mausoleum was closed for repairs. Frankly, I didn't feel we had missed very much. We then went over in front of the Hotel Metropol where little groups of people were talking. A big group soon gathered around me and fired rapid questions about the United States. I think I already described to you the gist of the discussions we had.

Henry called up the aunt of a friend of his from New Jersey; the aunt is an old woman who has been making her living coaching youngsters in English and German. She has relatives all over the world, and she has kept contact with most of them. After showing up at the hotel for tea, she invited us to dinner at her apartment, and we gladly accepted. The dinner was a typical Russian-Jewish feast, and we all had a wonderful time with her and her family. The usual questions about the United States were asked, plus the questions about Jews in the United States. They were wonderful hosts and obviously very glad to have us. Her granddaughter, whose parents were killed in Leningrad during the war, keeps house for the old couple while working as a music teacher, and she fed us royally. Of course the coming of our car caused quite a stir in the neighborhood, and at the very end, the old lady admitted that she had only made contact with us after enormous hesitation for fear she might be bringing down danger on their heads. It was moving, pathetic, and wonderful, all at the same time, to be with them and see how they felt.

After dinner, we set out on the Leningrad route for Kalinin, the capital city of the "oblast" (Russian word, roughly equivalent to the American state) north of Moscow. It is a weaving center, an ancient city which now serves mainly as an agricultural commercial distribution point and as an administrative center. We went into the hotel parking lot to find the night watchman dead drunk, oblivious to the whole world. I called the chambermaid, and she managed to snatch the keys out of his pocket and let our car through the gate. The next morning, I again made a blunder: I asked the chambermaid how the drunken night watchman was feeling. She angrily replied that they have no drunken night watchmen—that there were five wide-awake night watchmen sitting there over our cars all night!

Since we were outside the central cities for such a short time, I decided to try and meet some provincials, and I went away from the hotel for breakfast. Sitting down next to what looked like an intelligent face, I began to ask the usual questions and start the usual conversation. This guy turned out to be the assistant district attorney for the whole oblast. His job was to follow up all industrial directives that were issued in the area and make sure that none of them were against the law. If it turned out that any laws were broken, he had to notify the parties, who then had a certain number of days to rectify the situation. Only if there seemed to be major malice in a case would he submit it for legal prosecution. If any workers felt that they were being mistreated, they also came to him, and it was his duty to conduct an impartial investigation and supervise the needed corrections, if any. What he said sounded logical enough, but he said it in a very truculent, almost narrow manner, ending up with these words: "My duty is to see to it that not one single item of the law is contravened. If it turns out that even one was broken without my knowledge, I should be chased from my job!"

I felt that I somehow knew narrow characters like this, so I tried a little experiment. I asked him casually if he liked literature, and he answered yes. I then asked him whether or not he liked Tolstoy (who has some rather ironic comments on narrow court people); he hesitated for a minute, and then evasively said, "Public opinion considers Tolstoy to be a great writer." I told him that I was aware of this even before speaking with him, but public opinion interested me less than his personal opinion. He then said that he did not like Tolstoy; when I asked why, he replied that Tolstoy had put too many French words into his novels. I then said to myself that I really knew this character from beginning to end! When I told this story to other Russians, they had the same reaction, half amused, half shocked, that I did.

The assistant DA then went on to tell me something of his life. He had lost his mother and father when he was sixteen years old during the war, and he had received only a few years schooling before he had to go out and earn his living. He then went to night school while supporting himself and finally ended up, after years of struggle, with a legal education which entitled him to a good job. I then interpreted his narrowness in a somewhat different way than I had previously. It was rather amusing that at the end of his story, he reared up and said, "A career like mine, with a poor boy rising to a good job, could only take place in Soviet Russia!" He said this in exactly the same way as I have heard similar stories end, "Only in America could this happen!"

We then went on our travels to the city of Novgorod, a lovely old Russian city, which has been preserved as a sort of museum piece, in spite of the fact that it is now an oblast capital. The city was founded before the tenth century, and it has many old churches and an old kremlin fortress built by the old Russian princes before the day when Russia existed as a country. What that city has not seen in the way of cruelty! Again and again, it has been conquered and sacked until the streets ran red with blood—by Russian princes, Tatar princes, Russian tsars, tsarist police, and finally the Nazi Germans. In each case, the people have dug out and started all over again. The lovely old church work has been preserved, and there are many interesting works of art to see.

I latched onto a group of Russians who were looking at the monument commemorating a thousand years of tsarist history; it was built in the middle of the last century. Soon, of course, I was in a discussion with the Russians who were interested in the place, and we had a long, rambling talk. Some of them had never met an American before. We talked for some time about art, and it was clear that many of them are very much attracted by the concept of modern art, even though this practice has been almost entirely discouraged in Russia. It is a funny thing that the Communist bosses and the American congressmen are in complete agreement about what is right and wrong in the fields of painting and artwork. Nevertheless, Soviet youth are very much interested in the modern schools of painting, and the regime has begun to ease up its pressure against the new trends in this field. I got a lot of agreement from them when I said that art should not be completely controlled or judged by standards of politics but only by standards of art. This, of course, is heresy by Communist standards. They too have the feeling that control over art only stultifies its progress.

Early in the morning, because I couldn't sleep after 6:00, I took a long walk around the Novgorod Kremlin and the city's parks and churches. The Kremlin was beautiful at that hour in the morning, and I got a wonderful, fantastic view of the old walls and moats, even seeing the old princes in my mind's eye.

I also got a view of the local honor roll in the park: sketches of people who had been doing outstanding work in industry, agriculture, etc. Some of the faces, with big eyes, seemed most attractive. Others, with big mouths, seemed most unattractive. Few seemed in between. As I walked past a park bench, I noticed a young father at 7:30 in the morning with a sleeping infant, obviously his first, in his arms. I went over and told him in my professional father's whisper that I also have kids and know what it's like to soothe a sleeping baby. He was delighted to talk, and we sat down. The kid had gotten vaccinated the day before and had spent a restless night. Because the father was on vacation and his wife had to work, he had taken the baby out so that she could get some sleep and come to work fresh and on time. He treated the baby just like the usual crazy American father does with his first kid, and I was later favored with some smiles and gurgles after the son woke up. While we were talking, a procession of old ladies went through the park, and the fellow told me these were people on their way to church. Sure enough, I heard church bells in the background.

Later on, as I mused past the churches with their crosses on top, the ancient symbol of the Russian Orthodox Church, I remembered how the old Russians had seen this as an unchanging symbol of eternal Russia. For a thousand years, it ruled unchanged, and then, suddenly, was replaced with the Red Star and Red Banner, another symbol whose adherents consider it eternal. How does one explain these phenomena of history? What do people search for in these so-called eternal symbols? But the people in their daily lives just go right ahead. They make the necessary adjustments, and life, Christian, Communist, or otherwise, just goes right on, in many ways unchanged since ancient days.

We arrived in Leningrad, and I was put into the local fleabag hotel. I really didn't mind because it gave me a chance to see a very different class of Russians, unmixed with foreigners, at close range.

Love, Irwin

Tues. Sept. 13, 1960
Belmont, Mass.

Dear Mom and Dad,

Between threatening hurricanes, which left us almost untouched, and registering students, who never leave one untouched, I had to break off my narrative a bit. Let's get back to Leningrad.

My friend arranged for me to see her at the Hermitage before I went to the Pushkin House, the Leningrad literary branch of the Academy of Sciences. I went over to the Hermitage early in the morning and gave her a small present that I had brought, a copy of an ancient American-Indian vase found around the Mississippi River and probably dating back to the twelfth or thirteenth century. I know that she likes small aesthetic objects, and I was sure she would want another memento of her American trip. We greeted each other happily, and I also met the scientific secretary of the Hermitage, a fine, gracious old lady of the older Russian style. They all said they had heard good things about me from my friend, a compliment which I tried to parry as gracefully as I could. When my friend saw Brentano's efficient packaging, she laughed and asked if it was a small atomic bomb. She then promised to show me around her part of the museum in the afternoon, after I would be finished with work at the Pushkin House. I accepted gratefully, and that afternoon, I saw the magnificent exhibitions of quartz and other artistic minerals that are housed at the Hermitage. I also saw a movie of the Moscow Kremlin, which I was going to see the last day that I was in Moscow. The collection of the tsar's wealth is so fabulous and luxurious that it simply stunned my fantasy—for once, I came out of an experience with no feelings left to sort. It was later explained to me by a Russian professor that the rich tsar's collection is explained less by any excessive wealth than by the typically Eastern habit of holding onto every single piece of gold or silver ever received. The constant round of huge, pompously yet beautifully wrought gold and silver objects, rich materials, etc. just left me limp.

The next day, she introduced me to one of the most gracious men I have ever met, a relative of the famous composer, Glinka. This man showed me around the Russian history section of the Hermitage, including the last tsar's room, which my guide called the "best apartment in St. Petersburg"—he was right; it had a corner view of the most noble part of the Neva River. I also saw the rooms where the Kerensky government was arrested and the gates where the victorious revolutionary forces streamed through the palace. Everything was described with a nice sense of history's many ironies.

On the following days, I saw many, many artifacts from the life of Pushkin, and all of these things gave me a much clearer idea of his life style than I could ever have had otherwise. Some of them tend to over-romanticize Pushkin, to blot out the many foolish, weak, and silly deeds committed even by this genius of poetry and the beauty of language; nonetheless, it was all very impressive.

One evening, I had a dinner with my friend and her husband at their apartment. It was a marvelous evening, and we talked until two o'clock in the evening. They were fascinated by many of my experiences in Russia; it was obvious that an American's reaction to their country and their culture was a very deep and absorbing interest to them. It was a self picture which is a real rarity in Russia. Her husband is a very important architect and city planner in Leningrad. He is obviously a man of deep culture and sensitivity, and my first reaction to him was an extremely friendly one. He, too, is extremely proud of Soviet Russia, what they have managed to do in a patriotic way and how they have managed to rebuild and live through their war experiences. He was also very ironic about Soviet shortcomings, but only after he saw that I was willing to accept what was there in a reasonably objective manner. At first, he was very sensitive talking about such things as primitive-type toilets, until I made it clear that these were not the things in Russia of primary interest to me. He also told me a story which had shocked him very much: a German man, trained as a professor, had told him that he was working in a business firm because the business firm offered him more money. How, he asked me, could such a man do such a thing? I reassured him that there were also people in the Western world who worked in the academic world in spite of the fact that they could receive more money outside the university!

Both he and his wife had very favorable impressions of the United States and of individual Americans, but they had a difficult time envisioning the roles of money and income in the United States. I do not think it is fair to call the Russians less materialistic than we are: they glory in the philosophical title of "materialist," and they are anxious with every bone in their collective body to live as richly as we do, on the whole. But I do think it fair to say that the actual role of cash in an individual's life excuses less tyranny in Russia than it does in the United States. This is perhaps a snap judgment since I saw only a small part of Soviet Russia for a rather short time. It is, nonetheless, my honest impression.

They were very amused, particularly the husband, at many of the little crudities I had met, such as the assistant DA, who didn't like Tolstoy because the great writer used some French words, and the lathe worker who "explained" to me why modern French art is bad art. The husband walked me back to my hotel, and he was very surprised at the number of drunks on the street, after I had told him that in my opinion alcoholism was one of their most serious problems. He had earlier somewhat poo-poohed my statement, but he had to admit, rather sadly, that Nevsky Prospect was a lot more drunken than he had ever thought possible.

A few days later, when I was in the process of leaving Leningrad, my two friends came to the hotel to give me some presents for Viv and for the girl at Brandeis who had been so kind to the wife when she was touring Boston. They rode with me to the airport, saw to it that my baggage was properly labeled, and waved goodbye to me from the airport gate. I was very sad to leave them and owe them a great debt of gratitude for the kindness and frank understanding they showed me in Leningrad.

On Thursday evening in Leningrad, I went to see a Russian performance of Verdi's opera *Il Trovatore*. I sat down next to a fellow who made himself my friend for life by asking me if I live in Leningrad permanently or if I was just there on vacation. When I told him I was not a local boy, he asked, "Oh, are you from one of our republics?" I told him that I was not from one of their republics, but I was from a republic. When he learned that I was an American he was very pleased and anxious to talk, and it turned out that he was Jewish. He insisted that I visit his home and his family. I told him truthfully that I would be delighted but that my time was then all booked up. He asked how about Sunday, and I told him I had an appointment from 11:00 to the time I would have to leave the city.

He said, "OK, come over at seven in the morning." I saw that he was serious, and I accepted on the spot. It turned out to be one of my most moving experiences.

This man was a planning engineer, and his wife was a road building engineer. They have a nine-year-old son, and they live in an old apartment with his father, an old man about eighty years old. I gave the son a picture postcard of Boston with a picture of the new Boston expressway. When the mother, a road engineer, saw the picture, she confiscated it so she could have the picture of the good American road. I told the son not to fret, that I would send him another one without the road. They were all tremendously curious about Jewish life in America, and the old man was visibly moved when I could read some lines from a Yiddish book which he placed in front of me. He had kept the family from starvation during the Leningrad blockade by sewing as a tailor for the Soviet Army. He then brought out the Holy of Holies, the family album with about fifty pages of photographs of his brothers, sisters, cousins, nephews, etc. To my horror, he suddenly told me, after I had properly admired them, that they were all, to the very last man, dead—killed by the Nazis, some of them in France and the rest of them in Russia. Almost fifty people, individuals whom he had loved, all shot by the Germans. A little bit later, while I was drinking tea, he suddenly stroked my sleeve, put jam in my tea, and said, "You have to drink jam in your tea—after all, you are my son." It was all I could do to keep from crying on the spot.

They were very sad to see me go so soon, and I was sad to leave them. He loaded me with books for gifts, and I promised I would reciprocate from America.

Meanwhile, during the week, I had been going over to the Pushkin House to work on some literary materials held there. I met Dolinin, the famous Russian critic on Dostoevsky, and I had a wonderful time with him. He breathes the fire and the passion, the dark side and the inspiration that makes up the work of one of Russia's and the world's great writers. He is an old man and a wise one, and we had a common language to talk with. One amusing aspect of the interview concerned my face. Almost all Russians who had seen me previously, when they learned that I was American, looked at my bow tie and said, "Oh yes, I can see your

Anglo-Saxon features" (my face, with its stamped-on map of Jerusalem!). But Dolinin said, in a hurt tone, "Come on, buddy, you can't fool me, you're no American! What the hell are you, anyway?" I told him I was Jewish, and, much relieved, he airily dismissed the whole business and proceeded with the interview.

I also met an old lady named Mirateva, one of the old timers of work on the Gorky bibliography. She is a strange-looking old woman, sort of half witch and half angel, but she was very kind to me in spite of my un-Bolshevik views on Gorky, which probably offended her a bit. She led me to the current catalog of work by and about Gorky—it is a magnificent piece of work, and I could have used a year to work on it alone. I did the best I could in a few days to skim the cream that was there.

I was also ushered into the manuscript room of the Pushkin house, and they very kindly showed me the actual original manuscripts of works by Pushkin and Dostoyevsky. It was a little unreal, so much so that I had to pinch myself to believe it. The manuscripts are works of art in themselves, and I spent a most enjoyable time there. I was also told that they will put out a full academic edition of Dostoyevsky in the next few years, an edition which we will all welcome enormously.

I was then invited by the academician and his scientific secretary to spend a Sunday afternoon at his place in the country, to get some good herring, and to meet Zhirmunsky, one of the grand old men of Russian literary criticism, a man who has lived through very thick and very thin. I was of course delighted to accept the invitation. They extended it partly because they knew I was connected with Professor Lord of Harvard, whom they had met and esteemed very much. Two of these men have received invitations to come to Harvard and lecture on literature there. Both of them are dying to go, but they cannot decide the issue until their government gives them the cue.

I was driven out by both men and their chauffeur, Sasha, a man whom they obviously know and trust very much. Sasha was on fire to show me how quickly he could get me there, but the traffic cops along the way sadly crimped his style.

The country house was a piece of gingerbread out of a fairy story—all gabled roof and verandas. It turns out that the rich men are now forbidden to build more than five rooms into their houses to prevent some of the ostentatious luxury of previous periods. They get around this, to a certain extent, by building many closed verandas which can be used as rooms even when they are not called "rooms." The academician had had a fine house built. He was quite surprised when I went over it with my developed eye of the professional house hunter, and he was amazed at the details I picked up. Poor fellow, he never had a chance with a bastard who had been house hunting in Belmont and Cambridge for a year! They were delighted when I praised some of the carpentry, which really was first class, and they told me that their carpenter would be in seventh heaven to receive American praise for his work. I told them to be sure and tell him.

The academician's wife was of the old, hard variety of Russian women, very much in competition with her husband. She told me to be sure and tell her about Americans working on the Russian writer Uspensky. There were two daughters, rather charming ladies, one of them 29 years old, the other 14 years old. The younger was obviously the apple of her father's eye, and I would not be surprised if the older one suffered a bit from this. The older one was a student of English, and she was busily translating some American drama for the Russian stage. We had an interesting discussion about contemporary American literature, and I promised to send some material. Tennessee Williams is a hard one for them to comprehend.

The older daughter insisted on a strict British pronunciation of English and made fun, in a kind way, of my strongly accented American ways. She was really delighted when Zhirmunsky did not understand, later, an English phrase that I threw into the Russian conversation. It was "barnstorming"; Zhirmunsky only understood "bahnstuhming." He excused himself gracefully by saying that he had studied English well before the days of aviation. The younger daughter, on the other hand, was eager to learn American pronunciation of English, and she played some hot American jazz while her father left the house temporarily. It was explained to me that the father is embarrassed by such music, and he does not want it played while guests are in the house. I promised to keep the deep, dark secret.

The conversation with Zhirmunsky was a very moving one. He has signed a contract to come back to his early work (for which he has suffered much in the Soviet Union) and go through it again with the accumulated wisdom of age. I can only pray that he will live in good health to do it, for it could be a most important work. He seemed pleased that his work is known and admired by a wide circle of American specialists.

My hosts had urged me to take on board some Russian vodka in a round of toasts, but I had to excuse myself lamely since I knew one shot would make me horizontal. Half the company laughed and half came swinging to my defense, but somehow or other, I managed to beg off.

My friends did a pretty good job to a quart bottle, however, and I rode back with a slightly pickled scientific secretary. He told me some wonderful stories, and he also told me that American specialists should not take too seriously some of the scurrilous attacks out of the Soviet press. "You know what the people are who write these attacks?" he asked me. I said no, I didn't. "They are . . ." He used the Russian equivalent to an English four-letter word I shall not repeat. He then told me that seven years ago, he could not have talked with me the way he did and live the next day in Leningrad; in those days, he would have been reported by a spy and shipped the next day to a forced-labor camp.

"Old Jo, he didn't like jokes; no sir, Jo didn't like jokes!" He then turned to Sasha and said, "Isn't that right, Sasha?" Sasha fervently nodded his head and replied, "You are right; old Jo certainly didn't like jokes!"

The scientific secretary then told me that his work, of an archeological nature, took him up to the far north. In the old days, his journey would go past one forced-labor camp after another, but now, there is not a single camp in the area, he said. According to him, all the political prisoners still alive four years ago had been set free and sent home.

These people treated me in a very hospitable way, and I am deeply grateful to them for a fine day, as well as many useful contacts for my work.

I got to the plane from Leningrad to Moscow, accompanied, as I told you, by my kind friends. The stewardess got up in the forepart of the cabin and gave a stern little speech about the rules to be observed by all comrades in flight: no smoking on takeoff and landing, fasten seat belts, etc.

Back in Moscow the next day, I bade a rather sad farewell to the places with very friendly associations for me. I went shopping, and you should shortly receive the fruits of my tour. There are tea cozies for you, for Carolyn, for Marjorie, and for Viv's mom and sister. My shopping guide was an interesting bird. I saw the Kremlin, addressed one more crowd in front of the hotel in a kind of "swan song," had a good talk with a cabbie on the way to the airport, and then I was off into the wild blue yonder.

My last view of Russian soil was of an outstretched birch branch, white, pale, and graceful against the Russian soil. It seemed like a good omen and a fitting symbol of the feelings I had of the trip.

I don't know what you can make of these rambling, sometimes disconnected notes of a man on a trip. In any case, they will give you some ideas of what I was feeling and what I was doing on a trip I shall never forget as long as I live.

Love, Irwin

Index

pleasures of, 29–31
stock buying, 9, 11–12
World War II and life after, 21–24
Zionism and education, 19–21
Weil Brothers Funeral Home, 9, 40
White Army, 46
Wilson, Edmund, 180–181
Wise, Isaac Meyer, 10, 19
Wise Center Religious School, 41
Wise Center services, 42

Wohl, Rabbi Samuel, 10–11, 17–20, 26, 50, 76

Y

Yankees World Series game, 24–25
Yeltsin, Boris Nikolayevich, 182n28

Z

Zamyatin, Evgeny Ivanovich, 148n9
Zhegalov, Nikolai, 103

CPSIA information can be obtained
at www.ICGtesting.com
Printed in the USA
BVHW01s2044160118
505445BV00002B/131/P